Books by
Katherine Paterson

The Smallest Cow in the World (1991)

The King's Equal (1992)

Flip-Flop Girl (1994)

A Midnight Clear: Stories for the Christmas Season (1995)

A Sense of Wonder
   (combining *Gates of Excellence* and *The Spying Heart*) (1995)

Jip, His Story (1996)

The Angel and the Donkey (retelling) (1996)

Marvin's Best Christmas Present Ever (1997)

Parzival (1998)

Images of God (with John Paterson) (1998)

Celia and the Sweet, Sweet Water (1998)

Preacher's Boy (1999)

The Wide-Awake Princess (2000)

The Field of the Dogs (2001)

Marvin One Too Many (2001)

The Invisible Child (2001)

THE

INVISIBLE

CHILD

The
ON READING
Invisible
AND WRITING
Child
BOOKS FOR CHILDREN

KATHERINE
PATERSON

DUTTON CHILDREN'S BOOKS ~
NEW YORK

Some of the selections in this book first appeared in Katherine Paterson's *Gates of Excellence* (Lodestar, 1981) and *The Spying Heart* (Lodestar, 1989). These selections were later published in the author's *A Sense of Wonder* (Plume, 1995). The complete texts of the Newbery Medal Acceptance Speech (1981) for *Jacob Have I Loved*, the National Book Award Acceptance Speech (1979) for *The Great Gilly Hopkins*, the Newbery Medal Acceptance Speech (1978) for *Bridge to Terabithia*, and the National Book Award Acceptance Speech (1977) for *The Master Puppeteer* appear for the first time in this volume.

Library of Congress Cataloging-in Publication Data
Paterson, Katherine.
  The invisible child: on reading and writing books for children / by Katherine Paterson.— 1st ed.
    p. cm.
  ISBN 0-525-46482-4
  1. Children's literature—Authorship.   2. Children—Books and reading.   I. Title.
PN147.5 .P38 2001   808.06'8—dc21   2001032447

Published in the United States by Dutton Children's Books,
a division of Penguin Putnam Books for Young Readers
345 Hudson Street, New York, New York 10014
www.penguinputnam.com

Designed by Heather Wood
Printed in USA • First Edition • 10 9 8 7 6 5 4 3 2 1

For Sara Little and George Parker Winship, Jr.,
and in memory of Balmer Kelly and Inez Morton Wager

—K.P.

Acknowledgments

This book is dedicated to four teachers, two in college and two in graduate school, who had a profound effect on my thinking and my life. Though none of them imagined that I was going to become a writer of fiction for children, when that is what I became, all of them continued to encourage me and cheer me along my chosen path.

Although I spoke of them in the introduction, I cannot repeat too often my eternal thanks to my longtime editor Virginia Buckley and my even longer-time husband and first editor, John Paterson.

John not only made it possible for me to be a writer, but we also share the joy of four terrific children who have provided us with four terrific spouses and, to date, six amazing grandchildren. Since my family has graciously provided many of the stories I tell in these essays, I hope they feel properly acknowledged for these gifts.

A word of gratitude to all my relatives, friends, and acquaintances whose personal stories appear in this book. I cannot name you, each one, on this page, for fear of leaving out one of you or including someone who would rather remain unnamed. Still I know it is your lives that make these essays live. I hope I've told your stories in a way that will please you.

A special word of thanks to Alissa Heyman, who helped put this book together from my three previous books of essays and fistfuls of new material. Her perception and patience made the process a delight, rather than a drudgery.

Contents

Introduction

Looking over the speeches and articles in this volume is like going back through the thirty-six years of my writing life. I began to write seriously when I was asked by my denomination to write a book for fifth- and sixth-graders to supplement the church-school curriculum. I began that book when our first son was born in 1964. When it was published in 1966, we had two more children—a daughter by adoption and another homemade son—and I was feeling the need of something at the end of the day that had not been eaten up, soiled, or taken apart at the hands of a curious toddler. By the time we'd adopted a second daughter in 1968, I was madly scribbling away in five- to ten-minute snatches of time.

My first novel, *The Sign of the Chrysanthemum*, was not published until 1973, which meant that there were seven years of rejection slips, with, as I recall, two sales. The first was a short story to a Roman Catholic magazine, which folded immediately thereafter, and the second was a poem that I sold for ten dollars to another small magazine, which folded before my poem could be published.

You might wonder why I kept writing with so little encouragement. It was not that I knew in my heart that a writer was what I was meant to be. Most of my friends who are writers knew by the time they were ten that they would spend their lives writing. When I was ten, I couldn't decide whether I was going to be a missionary or a movie star. But, as these essays will show, I have always thought of myself as a reader. Indeed, I often say that one reason I became a writer was that I figured out that if you call yourself a writer, you can read all you want to and people think you are working.

Still, I kept writing. I had no guarantee that I would someday win awards for writing. Heavens, the only person during that time who seemed to think I could write something worth publishing was my loyal husband. But I always remembered the professor from graduate school who urged me to write and who had recommended me for that first writing assignment in 1964. When I protested to Sara Little that I didn't want to add another mediocre writer to the world, she gently reminded me that if I didn't dare mediocrity, I would never write anything at all.

Somehow, as timid as I am, I managed to dare to write. And I found that the real reward was not publication or even winning prizes but the process itself. As Anne Lamott says in the best book about writing I know, *Bird by Bird*: ". . . Writing has so much to give, so much to teach, so many surprises. That thing you had to force yourself to do—the actual act of writing—turns out to be the best part."

As I've said, before, success might have come sooner if I'd had a room of my own and fewer children, but I doubt it. For as I look at my writing, it seems to me that the very persons who took away my time and space are the ones who have given me something to say.

So here I am, thirty-six years later, holding forth on reading and writing books for children. My body of work, which began with that supplement to the Presbyterian church-school curriculum, now numbers more than twenty-nine books, though not all of them are still in print. Our four children are grown and married, and we have recently welcomed our sixth grandchild. I've moved during those years from New Jersey to Maryland to Virginia and come to rest in an 1830s Vermont farmhouse where I have now lived longer than I have ever lived anywhere.

My publishing address has changed as well, as one house has bought up others. There have been two constants through these many moves—my husband, John, and Virginia Buckley, who has edited all my novels, though under a variety of imprints.

The chapters in this book, most of which originated as speeches, are like stepping-stones across those years. The earliest dates from 1975 and the latest from 2000. I'd like to feel I've grown, that I've learned a lot since 1964. I do know I'm still learning.

One of the great joys of these years has been getting to know others from around the world who care deeply for children and their books—teachers, librarians, other writers and illustrators, members of the children's publishing community, and yes, even critics. As the son who was born the summer it all began has said: "Do you realize how lucky you are, Mom? You get to work with the greatest people in the world."

I do realize it, and I am very grateful.

Katherine Paterson
BARRE, VERMONT

THE

INVISIBLE

CHILD

In Search of Wonder

This speech, given at the Children's Literature New England Summer Institute at Silver Bay, New York, in July 2000 for a conference entitled "The Green Prehuman Earth," is based on the May Hill Arbuthnot Lecture given in Aberdeen, South Dakota, March 14, 1997. The original speech was published in Journal of Youth Services in Libraries, *vol. 10, no. 4, Summer 1997, pp. 378–391. May Hill Arbuthnot coauthored the popular Dick and Jane series of early readers and went on to edit a number of literary anthologies for children. She is the author of two influential textbooks in the field of children's literature:* Children and Books, *first published in 1947, and* Children's Reading in the Home, *1969. The lectureship was established by her longtime publisher Scott Foresman and is administered under the auspices of the American Library Association Services to Children.*

Last Saturday morning, our three-year-old grandson was lying on his stomach on our deck, waiting for a chipmunk to appear. I was nervous, knowing that three-year-old patience is limited and that chipmunks, unlike grandmothers, do not live to please. But his patience was rewarded. A chipmunk came scurrying out from under a rock and scampered across the yard into the woods. "Did you see it?" I cried. "Wow," Carter said, beaming. And added, because he is a literate three-year-old, " 'Wow.' Just about all he could say was 'Wow.' "

For those of you not as literate as my grandson, the quotation is from *Lily's Purple Plastic Purse*, by Kevin Henkes. I have been thinking of Carter and Lily and Mr. Slinger all day as I've listened to all the presentations. What a day! " 'Wow.' Just about all she could say was 'Wow.' "

During Tony Watkins's lecture this morning, I was reminded of a quotation from Leon Garfield that seems particularly important for what we are thinking about this week. "Edward Blishen," Garfield says, "has a good phrase for books that are right for children. What they have in common, he says, is a young eye at their center. No matter how beautifully observed an incident may be, if it is solely an adult's view of young behavior, it passes inches over a child's head and heart. *Gulliver's Travels* may be read by the young, while *1984* is not suitable. Both are satires; both are fantasies; yet Swift has a sense of wonder (a property of Mr. Blishen's 'young eye'), and Orwell has not. Swift has anger (again a property of youth), while Orwell has only bitterness.

"Is it, then, that the young reader requires optimism in one way or another and is bored or repelled by the lack of it? It is tempting to think that that is all there is; but optimism is not enough. There should also be a sense of wonder and a deep belief that, to the spirit, the possible is more important than the probable."[1]

In 1997, on a freezing dark Vermont night, I drove my little twelve-year-old Honda slowly up the hill to Vermont College. For me, raised in the South, the driving was bad. The snow from the storm earlier in the day had not been fully cleared, and more snow would be coming within the hour. I finally found a parking place on a precipitously steep side street, hauled my enormous drawing board and bag of supplies out of the trunk, and started through the dark and snow toward the lighted building. Shyly, I asked the young woman at the desk inside the entrance where Drawing 101 would meet.

The Japanese have an expression that, if you've ever lived in Japan, makes enormous sense. They say of a formidable place or occasion, "The threshold was too high." For me the world of graphic art, of drawing, has always seemed to have too high a threshold. When I was young, the world was divided in half—there were those who could draw and the rest of us. I was without any doubt one of the rest of us. The ability to look at something and reproduce it on paper so that it could be recognized—let alone admired—belonged to a fortunate few, a fraternity from which I was destined to be forever excluded. Now I had boldly plunked down my money, invested in a king's ransom worth of supplies, and was determined, blizzard or not, to enter a class full of people all of whom I was quite sure were bucking for immortality in the local gallery.

One of the first things the teacher asked us to do was to write down for her what our personal goal was in taking Drawing 101. This is what I wrote: "I want to learn how to see. I want to be able to draw what I see." And then I added—so she'd understand that I had no false expectations—"I want to have fun doing it."

What I hadn't said, because it would have sounded too pompous even to me, what I really meant was: "I've come in search of wonder."

When the board of the Children's Literature New England Summer Institute chose to meet at Silver Bay, New York, the place I love almost more than anywhere on earth, I was thrilled. And when I heard the topic we would center on, I was even happier. They had chosen a theme about which I could not possibly be asked to speak, "The Green Prehuman Earth." I have no scientific expertise whatsoever, not to mention knowledge of a world without people. People is all I know. But, as you can see, I was not let off the hook. "Okay," I said at last. "I've done a lot of thinking about wonder." That's fine, I was told. "I'll be repeating a lot of things I've said before," I warned. Words on wonder are worth repeating, they said. So here I am—not at all green and very human—inviting you to join me in this beautiful place in a continuing search for wonder.

Now I know that if I have eyes to see, I can find wonder almost anywhere. Often I don't need to search at all. It startles me on a bright summer morning when I go out on the deck of our cottage a couple of miles down the road from here and see that a spider has been up long before. The early sun dazzles the sticky silken threads. It is an enormous web—the radials extending from its hub look to be more than a foot in length, so that the web itself measures more than two feet across. It is attached firmly on my left to the Adirondack double chair that our son David rescued from a trash heap, but then, quite marvelously, the whole right side simply floats in the air. I know that is impossible. The bridge lines on the right have to be anchored *somewhere*, but in the morning light they are invisible. I creep up on the web, feeling somehow that I am intruding on a great artist who needs rest after a work of this magnitude, but I have to know how she's anchored this creation— and then I see a single bridge line stretching up to the deck rail nearly four feet away. There must have been a second, lower bridge line, but I could not see it. Or perhaps I stopped looking. I could hardly breathe after I found the first. I tried to imagine that tiny creature, leaping into space from the height of the rail—across the void— surely a hundred times wider than the length of her body—leaping to attach that tiny trail of silk to the chair across the deck so that she could build her incredible web beside it. Needless to say, no one touched that web. It disappeared, finally, as all webs do, but not by human agency.

The poet A. R. Ammons obviously shares my love of spiders. In his poem "Identity," he muses on the fact that you can discern the species of spider by looking at the center of a web—every species has its own trademarked hub and center—but around the periphery, where the spider must find anchor for her web, there is perfect freedom—to adapt each web to the setting available.

> if the web were perfect pre-set,
>   the spider could
> never find
> a perfect place to set it in: and
>
>   if the web were
> perfectly adaptable,
> if freedom and possibility were without limit,
>   the web would
> lose its special identity:
>
>   the row-strung garden web
> keeps order at the center
> where space is freest (interesting that the freest
>   "medium" should
>   accept the firmest order)
>
> and that
> order
>   diminishes toward the
> periphery
>   allowing at the points of contact
>   entropy equal to entropy.[2]

While I'd rather not think of our double Adirondack chair, not to mention our deck railing, as in the process of decay and as elements of disorder (my dictionary's definition for the word *entropy*), still, as points of contact for the spider's creation, they are so—those irregular disorderly features of the environment onto which she attaches the periphery of her web. She can use anything handy for that. It is in the center that she will show her true nature, reveal the order to which she belongs.

My search for wonder began early on. I cannot remember the first time I heard the Eighth Psalm read, but it so exactly expressed my childish feelings about the universe that I memorized it, King James language and all.

When I consider thy heavens, the work of thy fingers, the
moon and the stars, which thou has ordained;
What is man, that thou art mindful of him? and the son of
man, that thou visitest him?
For thou hast made him a little lower than the angels, and
hast crowned him with glory and honour.
Thou madest him to have dominion over the works of thy
hands; thou hast put all things under his feet:
All sheep and oxen, yea, and the beasts of the field;

The fowl of the air, and the fish of the sea, and whatsoever
passeth through the paths of the seas.

O Lord our Lord, how excellent is thy name in all the earth!

It is not politically or in fact theologically correct to speak of humankind's dominion of nature. We need, indeed the Scriptures instruct us, to see ourselves as stewards of the natural world, not controllers, not dominators. And yet it is wonderful to contemplate our role—a little lower than the angels, the Psalmist says. It gives us enormous responsibility as well as food for wonder.

I fed upon wonder as a child, and when I'm deprived of it, my inner life feels as sterile as a barren landscape and my outer life feels as bombarded with junk as a suburban mall. And it seems to me when I look at what children today are frantically occupying their lives with, that it might be that they, too, feel that inner starvation for a sense of wonder. Could this be the reason they have gone crazy over Harry

Potter? Is there something in J. K. Rowling's books that feeds their hunger?

At this point, perhaps, I should say what I mean and do not mean as I speak of wonder in the context of this talk, for the word *wonder*, as we all know, can be used in a number of ways.

Why, at this very moment, some of you may be thinking: I wonder what on earth she's going to say next.

Dr. Annabel Profitt, in an article on the subject of wonder, talks about three uses of the word. The first is wonder as curiosity. I wonder what makes a car go. Why do things work? David Macaulay has done much to satisfy children's hunger in that regard. Children do want to know how things work. They are curious. They do wonder why. I have a number of well-worn books on my shelf seeking to slake that kind of thirst: *The Why Book of Weather* or *Frequently Asked Questions About Nature*. It is this kind of wonder that has led to humankind's long love affair with the sciences—the hunger to understand. If only we could understand, then . . .

One morning while I was working on this talk, the banner headline on our newspaper read GENETIC CODE COMES TO LIGHT. J. Craig Ventner, the chief scientist working on decoding the human genome, said: "Today marks a historic point in the 100,000-year record of humanity. [The achievement] carries humankind across a frontier and into a new era." Dr. Francis Collins, the rival scientist working on the same project, said: "We have caught a glimpse of an instruction book previously known only to God."

Wonder, curiosity about human life led us into this exploration. We now have the knowledge we sought. Knowledge is power. And we want to be powerful. And here lies the danger. A thirst for knowledge of the building blocks of the universe led human beings to build weapons capable of destroying all life (with the possible exception of cockroaches); what will knowledge of the secrets of life lead us to do? "This is just the beginning," another scientist said. "We have blazed the trail, but we have not yet started to travel it yet and explore the vast natural resources that are along the way." But who is asking where that road will lead? Who is asking that we take a sense of caution and humility along on the journey? Curiosity has killed more than cats.

A second use of the word *wonder* is wonder in the sense of marvel—a wonder is something startling, extraordinary, not to be expected in the common round of things. A computer is a wonder the first few times you encounter one. Recently I saw a television special on the telephone. Alexander Graham Bell went to the Centennial Exposition in Philadelphia to show off this marvel, which is now in all our houses—as ordinary a piece of equipment as a cookstove, which 125 years ago was a wonder itself.

I remember when I came back to the United States after four years in Japan, the last two spent in a house in rural Shikoku. I went into my parents' bathroom and turned on the left-hand faucet, and out of it poured hot water. The idea of hot water pouring out at a touch seemed like a miracle to me. "I will never get used to this," I vowed. But of course, within a week or two I was turning on the left faucet with never a thought unless my sister's shower had taken too long and the left faucet was running as cold as the right.

As Thomas Green says in *The Activities of Teaching*:

Wonder aroused only by sensational things is satiable, because they have a disgusting way of becoming usual and ordinary. When men find occasion to wonder only at the extraordinary or spectacular, it is the surest sign that wonder is already dead.[3]

A few days after the words "Some Pig" appear in the web and save Wilbur's life, Charlotte, you will recall, calls a meeting of the animals. "I need new ideas for the web," she says. "People are already getting sick of reading the words 'Some Pig!' " Charlotte is a real student of human nature. Give people a miracle one day, and three days later they'll come looking for a bigger one.

One of the most disturbing elements of our society, it seems to me, is the demand for ever more and greater marvels and thrills. The car, the motorcycle, the jet plane soon pale. We want more, faster, more dangerous. Till the next thing you know, we're bouncing over an abyss, suspended from our ankles by a wide rubber band. I'm not sure what you do for a thrill after bungee jumping, but believe me, someone will think of something more idiotic soon.

Our movies must become more violent, more shocking, because what shocked last year no longer has the power to arouse in us that same level of response. We keep thinking that sometime the wall will be hit, but no, it seems there are unimaginable things yet to be exploited, which will become, by next year, ho-hum.

We decry the scary series books for children, murderous computer games, violent TV and movies, not to speak of actual violence and pornography, but maybe we should step back and look at what this lust for frenzied distraction is saying to us. Isn't the need for ever-increasing decibels of shock a scream for something else? Isn't there in this cry a hunger that continues to be unsatisfied because it is being offered the wrong food? Have our children asked for bread and been given stones? Have they asked for eggs only to receive scorpions? More and more of worse and worse or even more and more of spectacle and marvel will not, cannot ever satisfy the hunger for wonder. To continue the quotation from Thomas Green:

> The wonder that is ceaseless, that can never be exhausted, has always to do with what is usual and close at hand; for the marvel of a thing has less to do with its frequency than with its contingency.[4]

We are speaking here of another kind of wonder that would be bread and meat to our children but which, I fear, in the noise and clamor of our age can hardly be found, for this kind of wonder asks of us quiet and time and close attention.

One human being in *Charlotte's Web* seems to understand this.

> "Have you heard about the words that appeared in the spider's web?" asked Mrs. Arable nervously.
>
> "Yes," replied the doctor.
>
> "Well, do you understand it?" asked Mrs. Arable.
>
> "Understand what?"
>
> "Do you understand how there could be any writing in a spider's web?"
>
> "Oh, no," said Dr. Dorian. "I don't understand it. But for that matter I don't understand how a spider learned to spin a web in the first place. When the words appeared, everyone said they were a miracle. But nobody pointed out that the web itself is a miracle."[5]

Yes, wonder comes in many guises, many of them debased, but let me direct you to what your friend and mine, Margaret Mahy, had to say on the subject in a lecture she gave in 1989. Margaret tells how when she was a child, she read in a family encyclopedia the then "scientific fact" that the world had once dropped off the sun and that it would someday come to an end. She pompously asserted this fact in the schoolyard, only to find herself chased home by unbelieving, irate schoolmates who were intent on drawing blood. "Yet," says Margaret,

> . . . though the scientist who advised the editors of *Arthur Mee's Encyclopedia* about the beginning of the world had made what I now take to be a genuine mistake, it was a mistake that

fixed my attention in childhood, and (it is even tempting to think) enabled me to see something true which stayed true, even when the information turned out to be false. If so, the true thing was wonder . . . and so I have come to think wonder must be a part of truth, but a part which our physical systems are anxious to conceal. A perpetual state of wonder and desire (which seems to me the truest state to be in, confronted with the universe) is certainly not the most practical state to try and live in. We are biologically engineered to have the wonder filtered out of our lives, to learn to take astonishing things for granted so that we don't waste too much energy on being surprised but get on with the eating and mating, gardening, feeding cats, complaining about taxes, and so on.[6]

Yet if you know Margaret, you know that biology has failed to filter out the wonder. She is, I believe, one of the most intelligent people I have ever known, but this enormous intellectual sophistication is coupled with the most winsome childlike wonder. To be with her is to know the joy of constant new discoveries and a delight in the marvels of the everyday.

Margaret Mahy, Thomas Green, and Dr. Dorian are talking about the kind of wonder that Rachel Carson wrote about in her book *The Sense of Wonder*. It is the kind of wonder that is drawn to the everyday, the ordinary, and sees in the broken seashell the link to the mystery out of which we are born. This is the kind of wonder that is all about us here in this place. We just need to open the eyes of our hearts.

A child's world is fresh and new and beautiful, full of wonder and excitement. It is our misfortune that for most of us that clear-eyed vision, that true instinct for what is beautiful and

awe-inspiring, is dimmed and even lost before we reach adulthood. If I had influence with the good fairy who is supposed to
preside over the christening of all children, I should ask that
her gift to each child in the world be a sense of wonder so indestructible that it would last throughout life, as an unfailing
antidote against the boredom and disenchantments of later
years, the sterile preoccupation with things that are artificial,
the alienation from the sources of our strength.[7]

But the world is a bit short on good fairies these days. So who is to
take their place? Who is to make sure that our children's sense of
wonder grows indestructible with the years? We are. You and I. And
since our concern tonight is books for children, it is here in the books
we write for them, publish for them, buy for them, read to them, share
with them, that we can begin our search for wonder.

Let me suggest that there are at least three aspects of wonder that
we may find in a well-told story for children—not only in a children's
book, of course, but also there. There is the wonder of nature and human nature—we call it setting and characters. There is the wonder in
the telling—language, style—how the story is told. And there is the
wonder behind and beyond the story—the meaning of this story that
ties us to the mystery of the meaning of our lives and of all creation—
the story's shape, flow, and theme.

Most of you can remember as I can the experience of reading *The
Secret Garden*. Now, strictly speaking, this story is not fantasy, though
there is certainly the feeling of magical kingdoms about it. We, like
Mary, think of Dickon as being magical—but we know of children
like that. Some of you probably had children very like Dickon. I
know I did. No, what Frances Hodgson Burnett has achieved is a
sense of wonder that puts us in awe of ordinary things—not a sense
of magic. She makes us tremble at one of the most commonplace

experiences—the growth of a flower. And yet, ordinary as it is, it is wonderful. That dried brown oniony ball that holds within itself a hibiscus or hyacinth or daffodil or tulip comes to glorious life. Just as in my beautiful new grandson there is the wonder of the meeting of two microscopic cells that have become in a few short months a living, breathing, thinking, feeling human life—a person, a member of our family.

When a beloved theology teacher I had was near death, he said to me that people were always asking him if he believed in the next world. He looked at me, his eyes as wide as a child's. "I can hardly believe *this* world," he said.

The best books for children help us to look at the natural world with this same kind of awe. In his autobiography, *Surprised by Joy*, C. S. Lewis tells about his earliest encounter with Beatrix Potter's book *Squirrel Nutkin*. On reading it, he was filled with an enormous desire—for he knew not what. Perhaps, he writes, Milton's "enormous bliss" of Eden is the best way to explain the feeling that overcame him, which he says ". . . I can only describe as the Idea of Autumn. It sounds fantastic to say that one can be enamored of a season, but that is something like what happened . . . the experience was one of intense desire. And one went back to the book, not to gratify the desire (that was impossible—how can one *possess* Autumn?) but to reawake it . . ."[8]

Just as books can tie us to the wonder of the natural world, they can tie us even closer to the wonder of human nature. All of us know characters from books that are more real to us than most of the people in this room—Anne of Green Gables, Long John Silver, Ramona Quimby, Peter Pan, Harriet the Spy, Jo March, Natasha Rostov—you have your own list. As readers, we want to ask the authors, alive or dead: How do you create a character like that? A character so memorable that long after the memory of the plot has dimmed, the person is still so real that you could carry on a conversation with him or her?

But as a writer, that seems to be the wrong question. When I'm writing a book, I feel less that I'm creating a character than getting to know a person. When I was trying to figure out how to write the book that eventually became *Jip, His Story*, I was doing the kind of desultory research that seems the only kind I know how to do—reading this and that, trying to get a picture of the time and place, searching for stray facts that would give my story substance and verisimilitude. Because I had the notion that the book was going to be set on a nineteenth-century Vermont poor farm, I began to read old town histories, looking for references to poor farms.

In a history of the town of Hartford, I found one of those entries that taxes all the meanings of the word *wonder*.

A man named Putnam Proctor Wilson and his family came onto the town poor rolls in 1811, and they were at first cared for by various local families. In 1814 "it became necessary to place Mr. Wilson in irons," and the selectmen employed a Jonathan Bugbee to make a chain and foot locks for him. In 1816 the selectmen gave an order to a David Trumbull to saw planks to make a cage for Wilson, who was being kept at the time in a private home. Then, the records show, in 1832 the town contracted with a man named Lovell Hubbard to build a new poorhouse on some leased land. Hubbard was paid $518 to build the house and $55 extra to add an apartment containing a cage for Putnam Wilson, and that year the town's poor were moved into the new house, including Putnam Wilson and two others who were judged insane. "These men," according to the anonymous writer of *The Selectman's Journal*, which the town history quotes, "were raving crazy most of the time, and there caged up like wild beasts in narrow, filthy cells. The writer often saw them, and viewing their scanty, ragged attire, their pallets of straw, and their pitiable conditions, was impressed with the conviction that the inhuman treatment to which they were subjected, was sufficient of itself to make lunatics of all men. Poor old Putnam," he goes on, "had some rational moments and was always pleased to see children, to whom he would sing the old song, 'Friendship to every willing mind, &c.,' as often as requested."[9]

I salute the anonymous writer of *The Selectman's Journal* for his compassionate account of the town's poor and insane, but pity was not my reaction to his account. It was wonder—wonder that such a man as Putnam Proctor Wilson could be—a man so frightening that leg arms were not sufficient for the adult populace to feel protected from his ravings. He must be confined to a cage—and yet, this fearsome lunatic loved children, and children, somehow, were not so afraid of him. Why, they would come and listen to him sing and beg him childlike for their favorite songs.

It is of particular importance to me that several friends who have battled mental illness have told me how much they love Put. I do not believe that I have sentimentalized the terror of such a life, but I hope I have shared with readers the beauty—the wonder of the man.

Another gift we owe to children in books is the wonder of language. Sometimes we forget this in our eagerness for children to "understand." Thus we see easy-to-read versions of Beatrix Potter or simplified editions of *Little Women*. But understanding must always mean more than decoding. And often we understand with our hearts wonders we cannot precisely decipher intellectually. Her elegant language is one of the reasons Beatrix Potter has endured—the absolute beauty and charm in the way she tells her very simple stories.

Stephanie Tolan, Steve Liebman, and I did an adaptation of *The Tale of Jemima Puddle-Duck* for the stage. Plots are thin in Potter, as you soon realize when you are trying to adapt one of her stories dramatically, but the language is rich. For example, in the lovely scene where we find Jemima explaining to the gentleman with sandy whiskers that she is not lost but simply looking for a nesting place where her eggs will be safe from the farmer's wife, who always takes them away and gives them to a hen to hatch, we read: "Jemima complained of the superfluous hen." Both Stephanie and I whooped with delight. Superfluous hen, indeed! Now, the word *superfluous* does not occur in basic readers for first-graders, but what a delicious word, one I suspect that only Beatrix Potter would know to choose.

I'm always puzzled that so many people who review children's books think that they've reviewed the book if they've revealed the plot. This is especially annoying if you've tried to write a book with a few surprises in it. But a sketch of the plot rarely tells us what we need to know—which is if this is a story worth reading. One of my writer friends was complaining the other day that she never knows what to say when people ask her what her book is about. The best book in the world doesn't make sense when you try to tell what it's about, she said. For instance, it's about this runty pig that the farmer is going to ax, except his daughter throws a fit, but she wouldn't have been able to keep the pig alive very long if it hadn't been for this spider who can weave words in her web. So the pig lives, but the spider, she dies.

But listen to it in E. B. White's words:

> Mr. Zuckerman took fine care of Wilbur all the rest of his days, and the pig was often visited by friends and admirers, for nobody ever forgot the year of his triumph and the miracle of the web. Life in the barn was very good—night and day, winter and summer, spring and fall, dull days and bright days. It was the best place to be, thought Wilbur, this warm delicious cellar, with the garrulous geese, the changing seasons, the heat of the sun, the passage of swallows, the nearness of rats, the sameness of sheep, the love of spiders, the smell of manure, and the glory of everything.[10]

Yes, part of White's story is fantasy, but the wonder of it is grounded in the wonder of the natural world, the changing of the seasons, the marvel that a spider can spin a web at all, the cycle of birth and the inevitability of death. It is hard for a writer who cannot use words well to convince me, much less to delight and enamor me. But White, as no one needs to say, manages to tell his fantastic tale in language so simple that a child can read it for herself and so beautiful she will weep when she does.

The third aspect of wonder that we search for in books for children is the wonder beyond wonders—nothing less than the mystery of meaning. And for this we look to the story itself—to the unfolding of the plot toward a significant theme. Story matters to us human beings. Story is the way we make sense of life.

The spider will throw her bridge lines on whatever the world offers her, but from these disordered points she will weave a web that will tell us who she is.

In his book on the philosophy of religion, *Man Is Not Alone,* Rabbi Abraham Joshua Heschel lays out a task for the artist or writer as well as for the person concerned for a meaningful life: ". . . all things," he says, "carry a surplus of meaning over being—they mean more than what they are in themselves . . . It is as if all things were vibrant with spiritual meaning, and all we try to do in creative art and in good deeds is to intone the secret strain, an aspect of meaning."[11]

Is this what we are trying to do as we tell a story for children—"intone the secret strain, an aspect of meaning"? I think we are. Aren't we seeking to share a mystery beyond that of spider webs as an indication of poor housekeeping and pigs as potential bacon?

The true meaning of a story is not something one can extract from the story itself. The whole story—character, setting, plot, theme, language—is the meaning.

In Dublin, Tony Watkins told a Sufi parable about a Master who has just told his disciples a story—a story which, if properly apprehended, will open their minds to the next level of their training.

When he has finished the story, one of the students asks the Master what the story means.

In answer, the Master asks him a question. "Let us say that you have gone to the market, chosen an especially fine peach at a fruit stand, and paid for it, but instead of giving it to you the peach seller peels your peach, eats the flesh before your eyes, and then hands you the peeling and the stone—what would you think?"

The baffled student replies: "But Master, I don't understand. Please explain the story."

Whereupon the Master patiently repeats the story of the peach.

There are two impulses in the education of children that concern me today. One is the back-to-basics slogan, which sounds almost like the acquisition of knowledge for the sake of power: If our children don't master the basics, or math, or computers, or whatever, how will we be able to maintain our position as number one in the world? But we already know what happens when our goal is knowledge for the sake of power. The eugenics and efficient annihilations of an Auschwitz; the firebombing of a Dresden; the instantaneous vaporization of a Hiroshima. Knowledge has not made our world a safer place, much less a better place or a more beautiful place.

We must, as Rabbi Heschel says, ". . . go out to meet the world not only by way of expediency but also by the way of wonder. In the first we accumulate information in order to dominate; in the second we deepen our appreciation in order to respond. Power," he reminds us, "is the language of expedience; poetry is the language of wonder. . . . The beginning of our happiness lies in the understanding that life without wonder is not worth living."[12]

Then, as though it were the antidote for knowledge run to conscienceless power, there is a movement to teach our children moral values. Now, I am not opposed to moral values. I just don't think we're going about it the right way. If you saw the movie Shine, you've seen what happens to a man who worships family values. He nearly destroys his children. But even those who are not emotionally ill, as David Helfgott's father as portrayed in the film surely was, seem to think morality can be taught in sterile tales and nineteenth-century doggerel.

If knowledge without a sense of reverence is dangerous, morality divorced from wonder leads either to chilling legalism or priggish sentimentality. I am always nervous when some well-meaning critic applauds my work for the values and lessons it teaches children, and I'm almost rude when someone asks me what moral I am trying to teach in a given book. When I write a book I am not setting out to teach virtue, I am trying to tell a story, I am trying to draw my reader into the mystery of human life in this world. I am trying to share my own sense of wonder that although I have not always been in this world and will not continue in it for too many more years, I am here now, sharing in the mystery of the universe, thinking, feeling, tasting, smelling, seeing, hearing, shouting, singing, speaking, laughing, crying, living, and dying.

We are quick to think of the wonder of birth, but I think we need to share with children the wonder of death as well. In Wallace Stegner's final novel, *Crossing to Safety*, the character Larry Morgan, who is surely speaking for Stegner himself, observes that we are given a little space of time and place on earth for a short while so that we may enjoy this life with awe and gratitude and then leave this life to make space for those coming after us. In *Tuck Everlasting*, Natalie Babbitt beautifully shares with children the truth that the wish for unending life on this planet is not only hubris, but were we to attain this sort of immortality, it would be unlikely to bring us joy.

The Swedish oceanographer Otto Pettersson preserved his intense love of the cosmos and his childlike wonder at its workings until his death at age ninety-three. When he realized that he hadn't much longer to live, he said to his son: "What will sustain me in my last moments is an infinite curiosity as to what is to follow."[13]

Wonder has a vital ingredient, which so far I have been skirting but I cannot end this talk without stating. The wonder that we seek has its grounding in profound mystery. It is the mystery of meaning beyond the universe, but also the mystery that has formed the universe. So no matter our creed or lack of it, if we are in search of wonder, we will inevitably, I believe, bump into a mystery that is ultimately spiritual. When we ask, "What does this all mean?," we are asking a theological question. When we seek to compose a coherent plot—a story that has meaning—we are acknowledging, whether we admit it or not, that there is such a thing as meaning. We are saying that the universe is not the realm of blind chance and chaos— that, however turbulent our individual lives may be, they are not adventures down the rabbit hole, but life in a universe the ordinary workings of which are so dependable that we mistakenly call them "laws."

Meaning in a story reflects our belief that there is meaning in the universe, that no matter the disorder that frames our lives, in the center—in the place that reveals who we are—there is order. As Put knew even in his terror and heartbreak, there is a place where All is well.

I want to go back to A. R. Ammons's poem about the spider web. In the middle of this poem, the poet muses on the fact that the possible settings of the web are infinite while the center always keeps the spider's identity:

> it is
> wonderful
>   how things work: I will tell you
>   about it
>   because

it is interesting
and because whatever is
moves in weeds
    and stars and spider webs
and known
        is loved:[14]

The meaning behind a spider web, like the ultimate meaning of a story, is found in "whatever is moves in weeds and stars and spider webs and known is loved." And so for me the search for wonder is a search to learn to see, to hear, to smell, to taste, to touch the old familiar things of earth and to experience all the precious perishable treasures of earth, nature and human nature, including my own life, in the light of this underlying mystery of wonder that is the source of creation and the ground of hope—the wonder beyond wonder whom to know is to love.

Back in 1925, a journalist named Mary B. Mullett went to see a farmer in a village up in the northern corner of Vermont. "The house is a big one," she wrote, "too big for his purse. By daylight I had seen how badly it needed repair. A young couple—Bentley's nephew and his wife—live in part of the house. The Snowflake Man keeps bachelor's quarters in the other wing.

"Strange surroundings in which to pursue a Dream of Beauty! And the little man opposite me seemed yet more strange, in the role of interpreter to the Great Designer.

"Perhaps that is all that some of his neighbors can see: a strange little man, in an ill-kept house, spending his life in work that leaves his purse almost empty.

"They pass by that work as unheedingly as they, and we, trample with careless feet the snowflakes themselves. I dare say we all are doing the same sort of thing: going through the world, indifferent to its wonders, not even knowing they are there! More blind and deaf to the beauty of the lives that touch our own than we are to the mutely exquisite appeal of the snowflakes we crush in passing."[15]

"On Sunday . . . [t]he minister explained the miracle. He said that the words on the spider's web proved that human beings must always be on the watch for the coming of wonders."[16]

The Child in the Attic

I'm going to call him Walter, though that is not his real name. Walter began life in a family of modest means in a city on the East Coast—father, mother, then two younger brothers. Walter, a lively child, was less than enchanted with school, but somehow he scraped through the boring days, investing a minimum of effort. Life may not have been wonderful for Walter, but it was okay, it was normal. Then suddenly, one day, Walter's life turned upside down. His father walked out, leaving his mother with no marketable skills and three small boys to care for.

It was a time when the job market was flooded with veterans returning from World War II. Women who had worked to support the war effort left their jobs and went home to be the perfect housewives and June Cleaver mothers of the fifties. But Walter's mother had to go to work. There was, of course, no child care system in place—proper stay-at-home mothers didn't require it. Nor was there any government effort in place to track down deadbeat fathers and force them to pay child support.

It isn't hard to imagine what Walter's mother went through, working at whatever jobs she could find, worrying all day about what her three little boys were doing, worrying all night about how she was going to feed them and clothe them and keep a roof over their heads.

As summer approached, her worry increased. Even though the city streets might have been less dangerous in the fifties than they have become, she was a good and caring mother who didn't want her children running loose all day long. So when she heard about a farm outside of town where the farmer and his wife took children in for the summer to give them three months of fresh air and good food at no cost—oh, the children would be expected to help out with the chores, but they'd want to, wouldn't they?—when she heard about this opportunity, she jumped at the chance. As soon as school was out, Walter and his two little brothers went to spend an idyllic summer in the country.

You are already anticipating trouble. The farmer was a stern taskmaster. He expected the children to work and work hard. Quite soon, Walter's lively, not to say rebellious, nature landed him in trouble.

Punishment was called for. And the punishment the farmer decreed was to be locked up alone in the gloomy attic of the old farmhouse. Now we imagine an angry, homesick, apprehensive child climbing the dark staircase, hearing the door at the bottom slam shut and the key turn in the lock.

It is summer, so there is still a little light coming from the small window. I don't know if Walter is crying; if he is, it is probably tears of anger, but eventually, like any prisoner, he begins to look about his prison. And he sees that he is not alone. The farmer has also exiled to the attic Charles Dickens and Jane Austen, Mark Twain and Robert Louis Stevenson, Harriet Beecher Stowe and John Milton. Walter takes down a dusty volume, carries it to the window, and begins to read.

When I was invited to come to OSU way back in another millennium, of course I said yes. I love to come to this festival. I see so many friends. I get to hear so many authors I admire and meet new writers who will become the leading voices of this century. There is, however, always the problem of a speech. The first thing that popped into my mind as I was beginning to get ready for this week was the story of my friend Walter. "The Child in the Attic" seemed like a terrific title for a speech that I hadn't yet written.

Still, it gave me a beginning for my speech. You see, I am quite aware that most of you have been frantically working at home on all those things that have to be taken care of before you leave home and job for three or four days. Then you've had a long flight or drive and, I hope, a good dinner. You're tired and sleepy. I was thinking of all these matters, and it seemed to me that I could start and end with Walter's story, and that might keep most of you awake, afraid you might miss hearing whatever became of Walter. If you'll stay with me, then, I'll tell you more about Walter before I've finished, for Walter is a real, live person, even though the vision of him in that attic brings out all the fictional juices in my system. There is something so evocative about that image—the lonely, misunderstood, despised child, exiled to an attic.

Perhaps that is why fiction writers have chosen to present this image as well. The most famous fictional child in an attic is, probably, Frances Hodgson Burnett's Sara Crewe in *A Little Princess*. One of the most formative books of my childhood was Mrs. Burnett's *The Secret Garden*. I hardly know any female writers of my generation who weren't deeply influenced by *The Secret Garden*. Most of my contemporaries would also name *A Little Princess* as one of the formative books of their childhood. I, however, cannot. We lived in China, and although we owned *The Secret Garden*, we seem not to have owned *A Little Princess*.

My earliest contact with *A Little Princess* was the Shirley Temple movie based on the book, one of the few movies I saw while we were living in Shanghai. I remember loving the movie. I haven't seen it since, so I don't know if I would love it still or how closely it follows the rather remarkable book, but I still recall my gasp of utter delight when Sara wakes up to discover that her cold, barren attic has been magically transformed and there is a hot breakfast waiting on the table.

I say "remarkable book," and that's what I mean. I realize, of course, that Frances Hodgson Burnett was a true Victorian, and we let her get away with sentiments and sentimentalities we would never tolerate in a modern writer. There is, for example, the scene where Sara is saying good-bye to her father, who is returning to India:

> Then he went with Sara into her little sitting room and they bade each other good-bye. Sara sat on his knee and held the lapels of his coat in her small hands, and looked long and hard at his face.
>
> "Are you learning me by heart, little Sara?" he said, stroking her hair.
>
> "No," she answered. "I know you by heart. You are inside my heart." And they kissed as if they would never let each other go.[1]

But we forgive Frances Hodgson Burnett all manner of Victorian excesses because she is, despite all, a magical writer. I can remember all too well how hesitant I was to read *The Secret Garden* aloud to my own children. I was afraid they would scorn its sentimentality or, worse, that I in my late-twentieth-century cynicism would realize I could no longer tolerate, much less enjoy, one of the greatest delights of my own childhood. But I did read it aloud to my children. Of course I saw sentimentalities and overblown language that I would never let myself indulge in, but the magic was more powerful than the embellished prose in which it was couched. It burst out and touched all our hearts.

A *Little Princess*, which I came to later in life, has that same magical quality. If you begin to think about the premise of the book in terms of our current moral outlook, you're soon in trouble. Captain Crewe has raised Sara like a little princess in British-occupied India. Although the Indians in the story are beloved servants, they are still servants. And the fortune that comes to Sara at the end of the story is from colonial Africa in the form of diamond mines, and today we know all too well who worked those mines and under what unspeakable conditions. Becky, the scullery maid at Miss Minchin's school, is rescued in the end by Sara, but rescued not to be Sara's adopted sister but to be Sara's personal maid, which would have been considered the highest possible happiness for one who was, after all, a member of the serving class. So there are a lot of very troubling elements in this book that I'm not going to try to justify because I don't find them justifiable.

There is, however, one very important idea in the book that I believe makes it worth reading, even for today's children. Once Captain Crewe dies and Miss Minchin realizes that Sara is penniless, she turns her into an unpaid servant, feeling quite smug that she has not, after all, turned her into the street. Miss Minchin has never liked Sara. Sara is far too self-possessed for a child. She is clever and imaginative and can see right through Miss Minchin's pretensions and hypocrisy. Now Miss Minchin has Sara where she always wanted her—at her beck and call. She sells all the beautiful things in what had been Sara's luxurious suite and sends her to live in the bare, heatless attic.

At first Sara is disconsolate. She is mourning for her father and unable to adjust to her radically changed circumstances. But Sara is a great reader of fiction and nonfiction alike. Although Miss Minchin has confiscated her library, she cannot confiscate what is in Sara's mind and heart. Sara knows history. She decides to pretend that her attic is a cell in the Bastille where she is being kept a prisoner. She makes friends with the other prisoner—Becky, the scullery maid—and with a rat, remembering that prisoners in solitary confinement in the Bastille often tamed rats. She gives the rat the name Melchisedec. Perhaps this is Mrs. Burnett's joke, as Melchisedec was a kingly high priest in the book of Genesis to whom, we are told, the patriarch Abraham gave a tenth of all he possessed. Sara shares her crumbs with the rat, which is a large percentage of what she possesses.

Pretending, when she is in the attic, that she is imprisoned in the Bastille is just one step from her other imaginative coping device. She begins to pretend that she is a princess. "I can be a princess inside," she tells herself.

". . . It would be easy to be a princess if I were dressed in cloth of gold, but it is a great deal more of a triumph to be one all the time when no one knows it. There was Marie Antoinette when she was in prison and her throne was gone and she had only a black gown on, and her hair was white, and they insulted her and called her Widow Capet. She was a great deal more like a queen then than when she was gay and everything was so grand. I like her best then. Those howling mobs of people did not frighten her. She was stronger than they were, even when they cut her head off."[2]

Poor Miss Minchin. She cannot understand what's going on in Sara's mind. When she berates and belittles the child, she sees something "like a proud smile" in Sara's eyes. She cannot imagine what Sara is thinking, which the reader knows is:

"You don't know that you are saying these things to a princess, and that if I chose I could wave my hand and order you to execution. I only spare you because I *am* a princess, and you are a poor, stupid, unkind, vulgar old thing, and don't know any better."[3]

Oh, how I wish I had read those words before I was nine years old. I think of the people, adult and child, who made me feel belittled and humiliated—if only I could have imagined myself a princess in disguise who could at any moment reveal myself and cry "Off with her head!" Not a very Christian thought, but then, children are not born magnanimous, they are born small. They have to grow into persons large enough to be able to love their neighbors, not to speak of their enemies. We can't expect self-sacrificial love from persons who haven't yet learned to love themselves.

We marvel at a man like Nelson Mandela. How was he able to walk out of prison after twenty-seven years of torture and humiliation and lead a tortured and humiliated people into a nation that sought justice without vengeance? If ever we despair of the human race, here is a man who can inspire us once again to hope.

"But didn't you hate your captors?" an interviewer asked him recently. "Yes," he replied. "For the first thirteen years I hated them. But then one day I realized they could take away everything I had—except my mind and my heart. I would have to give those away. And I would refuse to do that."

Nelson Mandela is a miracle, a man who knew that he had a mind and a heart too valuable to surrender, so dear in fact that he would use his solitary sentence to nourish himself. So for the next fourteen years he grew his soul. For which the world will aways be in his debt.

I do not claim for a moment that any book could work that kind of miracle in most ordinary humans. But I think there is a gift that a book can give a child which bears some relation to Mandela's story. A book can give a child a way to learn to value herself, which is at the start of the process of growing a great soul. It is why I struggle so against the idea that characters in novels should be role models. Role models may inspire some children—but they didn't inspire any child that I ever was. They only discouraged me. Whereas that awful, bad-tempered, selfish Mary Lennox—who could admire her? Who could love such an unlovable creature? Yet she was given the key to a secret garden. Not because she deserved it, but because she needed it. When I read *The Secret Garden*, I fell in love with Mary Lennox. She was my soul mate. And because I loved her, I was able to learn to love myself a bit.

I am often accused of creating unlikable characters. Many a well-meaning teacher or parent has taken me to task for bringing Gilly Hopkins into the world. But I wouldn't give anything for Gilly Hopkins just as she is, and if given a chance to reform her, I would flee in the opposite direction. Because children love Gilly. It seems that the worse they are, the more they love her. Which means, I believe with all my heart, that loving Gilly, they can begin a little to love themselves, and children who love themselves do not not strike out at other people. They do not shoot their classmates or blow up their schools. I would like children to take from a book I've written something that helps them love and value themselves.

A teacher last month asked me about another of my attic children, Vile in *Preacher's Boy*. Vile reminds me a lot of Gilly Hopkins, she said, and yet you don't give us the same hope that Vile will be all right. You just let her go off with that drunken father of hers. I want to know that she'll be all right.

The teacher was referring to Robbie's lament toward the end of the book.

Vile and her father have disappeared with the coming of the first snowfall:

. . . I got a postal card from Vile at Christmastime written in smudged pencil. They had made their way as far as Massachusetts, hopping trains. Zeb was mostly behaving himself, she said. She herself was working in a mill, which she didn't mind at all since no one made her recite lessons in a mill. I mustn't worry. She had taken the primer that Pa had given her and was teaching herself. Couldn't I tell how much her writing had improved even without her having to go to school? She spelled *writing* as *ritin*. And that was about the best spelling on the card. I spent more than an hour puzzling out what she was trying to say. It made me furious that she didn't know what was good for her. She could have had a swell life here in Leonardstown with us, but she threw it away.

It made me sad, too. Even if she was happier in Massachusetts, she was like a buddy to Willie and Elliot and me. We all miss her. Now that I'm back to being a Christian, I pray she'll come back. She hasn't so far.

What can I say to defend myself? I'm not sure I can. When I look at my major characters, I seem determined to give them hope; when I look at the lot of many of my minor characters, I begin to resemble a child abuser. Well, I'm not Dickens. I can't make everything turn out rosy for all. There are a lot of Viles in this world who have trouble remembering that their real name is Violet. It seemed that in all honesty, the writer must acknowledge that.

Still, we do not ever know what a child will take and treasure from a book. Once after I had made a speech, a young woman waited until everyone else had left the room to tell me that *Bridge to Terabithia* had saved her life. It seems she was a victim of incest from the time she was very young and had kept the uneasy secret of her family locked inside herself until one day, inexplicably, someone had scrawled her name and the four-letter-word message of her hidden family shame on the sidewalk outside the school for all the world to read.

"I didn't know what to do when I saw it," she said. "Then people came up and began asking me what it meant. But I had just finished reading *Bridge to Terabithia*, and I remembered what Leslie said to Janice Avery—that if she just pretended she didn't know what they were talking about, everyone would forget all about it in a week. It got me through that terrible time. I wanted to thank you for that."

That wonderful young woman reminded me once again that there are a lot of children in our midst, locked up in all sorts of frightening or lonely attics. I don't think it is too much of an exaggeration to say that books can be a key to that locked door.

A Little Princess is a realistic book, and though it may feel magical to us, it is not fantasy. But fantasy has its own attic children, and none quite so charming as a boy named Harry about whom much of the known world has gone absolutely wild.

I have long ago learned not to take anything for granted. I mean, when I wrote *Jacob Have I Loved*, I assumed educated adults would immediately catch on to the biblical allusion in the title and not complain that there was no character named Jacob in the novel.

But I've learned better. Not everyone has read the Bible. But surely by now everyone has read all about Harry Potter. No? Then you are undoubtedly a Muggle. What, you ask, is a Muggle?

Time magazine last September offered three clinically tested signs of Muggledom:

1) You spot a boy or girl whose forehead is emblazoned with a paste-on tattoo in the shape of a purple lightning bolt and have no idea what you are seeing.

2) You still believe reading is a lost art, especially among the young, and books have been rendered obsolete in our electronic, hot-wired age.

3) You don't know what a Muggle is.

I'm not known to be in the vanguard of current trends, but I know what a Muggle is. And as Muggley as I may look to you, I had read all three Harry Potter books before the middle of last summer, which, you will note, was before volume three had even been published in this country. And how is it, you may well ask, that you were able to read them before most of the rest of us could get our hands on them? Because, I say smugly, my neighbor Kevin at Lake George, a non-reading, computer-crazy eleven-year-old boy, was so enamored of *Harry Potter and the Sorcerer's Stone* that he nagged his mother (who had the credit card) into getting on the Internet and ordering volumes two and three from England for him. When he learned I was also a fan, he kindly loaned them to me. I gobbled them down in a two-day orgy.

Later that week, surrounded by his buddies, he came sauntering up to me on the swimming dock and, in a voice loud enough to be heard by everyone around, proceeded to ask me a few key questions about Harry Potter, glancing back at his friends to make sure they were getting the point that he and I were having a literary discussion.

Exactly one year before, his very literate mother had been moaning to me about the fact that her son just wouldn't read anything. Now he was gulping down 300-page hardback books and bragging about it in front of his friends.

To those of you literalists out there who are mumbling under your breaths that the place of Harry's confinement wasn't an attic, it was a cupboard under the stairs, I will say, merely, that it had spiders. That qualifies it surely as a metaphorical attic. The attic—or, if you insist, cupboard under the stairs—in which Harry Potter finds himself is in the home of his Muggle relatives, the Dursleys. What Harry doesn't know, and what his wretched aunt and uncle are terrified might come out, is that Harry is actually a wizard. And not just any old run-of-the-mill trickster, either. In the world of Witchcraft and Wizardry he is a very famous, if missing, wizard, the infant who survived an assault by the arch-evildoer Voldemort—the proof is that strange, lightning-shaped scar on his forehead. We all know, or certainly should know by now, what happens, so I'll spare you a page-by-page retelling, though I doubt any of your children would.

The point I want to make in the context of this speech is why this particular attic child has conquered the reading world, as well as many whom we would have thought of as citizens of the non-reading world. J. K. Rowling has tapped into the secret heart of us all. Just as Cinderella, despised and unrecognized amongst the ashes, made us all hope that someday our prince would come and reveal us for the princesses we were in truth, so Harry Potter fulfills our dream that we are in truth magical and powerful, and if only we could wrench ourselves free of the Muggles of the mundane world who drag us down and lock us in cupboards, we would fly away on magic broomsticks and amaze even the denizens of enchanted lands.

I hurry on to say that J. K. Rowling has done far more than simply tap into our unconscious longings. She has created a marvelous, delightful, and deliciously scary parallel world. I think *Time* magazine is right when it compares her books with the classic fantasies of Tolkien, Baum, Carroll, and Lewis. I think Rowling's writing will also endure and will deserve to. The adventures of Harry Potter, which have pulled a generation of computer-crazed children away from the keyboard and into a series of great fat books—these adventures will enchant children for many generations to come.

As I was thinking about the differences between Sara Crewe and Harry Potter, it occurred to me that they exemplify for me the principal difference between fantasy and realistic fiction. It is not that one genre is intrinsically better than the other, either as literature or as food for the emotions. It is, instead, a matter of where the imaginative action of the book takes place and, therefore, what we take away from the book, what we remember.

In *A Little Princess*, as in most serious realistic fiction, the imaginative world is inside the central character's head. In fantasy, the imaginative world is outside the main character. So, although you can perhaps think of notable exceptions, it seems to me that what we remember most about strong realistic fiction is character, while what we recall most readily about fantasy is story. Thus what we take away from *A Little Princess* is Sara Crewe herself; what we remember most about *Harry Potter and the Sorcerer's Stone* and *the Chamber of Secrets* and *the Prisoner of Azkaban* are Quidditch, Botts Every Flavor Beans, Hogwarts Express, and all the amazing adventures that Harry encounters. The magic is on the outside rather than the inside.

Any adequate literary diet for growing children would contain both realistic fiction and fantasy, not to speak of books of biography and nonfiction, but it would be natural for readers to have different tastes and so generally prefer one genre over another. Which is simply to say that we need more good books, not fewer, and if a non-reading child like my neighbor has discovered the magic of books through J. K. Rowling, we may hope that he will go on to other books by other writers. Maybe, she says hopefully, maybe even to one of mine. But for this to happen, this child has to first discover what books can do that nothing else does quite as well.

I promised you at the beginning of this talk to tell you what happened to Walter, the child we left reading in the attic. During the rest of that otherwise dreadful summer, Walter contrived to get himself punished on a regular basis. But by the next time he was exiled to the attic, he had managed to secure a flashlight for himself, so that his reading would not have to stop when the sun set.

He went back to the city and back to school. School continued to bore him, and he was never more than an indifferent student. Yet at the same time his teachers were writing him off, Walter was hungrily reading everything he could get his hands on. During those nights in that attic, the world had opened up for him. He had learned that books could stretch his mind and heart as nothing else and no one else had ever done before. He could not get enough.

Those in authority were surprised when Walter, who had exhibited no academic ambition in high school, opted to take the SATs. When the scores came out, Walter was called into the office. He must have cheated. There was no other explanation for his phenomenal score. He would have to take the test again, but this time he would be doing so under carefully monitored conditions. Walter repeated the SATs with a teacher standing over his shoulder and again pulled down an astounding score.

Walter graduated from college and took an M.B.A. from Harvard. He became an innovative and successful businessman and, more important, a devoted husband, father, and then grandfather—a man not only of intelligence but of wisdom, compassion, and delightful good humor. Despite a full and busy life, Walter still reads widely and voraciously. "Books saved him," his wife says simply.

Suppose there had been no books in that attic. What would Walter's story have become?

I ask this question because in our world, our states, our towns, our schools, there are many children whose young lives are hard, whose spirits are starved, who are isolated, angry, and fearful and whose attics aren't furnished with books.

There are many both in government and education who feel that the deprivation of these attic children will be alleviated by just getting them wired onto the Internet. But, friends, surfing the Internet does not compare with wrestling with a book.

This past fall I spent an afternoon talking with a group of persons who work with children at risk. The question I had asked them to help me answer was this: Why do our children turn to violence? It was a question many of us have struggled with this past year.

These professionals were very concerned about the Internet. Today, they said, when a child behaves aggressively at school, the routine solution is expulsion. At the very time when a child is most vulnerable, most reachable, he is further isolated. Often he goes home to an empty house and spends time with violent video games or on the Internet, desperately seeking out connections, and whom does he make connections with? All too often with other desperate, isolated, self-hating individuals who confirm his belief that all his hatreds are justified and that violence is the only way to relieve his mortal pain.

Access to the Internet is not the answer for these attic children. They need much more than that. They need much more even than access to good books. Fortunately, what they need is precisely what you can give them—and that is yourself. "Every child," said the director of the program, "needs a connection with a caring adult."

Last month I was asked to speak to a group of teachers who would be taking their classes to see a production of the play version of *Bridge to Terabithia*. I spent more than an hour telling them about how the book came to be written and rewritten and then how Stephanie Tolan and I adapted it into the play their classes would see. There was the usual time of questions, at the end of which a young male teacher thanked me for my time and what I had told them that morning. "But I want to take something special back to my class. Can you give me some word to take back to them?"

I was momentarily silenced. After all, I had been talking continuously for over an hour; surely he could pick out from that outpouring a word or two to take back to his students. Fortunately, I kept my mouth shut long enough to realize what I ought to say—it is what I want to say to all of you.

"I'm very biblically oriented," I said, "and so for me the most important thing is for the word to become flesh. I can write stories for children, and in that sense I can offer them words, but you are the word become flesh in your classroom. Society has taught our children that they are nobodies unless their faces appear on television. But by your caring, by your showing them how important each one of them is, you become the word that I would like to share with each of them. You are that word become flesh."

What I want to say to that isolated, angry, fearful child in the attic is this: You are not alone, you are not despised, you are unique and of infinite value in the human family. I can try to say this through the words of a story, but it is up to each of you to embody that hope—you are those words become flesh.

The Invisible Child

Some years ago in some city at some convention or other—the place and time and occasion have gone into some irretrievable file in my cluttered brain, I was having a very pleasant dinner in a restaurant far from the madding crowd. There were only five or six of us at the table, all the rest of whom worked, as I recall, for Harper Junior Books. Charlotte Zolotow, the publisher of Harper Junior Books at the time, was our hostess. It was an outside table on a pedestrian mall where in the summer evening we were having a lovely quiet time, but, finally, the delightful meal was eaten, the coffee drunk, the bill paid, and it was time to leave. Reluctantly, we got up and, because we hated for the evening to come to an end, we began to stroll down the mall together.

Suddenly we heard a male voice shouting behind us. We turned to see the tall young waiter from the restaurant running to catch up with us. We were puzzled. Had there been some mistake in paying the bill—or perhaps one of us had left a purse behind? He was out of breath from the chase, but as soon as he could speak, he addressed Charlotte: "I am a graduate student at the university. I've been working my way through the program by waiting on tables. Tonight is my last night because tomorrow I'll get my degree. I just needed to say to you, that in all my time here, you are the first person who has treated me like a human being. I wanted to thank you for that."

Charlotte acknowledged this compliment in her characteristically warm manner, but after he had started back toward the restaurant she expressed amazement over the encounter. She hadn't done or said anything out of the ordinary to the young man to have prompted such a reaction. Of course she hadn't. She had just been herself. She had treated the waiter, as she treated everyone, with graciousness and respect. She had seen him. He wasn't invisible to her. She wouldn't have treated him any more kindly had she known that inside the tall waiter was a scholar struggling to emerge.

When I was asked to give the Charlotte Zolotow Lecture, this story of Charlotte and the waiter was the first thing that popped into my mind. And, although I find it a very awkward word, perhaps I should say "waitperson," rather than "waiter" or "server," in this context. For when Charlotte spoke to the young man attending our table, she saw the person, not the function. In the long-departed days of my youth I worked for three summers as a waitress, and believe me, we noticed those rare occasions when someone we were serving regarded us as human beings.

One reason we gather so joyfully to celebrate Charlotte tonight is because her life and work are all of a piece. Look at her wonderful books. The child, the real child, is fully visible in them, portrayed with respect and affection. It is no surprise that children love Charlotte's books. They see themselves in them, their own fears and foibles, but they are able to like the selves they see because the author has seen them so clearly and so obviously cares for them.

This is the task of the writer for whatever audience. As Joseph Conrad said in his often quoted statement to his readers:

> My task which I am trying to achieve is, by the power of the written word to make you hear, to make you feel—it is, before all, to make you *see*. That—and no more, and it is everything. If I succeed, you shall find there according to your deserts: encouragement, consolation, fear, charm—all you demand—and, perhaps, also that glimpse of truth for which you have forgotten to ask.[1]

When Katy Horning called me last summer to talk about details for this trip, I anticipated that dread request for a title. Somehow, with her sympathetic listening to my long-distance bumbling about on the nickels of the CCBC [Cooperative Children's Book Center], I came up with the title I've chosen to go with: *The Invisible Child*. I was initially going back and forth in my mind between Charlotte Zolotow, for whom we all seem to be visible, and Ralph Ellison, whose masterpiece of this century, *The Invisible Man*, made us see what it meant to be invisible as far as the dominant social group was concerned. But as I began talking over the topic in the car with John on one of the many trips to Lake George, where our daughter was being married, and Barre, where we ordinarily live and work, the title began to take on an additional flavor.

John began to talk about the fact that each character in a novel has a visible self and an invisible self. It is the peculiar nature of novels that they allow that invisible self to be open and available to the reader.

I've become acutely aware of this unique quality of the novel as my books have been adapted for the stage or screen. Children who have both read *Bridge to Terabithia* and seen the Wonderworks adaptation for the screen can readily understand what a novel can do that a film cannot. "I liked the book better," one boy said to me, "because in the book you knew what Jess was thinking and how he was feeling. In the movie, you just kind of had to guess. You couldn't know for sure."

Soon after I saw the film, I was asked to adapt the book for the stage. I agreed to do so, not because I knew so much about theater or drama, but because I thought I might be able to do a better adaptation than the filmmakers had. I did have enough sense to enlist the help of Stephanie Tolan, who, before she became a writer for young adults, was a poet and playwright. I figured Stephanie could help me understand what would or wouldn't work on the stage. Then I sat down to read the novel with an eye to adapting it. I nearly threw the book across the room. "You can't put that on the stage!" I yelped. "It all takes place inside a little boy's head." I didn't need Stephanie to tell me that *Hamlet*-length soliloquies probably wouldn't work in theater for today's children.

When we began to write, neither Stephanie nor I imagined the play as a musical, but the longer we worked, the more we realized that a character could sing thoughts he could not so readily declaim.

So Jesse sings a song that foreshadows the tragedy to come. The line in the book reads: "Sometimes it seemed to him that his life was delicate as a dandelion. One little puff from any direction, and it was blown to bits."

Steve Liebman's music echoes the sound of raindrops as in a minor key the invisible children inside Jess and Leslie sit on opposite sides of the stage and sing what they're feeling:

First Jess:

> "My life's like a dandelion
> Perfect today,
> But delicate as a dandelion

One puff blows it all away.
I'm king of a secret kingdom
A land built of magic and dreams
I'm king—What on earth could harm me?
Yet, sometimes suddenly it seems,
My life's like a dandelion
Perfect today,
But delicate as a dandelion
One puff blows it all away."

And then Leslie:

"My life's like a dandelion
Wanted or not
All my life long I bloom where I please
Golden and stubborn and strong . . .
I'm queen [she sings, echoing Jess's words]
What on earth could harm me?
Yet sometimes, suddenly it seems . . ."[2]

And from the opposite ends of the stage they both sing once more of the dandelion at the mercy of the breeze. Two children invisible even to each other made visible to the audience through a song.

Although the letter to Janice Avery remains the favorite of young theatergoers, adults and those children made old by pain love the dandelion song the best.

Recently a writer friend forwarded to me a discussion of *Bridge to Terabithia* and *Jacob Have I Loved* that appeared on the Internet in August. More than one of the children's-literature experts engaged in the discussion were deeply troubled by both of these books, declaring, in essence, that the books were depressing and offered no hope. (Of course, I can't give you the direct quotations, not being able to re-trieve old mail beyond a couple of days and not yet having learned to file things I want to keep.)

Joseph Conrad once said that he never read his reviews, he mea-sured them. So, I suppose by the length of the discussion, I should have been cheered, but of course I'm a reader, not a mathematician, so I was properly downcast. I rather pride myself on being a hopeful writer. Of course, I also think I'm a pretty funny writer, but few are they perceptive enough to pick up on that fact.

In my own defense, it seems to me that what these experts are calling "depressing" are what I would call "seeing the invisible child." Jess, when he realizes a bit too late that he might have asked Miss Ed-munds if Leslie could have joined them on the trip to Washington, can't suppress a "secret pleasure at being alone in this small cozy car with Miss Edmunds."[3] Such a thought is not admirable, and because we know the rest of the story, it proves to be tragically ironic, but I maintain that Jess's feelings here are true to childhood, true to human nature. When a death occurs, it is always these secret moments that the griever returns to and wrestles with and feels guilt-ridden over. If we play false in a story about death on such an important detail, then a grieving child will lose an opportunity for comfort that the story might have provided.

I long to ask these critics who find no hope in *Bridge* what would constitute hope for them in this story. Leslie's miraculous resurrection from the dead? Jess waking up *Dallas*-style to find the last twenty pages to have been simply a bad dream? Or a story in which Leslie never dies—which would be a quite different story from the one that, out of the tangled questions of real life, I was trying to tell.

I have just published a book in which the personality of the cen-tral character is so out front that he barely lets you see his invisible self, this despite the fact that *Preacher's Boy* is written in the first person. It is no secret that I do not like to write in first person. I find it limiting, but more than that I find it deceptive. No one can be trusted to give a true, unbiased account of his own life. And, indeed, neither Louise Bradshaw nor Robbie Hewitt can be regarded as wholly reliable narrators.

I remember an angry conversation I had with a librarian years ago about *Jacob Have I Loved*. "And besides," she said, bristling, "I don't even think Caroline is all that bad." "Neither do I," I said. I can't remember where the conversation went from there, but I remember my astonishment at the number of intelligent adults who seemed unable to realize that you can't count on a jealous person to render a fair account of events. I have been astounded at the number of critics who berate the Bradshaws for their favoritism—for loving Caroline more than they love Louise. Pish posh. But Louise is, at least, writing from the viewpoint of an adult, which makes her a more trustworthy witness than the eleven-year-old Robbie, who is still 90 percent bluster and brag. So how do I expect the young reader to see through all this into the hidden, the invisible Robbie? I think those who see themselves in Robbie will not be deceived by the personage. I truly believe my readers will see past the posturing into the heart of a little boy who longs for his father's approval—a child who loves his afflicted brother despite all and who is finally able to accept the grace that Elliot brings to the family.

> I grabbed Elliot's hand. "Can you believe it, Elliot? You and me? We're riding in a genuine motorcar!"
>
> "Is dat good?"
>
> "It's a miracle!" I yelled over the racket of the motor. "A genuine miracle!"
>
> "Wheeee!" cried Elliot. Then he leaned over and kissed my hand.

And do you know? From that very moment I stopped all pretense of being an apeist and signed on as a true believer for all eternity. How could I not? God had worked a personal miracle especially for me.[4]

I almost missed the miracle myself. It's not, as Robbie thinks and then relates—and as even I first thought—it is not the fact that God has sent him a motorcar. No, the real miracle is in that sentence that slips past the braggadocio into the narrative: "Then he leaned over and kissed my hand." It is here in Elliot's gentle act of affection that the healing begins to take place in the invisible Robbie whether he himself knows it or not.

I'm not sure how often I've been told that my characters are "not wholly lovable" or just plain "not likable." It always hurts me to hear it, as it does any mother who is told that her children are obnoxious. Because, you see, I peer deeper into their hearts than a mother ever could. I see the whole invisible child. In a real way, I am that invisible child, and although I must be truthful in my portrayal of these children, it only makes me love them more, not less, to know them as they are.

It is my hope, of course, that children will find these characters to be real children like themselves—that they will be able to see themselves in them and then as they come to love and forgive these people on the page to be able to forgive and love their own deepest selves.

My preacher husband used to have a motto hanging in his study which read: "Love is a hell of a lot of work." Well, it is; there is nothing easy or sentimental about it. It takes a Maime Trotter to do it right. We do well to be suspicious of love that comes too easily. I think of the children, handsome, bright, winsome, so doted on by their parents. But we must be wary, we who are blessed with such children. We must be careful to look at these children, not past them to some goal of our own, to some ego satisfaction we count on them to provide us with.

In the wonderful movie *Searching for Bobby Fischer*, the young chess genius senses that his teacher and even his father have become obsessed with his skills. The father, whom we have known as exceptionally loving and thoughtful, suddenly has become very much like his chess teacher—two adults who don't seem to care what is happening inside of Josh just so long as he keeps winning chess matches.

"So what if I lose?" Josh asks his father the night before a big match.

"You won't lose," his father says.

"I'm scared I might," the boy replies.

"You're the best," his father says. "All those other kids are scared of you."

The father has turned off the light and is about to leave Josh's bedroom when the boy says in the dark: "Maybe it's better not to be the best. Then you can lose and it's okay."

The next day Josh stops the madness the only way he knows how. He loses in the first round.

In the scene following this humiliation father and son are in the pouring-down rain outside the hall. Josh is sitting huddled against the building while his furious father paces up and down. "Seven moves. Seven! How is it possible to lose in seven moves?"

"Maybe I don't really have it," Josh says plaintively.

"That's not true. That's not why this happened. Think!" he demands of the unhappy boy. Did he disobey his teacher's instructions? Did he bring out his queen too soon?

"Maybe he's just better than me," Josh says.

"No, don't tell me that potzer is better than you!"

The camera closes in once more on the child's wet, pain-filled face. "Why are you standing so far away from me?" he asks his father.

His father stops in his tracks and takes a long look at his miserable son. "C'mere," he says. Josh runs to him and throws his arms around his father, burying his face against his clothes. His father strokes his hair. "It's okay," he says to the sobbing child. "It's okay."

And that is what our children want us to do—to look—to look at them as they really are and assure them that it's okay for them to be who they are.

Jip in *Jip, His Story* is different from any of my other characters. In the beginning, he is like any poor farm resident, largely invisible to the rest of the community. On the farm itself, the only time he is visible to the manager and his wife is when he isn't working, which is not very often. Then Put comes into his life and sees him. A little later Teacher, too, sees Jip, and what they see is that rare person whose insides match his outsides—whose visible and invisible selves are all of a piece. When, in the beatitudes, Jesus says "Blessed are the pure in heart," he is talking about people like Jip. Unlike most characters in novels, it is not so much a change in the invisible child that shapes the story but the change in the visible child. Jip finds out that his mother was a slave and that he is therefore considered black, though he has actually more white ancestors than black. He tries to figure out why, even though he looks the same and feels the same, he is not *seen* the same by those he has known.

How was he different from the boy Mrs. Wilkens had trusted, her Lucy to all last winter? She hadn't despised him when he was a waif fallen off a wagon. Now she's set to betray me—like I done her or her children bodily harm, he thought. He wished he could think that Lucy was lying—rather than believe her ma had said such awful things. But he knew the truth of it. In Mrs. Wilkens's sight, he was no longer just Jip but a thing to be despised. His heart was no different, his mind no better or worse. Nothing about who he was or how he looked had altered in the least, but, suddenly, in other people's heads he was a whole different creature.[5]

One thing books can do is help us to see past labels to the person. The reason Hitler demanded that the Jews wear a yellow star was the fear that their Jewishness might not be readily visible. Someone might treat them as human beings if they were not properly labeled. Skin color is so helpful to the bigot who lives in us all. You're not so likely to make a mistake as to how you ought to regard someone if her color makes it obvious how she is to be seen.

I was aware of this when our children were small. We had two homemade, obviously Caucasian, sons, and then these two girls who were, well, hard to figure out. I cannot count the number of times perfect strangers would approach us and ask us to solve the racial puzzle which our family posed. How could they think about us properly if they didn't know what they were looking at? Lin and I were remembering just recently an incident that occurred when she was about eight. I had all four children with me at a retirement home bazaar. Since the two oldest were small for their age and the youngest large, I was shepherding four children of approximately the same size but of different varieties. Despite the fact that at that moment all four were behaving themselves quite nicely, a strange woman approached me, bristling belligerence: "Are all of these yours?" she demanded. "Yes," I said. Whereupon she grabbed Lin, our Chinese daughter, by the chin and tipped her head up. "Oh yes, I can see. She's got your eyes." The five of us could hardly wait to get around a corner to explode into giggles.

This demand, *Tell me what I'm seeing*, is one quite familiar to the writer of books for children. It is not enough, for many adults, to have the writer show the characters—even the invisible soul of the character to the reader. According to some critics, the writer has failed to help the young reader if she does not spell out what the reader is supposed to see. But what the reader, even the young reader, will see is, I maintain, the reader's task and the reader's choice. To paraphrase the Good Book, He that has eyes to see let him see. If the book is good enough, the reader will see more on every reading, more, even, than the writer knows is there.

But the writer must see more than the book. No matter how devoted she is to getting the story right, if she expects to share this story with others, she must also, at some point, become aware of the reader. Usually, the reader is an invisible child. But not always.

Some years ago the state of Vermont realized that the largest percentage of school dropouts was coming from a small segment of the population—the children of the hired help on the state's dairy farms. These dairy workers had been classified as migrant workers according to the U.S. Department of Agriculture because of their frequent moves, which made money available, and the state set about to tackle the problem of the education of these children.

The Vermont Migrant Education Program was established and entrusted with the mission to discover why these young people dropped out of school and what might be done to encourage them to complete their high school education. Because of their frequent moves and their parents' work, most of these children saw school only as a place of ridicule and failure—to be fled from as soon as possible. Tutoring programs and special health and counseling services were put in place. And then those in charge had another idea. Why not ask Vermont authors and illustrators to produce books in which these children could see themselves? The books would be introduced to the children in the summer program and then placed in their school libraries. The dairy farm children would have already read the books in which children like themselves were featured. This, reasoned the leaders, would give them a special status in school that they had not before enjoyed.

Now I have never been one to believe that you should write books to address problems—or even a narrow audience. It has been my experience that the book you think is perfect to help a particular kind of child with a special problem is not the book the actual child would choose at all. But when I was asked "as a Vermont writer" to contribute to the program, I'd only lived in the state a few weeks and I was so flattered to be called "a Vermont writer" that I joyfully accepted the challenge.

Those in charge of the program knew better than to leave me to my own imaginative devices. They made me put on rubber boots and go to working dairy farms in several parts of the state, talk to the dairy workers, visit in their homes, meet and talk with the actual children, go to their schools and observe. Finally, out of the muck of the dairy barn, the coziness of the trailer homes, and the buzz of the classroom, Marvin and the smallest cow in the world emerged. I had one great advantage over most of the other writers—they may have known Vermont better than I, but I knew how it felt to move and move and move.

I was thrilled that the dairy farm children loved Marvin, but children who have never seen a dairy farm love Marvin, too. I think the secret is that those in the Vermont Migrant Education Project required me to do my homework. I was forced to look very closely at the children they served. Children who would otherwise have been literally invisible to me became visible in body and, to some extent, in spirit as well.

Even though I pride myself on not writing sequels, I seem to be hanging on to Marvin for dear life. I've just finished a third Marvin book—which I hope HarperCollins will let me continue to call *Marvin One Too Many*. It wouldn't take a genius to figure out that it deals with Marvin's invisibility at a new school—a painful condition that many of us remember all too well.

In the Marvin books I've found myself doing something that I really haven't approved of a writer doing—trying to write a book for a particular audience. Marvin aside, when I am asked, as I often am, "Who are your books for?" I have trouble not being flip. "I write for myself and then go look in the catalog to see how old I am," is one answer. "Anyone who wants to read them," is another. "The child within myself," is a third, not too disgraceful, answer. But the truth is I don't want a child, visible or otherwise, sitting in my study looking over my shoulder.

A middle schooler called me last spring and asked if she could shadow me on career day. "Does that mean you would come to my house and watch me while I write?" Yes, that was what she meant. "I don't think it would work," I said. "In the first place it would be incredibly boring for you to sit and watch me write, and in the second place I couldn't write if someone was watching me." Christa thanked me politely and went and found a more likely candidate for shadowing.

I was once asked to submit a short story to an anthology and fully intended to do so until I discovered, to my horror, that my story would be submitted to high school students for editing. I immediately withdrew my story. Apparently I was the only writer who raised any objection, and the compiler was puzzled and unhappy with my attitude. I had a similar, more public reaction later. A teacher asked me in a question-and-answer session if I had ever considered having a child design one of my book jackets. Three hundred people heard me gasp and recover myself enough to utter the one-word reply: "Never." I tried to go on and explain myself on the basis of the professionalism which a jacket demands and that a nationwide contest, which was what she was plugging for, might indeed encourage one child, but it would make hundreds of children see themselves as losers. I'm afraid, however, that my justifications fell on deaf ears. I sensed what had been up until then a sympathetic audience was fast concluding that Katherine Paterson for all her reputation as a children's writer did not want to be bothered with actual children. This is only confirmed when I have to confess that, no, I don't try out my books on real children—the occasional exception being children whose last names are Paterson or whose mother's name was once Paterson. But I wouldn't let my own children even know what I was writing about until I had a draft with which I was reasonably comfortable.

So you may want to label me a hypocrite when I maintain that the child reader must be visible to the writer who calls herself a children's writer. I do not mean that we should set out to find what the majority of American children fancy and tailor our stories to pander to current fads. That wouldn't work. A book takes too long in the making. You'd be several fads out of fashion before you got the book into stores, much less into libraries and into children's hands. Nor do I believe I could, even if I should, consciously write a book for a child with a seven-minute attention span. Books are not TV or, heaven help us, MTV or the Internet. I suppose it would be possible to write a book whose plot jumped around like a frog on pep pills, but that's not what books are about. If that's the kind of writing you want to do, I think you should be in a more hectic medium. Books are meant to be read slowly and digested. These days people don't pray much or go to services of worship, they don't commune with nature—why, they hardly go to a national park without a TV set, a laptop, and a cell phone. The book is almost the last refuge of reflection—the final outpost of wisdom. I want children to have the gifts that books can give, and I don't believe they can get them from a book that attempts to imitate the frantic fragmentation of contemporary life.

Let us pause here to pay tribute to Harry Potter. This is a children's book for whose author children are truly visible. What's more, she has somehow seen straight into the heart of the eleven-year-old non-reading male and given him what he always wanted and never knew—until he met Harry—that he did. He thought, our young non-reader, that he hated books. He thought that books were boring. When you could access the world in nanoseconds, when you could engage nightly in virtual life-or-death struggles, killing and being killed, why would you sit quietly for hours and turn the page? Well, you wouldn't, unless what you found there was better than the alternatives, and our eleven-year-old found Harry Potter more fun, more exciting, more suspenseful than all the alternatives open to him. He also, being computer literate, knew he could order the second and third volumes from England before they were published in this country and be the envy of his neighbors no matter what their gender or age.

So here's to you, Harry Potter! You've taught that boy who was slipping away from the rest of us the delight of the printed page. Long may you wave your wand!

When the rest of us who write for children can tear ourselves away from the market envy we experience when we check your position on *The New York Times* best-seller list, and the prestige envy we feel when we see the review of your third volume has been given a full page among the grown-up books and not confined to a few inches in the ghetto of the monthly children's section, when we can turn, I say, from our not inconsiderable envy of you, what are we to learn from you that will make us better writers for the young?

Perhaps we can't hope to imitate your playful creativity, your inventive plots, your delightful characters, your charming language, but I think we can learn to look once more at the invisible children for whom we say we are writing. And sadly, many of those children are quite different from my eleven-year-old next-door neighbor who loaned me his volumes two and three hot off the airplane. We have to see them as well.

The morning I was working on this part of the speech I heard a commentary from a Vermont writer who worked as a volunteer in a program for children that her local school had decided were children at risk. She said that studies had revealed that school victims and school bullies, both of whom are regarded as children at risk, share many of the same characteristics—headaches, sleeplessness, feelings of sadness—in short, the classic signs of depression. As many bullies admitted to suicidal thoughts as victims, and most of the bullies were known to have been victimized at school, but more often at home.

The commentator told about the program she took part in. All except one of the children in her particular group had been identified as victims. But the one girl labeled as a bully didn't seem so different from the victims. All the children wanted the volunteers to like them. Sometimes they would confide family secrets. One of the children who on the surface seemed quite cheerful and well-adjusted told the commentator that she had been warned that her baby brother would suffer the consequences if she revealed to anyone what went on at home.

The volunteers were never told anything about the children; even their last names were kept confidential. When the program was over they were ordered not to try to contact any of the children, and there was no realistic way they could do so. However, one day, several months later, the volunteer had gone to a lake with her family and to her surprise spotted the one girl labeled a bully playing volleyball on the beach. "I was thrilled to see her," she said, "and she apparently was glad to see me. She left the game and came running over to say hello. 'How are things going?' I asked her. The girl shrugged and then, still smiling at me, ran to rejoin her game."

The commentator mused on her feelings of helplessness, her frustration at not being able to rescue any of these children of abuse. "But," she said, referring to the program of which she had been a part, "if we cannot defeat despair—sometimes we can interrupt it."

There are so many of these children and young people, invisible to most of us until they erupt into acts of destruction against others or, more often, against themselves. When I really look at these children I have to ask myself, is it possible to write a book for them that might interrupt despair?

In the last few years there have been a lot of books about such children. Indeed as chair of the National Book Award jury for Young People's Literature in 1998, I began to wonder if there was a good writer in our country who *wasn't* writing a book about an abused child. We the jurors began to long for a story in which the mother was caring and the father was something less than a monster. And as much as I admired the artistry of a number of these books, I am not sure I would have given them to an actual abused child already surfeited on despair.

But should a writer be dishonest? Should a writer administer hope like a dose of Prozac? Surely not. Then what are we to do?

After the Columbine tragedy I happened to hear a National Public Radio interview with the writer Stephen King. King, it seems, had written a book several years ago in which a disaffected high school student takes a gun into his school and begins shooting. After one of the school tragedies in 1998, this book had been found among the possessions of the young killer.

The interviewer asked that hackneyed question: "How did you feel, Mr. King?" To which Stephen King replied: "I immediately called the publisher and had every unsold copy of the book recalled from bookstores and destroyed."

I was torn between amazement and admiration at such a response. But I'm still not sure if I agree. The truth is, we have no way of knowing what will trigger a violent reaction in a sick mind. On the basis that some part of the text might lead a sick mind into tragic behavior, every unsold copy of the Bible should be recalled and destroyed. So what kind of responsibility do we have—what limits should we place on ourselves—we who seek to write for the young?

When I was in Australia last year, I got into a chance lunch-table conversation about contemporary, realistic fiction. Most of the people at the table were teachers or librarians, concerned about the spate of new Australian books, which seemed terribly depressing to them. Should children whose lives are bleak anyhow be subjected to such books? they asked the two social workers who happened to be sitting with us. The social workers talked soberly about their clients, and then one of them turned to me and said: "Our kids love *Gilly Hopkins*." "But I don't understand that," I said. "You've just been telling me about the horrendous problems of sexual abuse the children you work with have to deal with. Why should they like Gilly? She's never even been physically abused. By *their* standards of experience her life must seem totally unrealistic."

"Yes," the woman answered, "her life is a lot easier than theirs, but they recognize the kinship. Isn't it," she said thoughtfully, "something like the essence from which you make perfume? All you need is a drop or two to get the aroma. You wouldn't want to put in too much."

I think back on that conversation a lot, and I think that social worker is right. If we want to interrupt the despair rather than add to it, we can't fake the essence, we need the real stuff, but we must use it sparingly. A drop or two goes a long way. As Emily Dickinson instructs us:

> Tell all the Truth but tell it slant—
> Success in Circuit lies
> Too bright for our infirm Delight

The Truth's superb surprise
As Lightning to the Children eased
With explanation kind
The Truth must dazzle gradually
Or every man be blind—

Above all, it seems to me, if we are to write for children, we must forget our fame, our skill, our cleverness, even our personal catalog of pain and grief and become once more in our heart of hearts invisible children reaching out to the rest of the invisible people in our world.

In Han Nolan's *Dancing on the Edge*, a girl named Miracle is given in the hospital a copy of Emily Dickinson's poems. One night she finds one that goes like this:

I'm Nobody! Who are you?
Are you—Nobody—Too?
Then there's a pair of us!
Don't tell! they'd advertise—you know!

How dreary—to be—Somebody!
How public—like a Frog—
To tell one's name—the livelong June—
To an admiring Bog!

Miracle says: "I read the first lines again: 'I'm Nobody! Who are you? Are you—Nobody—Too? Then there's a pair of us! Don't tell! they'd advertise—you know!'

"I tossed the book down and cried out. I didn't know if it was in shock, or pain, or joy, or fear. I just cried out. For the first time in my life I had recognized my reflection."[6]

A few weeks ago I was invited to talk about *Preacher's Boy*. In response to a question, I spoke about Robbie's tangled attitude toward his brother, Elliot. How could his parents love Elliot so much? He, Robbie, was bright, funny, handsome, everything a parent could wish for. Shouldn't they love him more than they loved his damaged brother? Wasn't he more worthy of their love?

Later, when no one else could hear her, a lovely, articulate fifth-grade girl spoke to me. "You know what you said about Robbie and Elliot? My brother is autistic. I know just how Robbie feels."

So although, like other writers who live in the small pond of children's literature, I sometimes catch myself in the role of the self-important Frog who sings out his own name to the admiring Bog, that is not what I want to be—and those are not the books I want to write. The book I always hope to write is like a secret one Nobody whispers to another Nobody—one invisible child passing along to another invisible child the gift of sight.

Missing Persons

Namaste [Greetings]. There are many people that I want to thank tonight. First of all, our Indian hosts for all their hard work and gracious hospitality which has made this congress possible. Thanks, too, to Carmen Diana Dearden and IBBY [International Board on Books for Young People], especially Leena Maissen and her helpful and capable staff. Thank you, Rudine Sims Bishop and USBBY [United States Board on Books for Young People], especially Barbara Barstow and the members of her committee, for once again nominating me for the Andersen Award. I must also thank my publishers, Clarion, represented here by Nina Ignatowicz, and also HarperCollins and Penguin Putnam for making it possible for my husband, John, to be here in New Delhi with me. I am very grateful for that, as he has been an important person both in my life and in my work. And, of course, to Peter Schneck and the Andersen jury, who made it possible for me to be here.

I hope you are half as glad to be here tonight as I am. Can you imagine how thrilling and how overwhelming it is for me to stand here in New Delhi to be told by you who know what literature is and who care deeply for children that I have written books that will truly matter to children around the world? There is no way I can express my gratitude for this, the greatest honor of my life. As I told Leena Maissen and Peter Schneck, when I received the news, I broke into tears of joy.

But tonight that joy cannot be complete because there are people missing from this room who I wish were here: Tomi Ungerer, with whom I share this wonderful award. Virginia Buckley, my editor of nearly twenty-eight years, who was planning to be here but whose health did not permit it. And Dorothy Briley, who served IBBY and USBBY over the years and who had lately become my American publisher. It was Dorothy who gave me the news in April that I had been chosen for this wonderful award. As you probably know, Dorothy died very suddenly in May. We cannot measure the loss either to children's publishing in America or to the world of children's books. I would like to tell you, though, that a lectureship has been established in her honor. The Dorothy Briley Lecture will be presented every two years at the U.S. regional IBBY Conference by a writer or illustrator from another country. It seems a very appropriate honor.

Ever since Dorothy's phone call in April, I have been receiving congratulations—and also questions. The most worrisome one was: Have you written your speech yet? Oh, no, I answered. I'm working on a book. As soon as I finish it, I will think about the speech. Then finally, at the end of August, I had to face two facts. First, the book was still not finished. Second, I would have to put it aside and start on the speech.

I do not think of myself as a procrastinator, but why did I think that before I could begin to work on such an important speech I must first rearrange my bookshelves? The picture books, in particular, were overflowing the bookcase and piling up on top of the case and onto the floor.

In Vermont at this time of year many people have yard sales where they sell all their junk and discarded furniture to their neighbors who, in turn, have a sale the following week and sell all their junk and old furniture. I went to a yard sale around the corner and bought an old bookcase for the picture books. When I got the bookcase home, I found that the shelves weren't tall enough for most of the picture books, so I had to decide which of my other books should be moved to the newly purchased bookcase in order to make room in the tall shelves of the built-in bookcase in the living room for the picture books. It was rather like rearranging an elephant.

Anyhow, in the course of all this activity, which was serving its main purpose of preventing me from worrying about what I should say tonight, I came across a very worn book. Its cover was torn and its spine was broken. It obviously dated back to the days when our four children were small. As I opened it, I found that the poor book had been bound upside down. In those days we had more children than we had money, so I suppose I was able to buy this upside-down book very cheaply. But I could tell from the way it was nearly worn to pieces that it was a much-loved book despite the faulty binding. I turned it upside down and around to find the title page. There, staring out at me, was a large green octopus, two of its eight arms folded across its chest in a very self-satisfied manner, the other six trailing casually behind. The upside-down, well-worn, much-loved book was, of course, *Emile*, by Tomi Ungerer.

I sat right down on the floor and read *Emile* from beginning to end. (My mother used to say that no one who is literate should ever try to clean house.) It is no wonder that my children loved Emile. Emile is a charmer—a talented musician, a marvelous swimmer, an amusing contortionist, a selfless and resourceful hero with eight arms besides. Alas, I thought, I am none of those things. When I had four children under the age of six, I often wished for eight arms, but I have always been very ordinary and very human.

Perhaps this is why I write the kinds of books I do. As a child I was fearful, untalented, awkward, and anything but a hero. When I became a writer, I wanted to write books for children like me who were often discouraged and afraid—who needed encouragement and hope. I was born in China, one of five children. My older brother and sister were friends, and my younger sisters had each other to play and quarrel with. And there I was, stranded in the middle. Because of World War II, by the time I was eight, we had twice fled as refugees and finally settled in America, which was the land my parents called home, but a place where I was an alien, with cast-off clothes and a strange way of speaking. There were plenty of bullies in my early years in the United States but no friends—except the friends I found in books.

Eventually I became less strange to my classmates and was able to make friends off the printed page, but by the time I had to move again (I moved more than fifteen times before I was eighteen), I had learned that books can give you friendships that your own life, limited as it is by time and space, is too narrow to provide.

When I was about eleven, I read a book called *Struggle Is Our Brother*. It was the story of Russian children in Stalingrad facing the Nazi destruction of their city. As I shared the struggles of those Russian children, I became their sister in the struggle. And when, a few short years later, I was told that I must hate and fear the Soviet Union, I could not, because *Struggle Is Our Brother* had given me friends in the Soviet Union—friends that I cared about and could not bear to see harmed.

When I became a writer, I began by writing about Japanese young people. As a child in China, I considered the Japanese my enemies.

But I grew up and I lived for four years in Japan and made friends there that I will love until I die. I wanted to give American children friends in Japan—friends in another time and place that they would care about—a sort of shield against propagandist lies and cultural and racial prejudice. Now it is my hope that I can give your children American friends who will cause them to question the image of my country that Hollywood presents or nationalistic bias might construe.

When I look at the library shelves in America, I am acutely aware that so many American children's books are published that we often fail to realize our need for books from other countries—that we *must* give our children friends in Iran and Korea and South Africa and Serbia and Colombia and Chile and Iraq and, indeed, in every country. For, when you have friends in another country, you cannot wish their nation harm.

Rabindranath Tagore, the great Indian poet and winner of the 1913 Nobel Prize, has written:

> Where the mind is without fear
> and the head is held high;
> Where knowledge is free;
> Where the world has not been broken up into fragments by
> narrow domestic walls;
> Where words come from the depth of truth;
> Where tireless striving stretches its arms toward perfection; . . .
> Into that heaven of freedom, my Father,
> let my country awake.[1]

Let all our countries awake.

I began tonight speaking of the people who are missing from this room. The most important people who are missing are the children to whom you and I have devoted our lives. Years ago when I was asked why I wrote for children, I gave a flip answer: "I don't write for children," I said. "I write for myself, and then I go to the publisher's catalog to see how old I am."

But I don't write just for myself, I do write for children. I should never be flip about that. I owe children respect. Neither can I be sentimental about children. The only people who can be sentimental about children are the people who don't know any. Those of us who are parents or teachers or librarians living and working day in and day out with children know that they can be infuriating as well as delightful, malevolent as well as innocent, cowardly as well as heroic, depressed as well as joyful. They are, in short, human with all the glory and the anguish the word implies. But they are humans with less experience and a narrower perspective than we have. They are, therefore, more vulnerable to injury and, to a heartening extent, more resilient and more teachable than we who are older. But to write for them is an enormous responsibility, and the writer for children must never be allowed to forget this fact.

A few weeks ago I received a letter from a man who for many years was a child-care worker in a hospital for emotionally disturbed children. Tim Smith told me about an experience he had reading aloud my book *Bridge to Terabithia* to one of his patients. When he got to the chapter in the book where Leslie Burke dies, the boy began to cry. Mr. Smith was surprised. Until that time Jimmy had either refused to acknowledge his feelings or would project them onto someone else. Mr. Smith stopped reading the book, not wanting to distress his young patient further, but Jimmy insisted that he go on. "That night," Mr. Smith wrote, "we finished the book together, both of us sitting up on his bed with our backs against the wall, our feet dangling off the edge of the mattress, and tears welling up in our eyes." What Mr. Smith had not known before that night was that Jimmy had also lost a close friend in an accident and had never been able to deal with his loss.

As they talked about the story, Jimmy decided that it must be a wonderful thing to be an author and be able to put your feelings into books. He was not yet able to write well himself, so he began to dictate stories to Mr. Smith, who would write them out. Jimmy illustrated each story, gave it a title, and signed his name. Mr. Smith would then give each book an imaginary ISBN number, and Jimmy would insist that the publisher be Thomas Y. Crowell—the original publisher of *Bridge to Terabithia*. Jimmy remained in the hospital for a year, but from that time on, his therapist and his parents read Jimmy's books and could know from them the turmoil he had not been able to express before.

The Jimmys of the world, the needy and broken children among us, may be missing from this room tonight, but they must never be shut out of my room when I am working. No matter how lost I become in the story I am telling, before I am through I must remember that I write for these children—so I must do so with honesty, respect, and compassion. At this conference we will seek to understand how children's books may serve to make peace among nations, but books can also help to make peace within a child's troubled heart. We must be brave enough to give children books that have the power to heal.

In the Andersen Award you have given me a great honor, but you have also placed upon me a tremendous trust. I want to promise the members of the jury who chose me and you who represent the world of children's books that I will spend the rest of my life seeking to live up to the trust you have placed on me tonight.

An old Chinese philosopher, when asked what had been his greatest joy in life, replied: "A child going down the road singing after asking me the way."

Confusion at the Crossroads

Anne Carroll Moore, who served as the Superintendent of Work with Children at the New York Public Library from 1906 to 1941, was arguably the most influential voice in children's books during the first half of the twentieth century.

Back when I was a more self-confident—read *pompous*—person than I am today (which takes us back nearly fifty years), I wrote a poem that began like this:

> I am youth, standing at the crossroads of eternity.
> Which path shall I take?

You'll be relieved to know that I cannot remember another word of this poem, and that in the many moves I've made since 1949, it has been safely lost and will, I profoundly hope, never turn up to torture posterity.

Indeed, I really hadn't thought of "Youth at the Crossroads," as I think that poem was called, for many years—one does indeed try to block out the fact that as a writer one seemed to have shown so little in the way of early promise—but in trying to think of what to say today in a lecture to honor Anne Carroll Moore, the image of roads seems inevitable, and thus emerged the ghost of my early work.

Grace Greene loaned me the Vermont State Library's copy of Miss Moore's autobiographical *My Roads to Childhood*, which I found, as I was beginning to write this speech, to be a first edition. On the half-title page, an elegant hand has added a message under the title. "*My Roads to Childhood*," Miss Moore has written, "lead to the heart of Vermont. With the best of good wishes and happy memories of July 11–12–15, 1940. Anne Carroll Moore, Burlington."

Now I'm not a person who routinely prizes either first editions or autographed copies—I have too realistic a notion of what my own are worth—but there was something about having those words in Anne Carroll Moore's own handwriting sitting next to me as I wrote this speech that I found surprisingly cheering. Surprising, because, of course, I quake to think what her critical voice would have done to my books. Would any of them have ever made the sacred Christmas list? Would they have been hailed like *When We Were Very Young* and *Skunny Wundy*? Or lamented like *Stuart Little* and damned with an eyedropper of praise like *Charlotte's Web*? I have a funny feeling that E. B. White (with Ursula Nordstrom at his elbow) was in a better position to withstand Miss Moore's withering gaze than I, but, of course, if my titles included *Stuart Little* and *Charlotte's Web*, I might feel less threatened myself.

It is easy to caricature a woman who was less than enthusiastic about *Charlotte's Web*, the book that is perhaps the most loved of our century—a woman who invested a doll with almost human significance. But that is to miss a woman who from childhood on was racing down the road far ahead of most of her contemporaries.

In *My Roads to Childhood* she quotes a letter from her father, sent to her when she was at boarding school, so she must have been just a little older than I was when I wrote that dreadful poem cited a minute ago. "This life," Mr. Moore said to his young daughter, "is a great mystery. It is a great thing to live at all and more to live well. It's a puzzle to know what to do, what to fit yourself for but whatever it may be you must put your heart as well as your mind into it. I want you to have the best we can give you, but you and not we, must determine what is best for your *own* time."[1]

"It was," Miss Moore concludes, "a generous and an understanding letter for a girl of the 1890s to receive." Indeed.

Luther Moore died just a year after his daughter graduated from Bradford Academy, so her first great crisis at the crossroads occurred when she, no longer able to study law with her wise and beloved father, had to decide which road would be best for her own time. We can only be grateful that she chose to give her heart and mind to bringing books, the best she could find, to the children of New York City and thus to children of the whole country.

I think of the strong personalities and great minds that have so shaped our understanding—who came to us through the New York Public Library system and Anne Carroll Moore—among them Margaret McElderry, Augusta Baker, Frances Clarke Sayers, Ethel Heins—grateful that Margaret is still such a force among us and wishing that all these women were standing with us today as we confront our current crisis at the crossroads.

It isn't as though we were simply standing at the crossroads wondering what path we should take. It is more like we've been grabbed by the ear and dragged down a road we had never meant to travel.

Early this month I was visiting with a friend of mine who is a school librarian. She works in one of Vermont's wealthiest towns— but a town that does not feel it can afford to hire a full-time librarian in the elementary school, so Anne works there four days a week, and one day a week she works in a tiny town nearby. Actually, Anne says, the needs in both towns are the same, but the hungers are different. Over the summer the school board in town number one panicked over a perceived crisis in costs. They didn't touch the Internet budget, but they froze the book budget, so Anne hasn't been able to buy a single new book since June. This is what happens when citizens consider the Internet a necessity for the education of their children and books a frill.

On Fridays, Anne goes to the tiny school whose library is missing such basics as *Goodnight Moon* and *The Three Billy Goats Gruff.* But they are trying hard to do better. Someone recently gave the library a memorial donation of $1,000, designated for books. Anne rushed to Burlington to the huge Barnes & Noble to spend this largess. And came away deeply discouraged. The largest bookstore in the area had so few of the truly basic books she felt the tiny library must own that she was able to spend only a fraction of the gift. "It was nearly all pop junk," she said. "I couldn't spend the money on junk." This is what happens when people in charge of children's publishing and marketing do not respect the hearts and minds of children and regard children's books as perishable products to be sold quickly while fresh and at the end of the season to be relegated to the dumpster in order to clear the shelves for next season's fresh produce.

Earlier this month I was asked to address the topic "What Is Literature for, Anyway?" The fact that we ask the question means that we've moved from the Golden Age of Children's Literature into the Age of Confusion. And the Confusion makes it hard to withstand the gale winds of technology and merchandising, which are rapidly blowing us in directions we are going to have difficulty returning from.

But as mired as we are in the confusion of our own age (and I supposed the confusion of metaphors in these last two paragraphs are indicative of my confusion), I think it well behooves us to realize that we are not the first generation to fear the changes that seem to engulf us. Plato, lest we forget, argued in the Dialogues that if people learned to read and write, poetry would disappear, for it was only in the oral tradition that poetry could be preserved properly.

I was made aware of this earlier crisis at the crossroads in 1995 when John and I went to the island nation of Fiji to be part of a conference of Southeast Asian teachers. I worried excessively about the speech I was supposed to give. But when I'd mention my anxiety to others, they'd pooh-pooh it. But you don't understand, I'd say, these teachers don't even have pencils and paper for their classrooms, much less books. What can I say to them? Just tell stories, someone said. But all my stories are about books, I'd say. Mostly my own books, which there was very little possibility these teachers had ever seen.

It didn't help that the first major speaker was a Fijian professor at the University of the South Pacific who spoke on the dangers of literacy. Quoting Plato's Socrates, he argued eloquently that the rise of reading was destroying poetry and the oral tradition from which it arose. Once people began to read, he said, they could no longer keep in memory the poetry, the stories, the wisdom of their tradition.

Of course the fallacy in his argument lay in the fact that if he himself had been unable to read, he could not have made the argument from Plato.

But nevertheless I was not comforted. What were these several hundred people in their beautiful sarongs and wise brown faces going to make of a speech by a pale American who had spent much of her early life, nose to page, and much of her later life, fingers to keyboard?

Fortunately, my speech came late in the week when I had gotten to know many of the folks in the audience. I had gone every noon to the storytelling sessions and sat, entranced as a child, listening to stories from island nations whose exotic names I had never heard before. I saw homemade books made out of old newspapers covered with white paint so text and pictures could be painted boldly on the newsprint in a size that fifty children in a village school could read along.

As I spoke to these teachers from whom I'd already learned so much, telling them, as I had to, stories about books they had never heard of, I felt something I could not describe—a powerful sensation from the audience that pulled from me what I knew was one of, or maybe, the best speech I had ever made. I couldn't understand what was happening, but I sat down afterward, nearly overwhelmed. My husband had felt it, too. We just looked at each other with dazed expressions on our faces.

Later we tried to analyze what had occurred, and this is what we decided. I had never spoken to an audience before who, having grown up in the oral tradition, truly knew how to listen. The thing that was happening in that open-air auditorium that day was *listening*. The listening was so focused, so powerful that it was palpable.

When Western civilization made the decision to set down in writing the treasures of literature and the scientific imagination, something precious was lost that, as a people, we will never in all probability retrieve—the power of corporate memory, and, perhaps more importantly, the ability to truly listen to the spoken word.

But in the public libraries of this country something of this valuable aspect of preliterate civilization has been preserved. For Anne Carroll Moore, storytelling was a vital element of services to children almost from the beginning of her tenure here. I have heard Ethel Heins describe her fear and trembling at being asked to demonstrate for Miss Moore her storytelling skills, for no one could become a steward in ACM's kingdom unless she or he was a good storyteller. As we know, Ethel passed the test and went on to become one of the best.

I take great hope in the resurgence of storytelling in our country. There is obviously a hunger today among people, young and old, to listen to the well-told tale. Plato would be pleased.

There was another crisis several millennia later. This was the crisis that occurred in Western civilization when the printing press was invented and came into popular use. On the final Sunday of October every year, we Protestants are reminded of this crisis. On October 31, Martin Luther, an unknown professor of theology, nailed on the door of the Wittenberg Cathedral a list of ninety-five objections to the prevailing practices of the Roman Catholic Church. Now this whole matter might have been quickly hushed up—except for the printing press. Within weeks, copies of the ninety-five theses of Luther had spread all over the nation. The printing press also made it possible for the Bible, which heretofore had belonged in gloriously illuminated hand-copied editions in church or monastery, to infiltrate even the humblest of homes. And those printing presses weren't just printing Bibles and religious theses, they were printing the classics of Greek and Rome. Wouldn't Plato have had mixed feelings about that?

And of course trouble ensued. Not only the Protestant Reformation and the splintering of Christendom but the questioning of the whole social order. For wherever people can read freely and widely, they begin to think and question, and there is nothing the established order dreads more than a thinking, questioning populace.

Erasmus, an orphan boy, took the only path out of poverty open to him, becoming a priest. But secretly he read those forgotten classics. "A heathen wrote this to a heathen," he marveled when he read the Dialogues of Socrates as written by Plato, "yet it has justice, sanctity, and truth. I can hardly refrain from saying, 'St. Socrates, pray for me.' "[2] And so the enlightenment was born.

In his wonderful book about books, The Gutenberg Elegies, Sven Birkerts reminds us that with the advent of the printing press and the consequent proliferation of books and reading material, the nature of reading itself changed. Just as poetry changed radically when it was no longer primarily memorized and declaimed, so there was a sea change in the act of reading itself. In the Middle Ages and until about the middle of the eighteenth century, very few people owned books at all, and the average book owner had very few books—a Bible, a devotional tract or two, perhaps an almanac—all of which were read over and over again. So the act of reading was necessarily intensive. But by the early nineteenth century those people who could read were, by and large, reading extensively. In addition to books, all kinds of journals and newspapers were available, so the reader read a page or an item only once, racing to get to the next bit of reading material.

In our day, adults who read generally read this way, although today's pace in relation to the pace of the past century is like that of a fast-forwarded cartoon to a painting on the wall of a cave. There is so much more paper coming into our houses and places of business these days that to glimpse at a page of print is to read.

And this is where we who write for children still have the advantage. For the child who reads today seems still willing to take the time to give a book, in Robert Louis Stevenson's felicitous phrase, "a just and patient hearing." I increasingly feel a sense of pity toward my fellow writers who spend their lives writing for the speeded-up audience of adults. They look at me, I realize, with a patronizing air, I who write only for the young. But I don't know any of them who have readers who will read their novels over and over again, who will create their own Terabithias to play out endless repetitions of beloved passages.

These are readers who tell the writer things about her story that she didn't know herself until the intensive reader reveals them to her. A fifth-grade boy asked me once in a school visit, "Did you name Jesse Aarons after Jesse Owens?" Of course I had—a young boy who wants to be the fastest runner in the fifth grade has a name that sounds almost exactly like that of one of the greatest runners of all time. Of course I had named my Jesse after the great one, but I didn't know it until an African-American child who was also an intensive reader asked me that question.

Many parents and other adults seem to have forgotten that chil-

dren who read are by and large still like the intensive readers of another century. "Oh, I know he likes that book, but why buy it for him?
He's already read it," they say in the bookstore.

When we had four young children and very little money, I chose
books for them by the number of times they had checked a book
out of the library to reread it. On about the sixth reading, I acknowledged the child's need to own the book and went out and plunked
down some of our scarce family budget for a copy the child could
keep always.

I have not mentioned the adults among us, those babies bottle-fed
on the electronic tube, who scarcely read at all. One story will suffice.
It comes from a book about the making of the BBC television adaptation of *Pride and Prejudice*.

I was telephoned [one of the producers writes] by a potential backer . . . The call went like this:

"We're very interested in putting £1 million into *Pride and
Prejudice*. Can you tell me who's written it?"

Assuming that, if they were prepared to invest so much
money, they would have already read the book and just
wanted to know who had adapted it, I said: "Andrew Davies,"
and then added as an afterthought "from the novel."

"Novel? What novel?"

"Er . . . the novel. By Jane Austen."

"How are you spelling that?"

"A.U.S.T.E.N."

"Is she selling well?"

"Er . . . yes. Very well."

"How many copies has she sold?"

"You mean altogether?"

"Yeah. Since publication."

"Since . . . er . . . 1813?"

There was a long pause. "You mean she's dead?" (Another pause) "So she wouldn't be available for book signings?"[3]

The communications revolution, which began with the printing press, has speeded up to the extent that once more we have a crisis at the crossroads. Sven Birkerts, who is my authority in these matters, says that the great danger in this particular crisis is that most people are oblivious to it. You mention your concern with what television, video, computers, the Internet, the World Wide Web is doing to our society and you are dismissed as a Luddite.

By the way, you know what a stupid person is, don't you? Someone who doesn't know today what you found out yesterday. Well, what I found out almost yesterday was where the term *Luddite* originated. My *American Heritage Dictionary* defines a Luddite as "any of a group of British workmen who, between 1811 and 1816, rioted and destroyed laborsaving textile machinery in the belief that such machinery would diminish employment. [After Ned *Ludd*, a legendary leader]."

Naturally, I wanted to know more. I happen to own two encyclopedias on CD-ROM. I consulted the first. It had one sentence about the Luddites, no mention of our man Ned, and no bibliography. The second only mentioned the Luddites in passing in a long article devoted to the Unabomber in which some historian had compared the Unabomber's manifesto with the ideas of the Luddites.

Not fair, thought I. One must tap into the vast riches of the World Wide Web. So I typed in "Ned Ludd" and got a choice of 10,000-plus entries, among them notice about the opera of the same name in a distant city, an opportunity to take a "terrible hippy Luddite test" (which I declined), a Spanish-language site offering information as best I could make out on Quixote of la Mancha, and, more promising, that familiar one-sentence description of the nineteenth-century Luddites. I checked the "more like this" button and was offered the chance to read about the new Luddite Society and several opportunities to check out "Is It O.K. to Be a Luddite?" by Thomas Pynchon.

There may have been a way to get the information I sought, but being something of a Luddite, I gave up after many minutes of this, went down to the den, and fetched up volume 14 of my thirty-five-year-old *Encyclopaedia Britannica*. The *Britannica* devotes almost seven inches to the Luddites, explains about the legendary Ned, and includes an annotated bibliography for those who hunger for more. So you see what will happen if I get rid of my *Britannica* and rely on my computer. And, more ominously, what is happening in our school libraries, which nationwide as of this year are spending more of their limited budgets on technology than books.

As I have said before, and this recent experience seemed to prove to me, the Internet is as wide as the ocean and about one inch deep. A wise man told us long ago:

> A little learning is a dangerous thing;
> Drink deep, or taste not the Pierian spring:
> There shallow draughts intoxicate the brain,
> And drinking largely sobers us again.[4]

The Pierian spring, incidentally, for those of you whose memory of mythology, not to mention Pope, is as faulty as mine, is the Macedonian spring from which the muses drank—in other words, the source of inspiration for the arts and sciences of ancient days.

There is a powerful essay in the September issue of *Harper's Magazine* by Earl Shorris entitled "Liberal Education as a Weapon in the Hands of the Restless Poor."

Mr. Shorris set out a few years ago to write a book about poverty in America and ended up writing quite a different book than he had intended. "The poor themselves," he writes in explanation, "led me in directions I could not have imagined, especially the one that came out of a conversation in a maximum-security prison for women. . . ." In the prison Shorris met an African-American woman called Niecie who was a high school dropout but who had, in her years of incarceration, not only finished high school but begun college. Her special love was philosophy.

When Shorris asked a group of women in the prison, "Why do you think people are poor?" the conversation centered around the abuse of women until Niecie, with something of a sneer on her face, broke in: "You got to begin with the children," she said. "You've got to teach the moral life of downtown to the children. And the way you do that, Earl, is by taking them downtown to plays, museums, concerts, lectures, where they can learn the moral life of downtown."[5]

At first Shorris didn't understand what Niecie was getting at, but as she explained it further he realized what she was saying. "Although," he says, "she did not say so, I was sure that when she spoke of the 'moral life of downtown' she meant something that had happened to her. With no job and no money, a prisoner, she had undergone a radical transformation. She had followed the same path that led to the invention of politics in ancient Greece. She had learned to reflect. In further conversation it became clear that when she spoke of 'the moral life of downtown' she meant the humanities. . . . If the political life was the way out of poverty, the humanities provided an entrance to reflection and the political life . . ."[6]

And so with Niecie as a sort of educational consultant, Shorris organized a school of the humanities for the poor, believing what Niecie believed and the University of Chicago's Robert Hutchins had practiced—that "the best education for the best is the best education for us all."

I can't stop without telling you a bit more of what happened in the Clemente course in the humanities. Shorris's first attempt to recruit students for the school was a total failure. He was urged to aim lower, but he refused. Instead he tried a different approach. "You've been cheated," he said to a group of potential students in the Bronx. "Rich people learn the humanities; you didn't. The humanities are a foundation for getting along in the world, for thinking, for learning to reflect on the world instead of just reacting to whatever force is turned against you . . ." He explained to them Thucydides' idea of politics. "Rich people," he went on, "know politics in that sense. They know how to negotiate instead of using force. They know how to use politics to get along, to get power. It doesn't mean that rich people are good and poor people are bad. It simply means that rich people know a more effective method for living in society . . ."[7] He got fifty applicants for the thirty positions in the course, which included philosophy, poetry, art history, logic, rhetoric, and American history—all taught on the highest university level by eminently qualified professionals.

It was Niecie who told Shorris how to begin his first class. When he told her he was going to teach moral philosophy, she asked him what that would include. He told her that they'd begin with Plato: the *Apology*, a little of the *Crito*, a few pages of the *Phaedo*. Then they'd read Aristotle's *Nicomachean Ethics* and Thucydides, particularly Pericles' Funeral Oration, and end with *Antigone*.

"There's something missing," said Niecie, the former addict and HIV-positive prisoner.

"And what's that?" asked Shorris.

"Plato's Allegory of the Cave. How can you teach philosophy to poor people without the Allegory of the Cave? The ghetto is the cave. Education is the light. Poor people can understand that!"[8]

And so the course began—there were losses along the way, but sixteen of the original thirty graduated—from a course as tough as any they would have taken at one of our Ivy League universities. These students recognized that the humanities were the door into a different quality of life. And they were willing to work like the Greeks of old to get through that door.

Now I contend that Earl Shorris's course couldn't have been taught by computer. It took intensive reading of difficult texts. Reading in this fashion is, simply put, hard work. It demands not merely the skill to decode, it demands time and thought, it demands reflection. And out of this reflection comes wisdom. And wisdom is in short supply in our society.

"My core fear," says Sven Birkerts, "is that we are, as a culture, as a species, becoming shallower; that we have turned from depth—from the Judeo-Christian premise of unfathomable mystery—and are adapting ourselves to the ersatz security of a vast lateral connectedness. That we are giving up on wisdom, the struggle for which has for millennia been central to the very idea of culture, and that we are pledging instead to a faith in the Web . . ."[9]

Well, back to our own crisis—the confusion in the world of children's books. It is not unrelated to all I've been saying. It has been my experience as I speak in schools and hear from young readers that there are still intensive readers among our children, but for them a more frightening crisis than technology looms. While computer capacity expands unbelievably, the books that children who read intensively will want to read eighteen times and reflect upon and pass down to their own children are rapidly going out of print. There is no lack of books, but these are, for the most part, books they will be pleased to read once and pass on.

Hence my librarian friend's lament. It is certainly all right for children to have books that they will read only once—it develops both fluency in reading and the habit of reaching for a book instead of a remote, but how can we be content to give children only the books that will be raced through and deny them the books that they might return to over and over again—the books that will shape their thinking and change their lives?

When my two granddaughters were, respectively, two and not quite five, I bought them each a paperback copy of *Tom's Midnight Garden*, by Philippa Pearce. No, this classic of our century is not a book that anyone would choose to own only in paperback, but it was out of print in hardcover, and I was afraid that if I didn't grab those paperbacks two years ago, by the time my granddaughters were old enough to love the book, it wouldn't be available at all.

If there's a single chorus I've heard over and over again, it is the line "I don't care what my children read, as long as they are reading." I'm not going to argue with certain elements of that statement. As I said earlier, there is value in books or periodicals or train tables or the sports page—simply in their ability to hook young readers into the pleasures of reading. For let's not get confused here—without pleasure, the reading experience is a mighty dry desert.

But there is a deep pleasure that can only be experienced in the intensive reading of a rich book that I do not want my grandchildren to miss. And they will only have this pleasure if they do the harder work of reading books that matter. And it matters to society, to the world, to the future of society in the world, if my grandchildren are given the chance and take the opportunity to pierce the glitzy facade of our age and enter into conversation with the wisdom of our race.

Wisdom, as Sven Birkerts reminds us, is "predicated on the assumption that one person can somehow grasp a total picture of life and its laws, comprehending the whole and relation of parts . . . We once presumed that those parts added up, that there was some purpose or explanation to our being here below."[10]

But today, he goes on to say, we are "inundated by perspectives, by lateral vistas of information that stretch endlessly in every direction" and thus "we no longer accept the possibility of assembling a complete picture. Instead of carrying on the ancient project of philosophy—attempting to discover the 'truth' of things—we direct our energies to managing information." But wisdom is not the assembling of facts or the managing of information—it is the ability to see through the facts—to "perceive the underlying laws and patterns." And yes, to believe that it is worth the struggle—that beyond the facts there is a comprehensible whole.[11]

But the vertical piercing of the horizontal mass of facts is hard work for us today who live in the confusing onrush of incoming data. The quiet depth survives, Birkerts maintains; we can find it in art and literature, but experiencing the depth—some part of that which we call wisdom—is hard work—we must give to the task time and energy and reflection.

I dare to think most of us who have troubled ourselves to gather to honor Anne Carroll Moore would agree that wisdom is worth the work. And at the crossroads of eternity, it is the narrow rocky path into the heart of wisdom that we aim to follow.

I want to share one thing about Anne Carroll Moore that I did not know when I agreed to do this lecture. I learned it when I read her biography in the *Dictionary of American Biography*. Until that moment I had had a rather mixed view of this enormous figure in the history of children's books in this country. I think you can tell by some of my earlier remarks some of the ingredients of that mixture. One thing I haven't mentioned so far is Anne Carroll Moore's concern for the children of the poor and the many immigrant children who crowded the slums of the city in her time as well as ours. She believed that libraries had a special obligation to these children. Her concern dated back to her earliest days as a librarian at the Pratt Institute Library in Brooklyn before the turn of the century.

Among the immigrant children who came to Pratt was a little

Jewish boy named Leo Max Frank. Frank grew up and moved to Georgia, where he became relatively prosperous as the owner of a small factory. But one terrible day, he was accused of assaulting one of the young women who worked for him and then murdering her to cover up his crime. Facing execution in an Atlanta prison, Leo Frank wrote to the librarian he had known as a child and asked for her help. Miss Moore was convinced of his innocence, spoke out in his defense, and traveled to Georgia to visit him in prison. Leo Frank was eventually exonerated, but the proof of his innocence came too late. He had been dragged out of that Georgia prison and lynched by an angry anti-Semitic mob.

I had read a book about this tragic event years ago, but I didn't know until this fall the connection between Leo Frank and Anne Carroll Moore. The correspondence between the librarian and the prisoner, dated between 1914 and 1915, is preserved with his papers in the American Jewish Archives in Cincinnati. I readily forgive any number of eccentricities to a woman of such courage and such compassion.

And courage and compassion are what we need today. It takes courage to live in a way that society despises. In a world where profit is king and technology its slave, to act as a free seeker after wisdom means taking risks that will probably not reap great financial benefits or media applause. It has been known, rather, to get the seeker into a lot of trouble, or at the least lose him or her a lot of fair-weather friends. I know a lot of pretty lonely librarians and teachers around the country, and in our large publishing houses, the casualty rate among seekers after wisdom is growing by the day.

But we who care about children and ultimately about wisdom must do what Earl Shorris sought to do in this city—share, with those who do not know, the riches and depth of human experience—with the hope that in drinking deeply of the Pierian spring, they may become wise leaders for the confused masses milling at the cross-roads.

In her wonderful essay "Lose Not the Nightingale," Frances Clarke Sayers summed up the task a generation ago:

> The power of responding to the intuitive and the poetic is greatest in childhood. Rob children of this power, and you rob them of an everlasting anchor and refuge. . . . If we let go the fashions, the theories, and the trends in reading; if we read and reread the great books; . . . if we lose no opportunity to share with children these books that have possessed us, irrespective of their ages, their seeming ability, or disability, trusting in powers beyond tests and measurements . . . the power of the writer, the power of our own sincere, spontaneous enthusiasm; if we demand of publishers and writers and artists the best they can give; if we can wake in children a response beyond their immediate need—if we organize to accomplish these things, we shall never, never lose the nightingale."[12]

In the course of writing this speech, the last two lines of my adolescent poem suddenly came back to me unbidden. Had I solved the confusion at the crossroads? Was I headed up the right path toward some shining goal? Surely I had not allowed my generic youth to chose the low road to degredation, sloth, or greed?

> Well, here are the last two lines:
> I am youth, standing at the crossroads of eternity.
> Which path shall I take?

Confusion apparently reigned for me at sixteen. But you and I are charged with giving the best that is in us to that confused and clueless, perhaps frightened youth. Like Anne Carroll Moore and those mighty women in her train, we know, don't we, what is best for our time. We know that the mechanical nightingale chirping out its metallic tune to order can never replace the wild creature filling the quiet woods with its heartfelt melody. With compassion and courage we must do our best in our own time to help those who must decide when they come into maturity what will be best for their own time.

NOTE: *An abridged version of this speech appeared in* School Library Journal, *May 1998, pp. 34–37.*

Still Summoned by Books

Frances Clarke Sayers served as an assistant to Anne Carroll Moore, succeeding her as Superintendent of Work with Children at the New York Public Library. She also served as librarian at the University Elementary School at University of California, Los Angeles, and later taught children's literature in the Department of English there. From 1960 to her retirement in 1965, she was a member of the faculty of the UCLA School of Library Science. She was an eloquent and outspoken advocate for excellence in children's literature.

I've been what I consider a serious writer now for nearly thirty-two years. I can date it with confidence because my career as a writer coincides almost exactly with the birth of our son John. I was asked when I was great with child if I would write a book for my denomination's church-school curriculum. Three moves and three children later, my book for the church was published, and I made the decision to keep on writing. It was seven years and another child, with all four of them in public school, before my first novel was finally published, but all those years of frustration and repeated rejection were not wasted. I was learning how to write. Thirty years later I'm still learning.

One of the books given to me fairly early on by a writer friend to help me in this never-ending process was Frances Clarke Sayers's classic, *Summoned by Books*. Ms. Sayers was a mythic figure to a writer struggling to write for children. She knew what excellence was. You had only to read her literate and loving descriptions of the two great

Eleanors, Estes and Farjeon. I couldn't believe that she would have ever noticed me, much less approved, but no matter, she had, in my mother's words, gone to a better land and would never cast her piercing gaze on my feeble attempts.

Then, unaccountably, my books began to win a series of unbelievable prizes. Perhaps it should have filled me with confidence. It never did, but it made me bold enough to include a quotation from the lofty Ms. Sayers in my Newbery acceptance speech for *Jacob Have I Loved*, hoping she would look down from above with some degree of tolerance. After all, I was trying as hard as I could to meet her standards.

Just before I was to deliver that speech, Ethel Heins, who in those days was the editor of *The Horn Book*, which was scary enough, told me that Frances Clarke Sayers would not, metaphorically speaking, be looking down on me as I spoke, but looking up from the first tier of the audience. "I thought she was dead," I squawked. Whereupon Ethel informed me that she was not only very much alive but at that exact moment in the same San Francisco hotel where this conversation was taking place.

I don't know how Ms. Sayers graded me in her heart of hearts, but she was wonderfully gracious to me that evening, and I will cherish the memory of her presence as I tried to explain, using her words, what I thought we writers for the young are about. "We know," I said, "that those of us who write for children are called, not to do something to a child, but to be someone for a child," and then added, " 'Art,' in Frances Clarke Sayers's wonderfully passionate definition, is 'a controlled fury of desire to share one's private revelation of life.' And she, the librarian, summons us who are writers to the service of art—to give the best that is in us to (again quoting Ms. Sayers) 'the audience that lives by what it feeds upon.' "[1]

The tribute that I gave to the Frances Clarke Sayers who sat looking up at me from below, I am honored to repeat to the one now looking down from above. I'm still trying, Ms. Sayers, to give the best that is in me to the audience that lives by what it feeds upon. And no matter what dire analyses and predictions I am given of the present day and the children of this day, I believe that they still can be summoned by books which, again in your words, give "the shattering and gracious encounter that all art affords."[2]

When I think of that shattering and gracious encounter, three scenes come to mind. In the first, my older brother and sister and I are snuggled up to our mother on the parental bed in Hwaian, China, and she is reading to us. Now Mother might be reading any number of things from *Egermeier's Bible Story Book* to *The Wind in the Willows*. But in this picture she is reading Kipling's *Just-So Stories*, because I love to watch the way her Georgia mouth wraps itself around those very British-sounding words. "In the High and Far-Off Times the Elephant, O Best Beloved, had no trunk" and the oft repeated instructions to the Elephant's child, who filled all Africa with his 'satiable curtiosities: "Go to the banks of the great grey-green, greasy Limpopo River, all set about with fever-trees, and find out . . ."

Then I have a picture of myself on the bed in the back bedroom in Takoma Park, Maryland, with our four children—a boy and a girl on either side so the boys won't poke at each other. Again, I could be reading any number of things, but in this picture I am reading *Charlotte's Web* for the umpteenth time, and we are approaching page 171 and John, who is about six, begins to call out: "Don't cry, Mom, don't cry. You ruin it when you cry!" And I determine for the umpteenth time that I will get through without crying. After all, how many times have I read this now? I know it nearly by heart. But by the time we get to page 171, I am weeping uncontrollably, so I hand the book to John and he reads: ". . . The infield was littered with bottles and trash. Nobody, of the hundreds of people that had visited the Fair, knew that a grey spider had played the most important part of all. No one was with her when she died." Now there's a shattering and gracious encounter for you. The only reason I can get through that passage this afternoon is that I have no child beside me to hand the book to.

The third picture takes place last spring. The grandchildren are visiting, and both of them have been sick during the night. Katherine, who is four at the time, feels rotten and (though it is hard for such a wonderful child to act rotten) let us just say she is not being her usual peerless self, so her father has exiled her to the living room. A little bit later my daughter Lin goes in to check on her unhappy child and then comes out and says to me: "Mom, Katherine needs a visit to the Bunny Planet." So I take Rosemary Wells's three little books and sit down on the couch with a very sad, silent little Katherine and read them all straight through. When I finish she is cheerful enough to speak. "Now," she says, "let's read them again, Nana. You read *The Island Light* and *Moss Pillow*, and I'll read *First Tomato*. So, obediently, I read the two books assigned to me, and then Katherine, in the manner of children who have been read to since birth and are just on the verge of breaking into reading on their own, opens *First Tomato* and, in absolutely perfect cadence, recites the much loved book.

For those of you not yet acquainted with the Bunny Planet books, *First Tomato* tells of poor Claire for whom everything goes wrong, including getting snow in her shoes and having math class go on for two hours, concluding with "At playtime Claire was the only girl not able to do a cartwheel. Once again the bus was late. Claire needs a visit to the Bunny Planet." Then Katherine turns the page and the magic happens. You can hear it in her voice, which turns from the sodden prose of Claire's tribulations to the poetry of her deliverance: "Far beyond the moon and stars / Twenty light-years south of Mars, / Spins the gentle Bunny Planet / And the Bunny Queen is Janet. / Janet says to Claire, 'Come in. / Here's the day that should have been.' " And

Queen Janet gives poor little Claire the day that should have been—the day when her mother takes the first ripe tomato, which Claire has picked, and makes it into First Tomato soup "because I love you so."

By now Katherine has made six voyages to the Bunny Planet, and when she returns with Claire from this final trip, child and bunny are both healed and happy.

And so the encounter is passed down from my mother to her great-grandchild, whom she never saw, but whom she would love with all her heart and would have read to every chance she got, just as she read to me and my brother and sisters. So that I read to my children and my daughter and son-in-law are reading to their children.

In our family, books have created a shattering and gracious encounter of illumination and healing. It was my love of stories that led me to writing them. I didn't know when I started if I had any talent or ability. I only knew that I had been summoned by books and wanted not only to read them but to take part in their creation.

That is why I have entitled my tribute to Frances Clarke Sayers *Still Summoned by Books*. In our day and time, there are many places where that word *still* is not taken for granted as it is in my house and yours. There is a far greater push these days to get a computer in every classroom than there is to make sure that the library is overflowing with a great variety of books of knowledge and imagination that have the power to summon children from the myriad distractions of their lives to the wide and nurturing world of the printed word.

In preparation for this speech I went back to reread Jacob Bronowski's *The Ascent of Man*. The final chapter of this marvelous book, which is connected, of course, to the public television series by the same name, is entitled "The Long Childhood."

What is it, Bronowski asks, that makes human beings unique? Is it the opposable thumb? The ability to make tools? No, it is the ability to create language—not just give cries of greeting or alarm—but to name things. To construct words and rearrange them, so that the same words can take on varieties of meaning. This unique human ability has given rise in every human society to both science, by which we mean knowledge, and art, by which we mean works of the creative imagination.

We all know that there is a difference between the skull of early humanoids and our own skulls. Our egg-shaped foreheads have replaced their sloping ones. And in that enlarged space, are the frontal lobes, which allow us to do something else animals cannot do. They enable us to plan actions and wait for rewards that are not immediately evident. We out of all creation can plan for the future. This unique human development, Bronowski says, "means that we are concerned in our early education with the postponement of decisions." Therefore, before the human brain is an instrument of decision, he says, it is an instrument of preparation. We need, as human beings, a long childhood and adolescence. We have to delay decision making, because we need first to acquire the knowledge our future decisions will demand.

What happens during this period is crucial to what the person will become. We know now that our children are born with their brains wired for acquiring language, but science has also taught us that in order actually to acquire language, any language, a child has to learn some language quite early on. A baby is born with a brain receptive to language, but if she or he is not spoken to, played with, read to, those areas of the brain simply do not develop as they are meant to. Recent studies prove that the children of deaf parents begin to babble in sign language at the same time children of hearing parents begin to babble orally. It doesn't matter, it would seem, what language a child is early exposed to—just that he or she is given a rich experience of human language in those early months and years of life.

Then there is the matter of time. Bronowski speaks of the long childhood of Western civilization, but in truth childhood is too short to waste. We can't snatch these empty-caloried books from our children's hands, indeed, that would make them all the more desirable, but somehow we must make sure early on that they have books that will truly nourish them, that will enlarge their minds, that will prepare them to make wise and compassionate decisions when they are grown.

The child who has the finest literature as a touchstone can read trash and not be damaged, but many children have no means of comparison. I may have devoured comic books when I was eleven, but my mother used her scarce dollars to buy me a copy of *The Yearling*.

"But my children don't want to be read to anymore," a parent will complain. And here teachers do have the advantage. Whereas, your eleven-year-old might complain if you dragged him from the computer game he was engrossed in to read him a story, I have never heard of a school class complaining that they'd rather do duplicated work sheets, thank you, when the teacher pulled out a story at the end of the day. A number of families I know read in the car on long trips or read by the campfire. But I think the secret of reading as a family lies in starting at birth and never stopping. I can remember my two older ones, who thought they had grown too old to be read to, coming and standing at the door while I read to the younger two, and often the stories they returned to hear were the same stories they had heard many times before.

When our youngest was a junior in high school all her siblings had left home, and she was desperately lonely for them. She was angrily recounting one day her long list of adolescent grievances against the universe in general and her mother in particular when suddenly she summed it all up in one great dramatic flourish: "And besides," she said, "you never read to me anymore." I was both stunned and delighted. This was my child who read *War and Peace* for pleasure, and she wanted her mom to read aloud to her? This was a character defect

I could absolutely and gleefully repair. Reading aloud was something I knew I was good at.

A year later this same child was deep in the spring agony of waiting for college acceptance. I found her one Saturday morning curled up in the big armchair engrossed in a book. I turned my head upside down to see the title. To my astonishment, she was reading *Charlotte's Web*. I couldn't resist. "Oh," I said, "I see you're reading a good book." She looked up and said fiercely, "This is a *great* book."

There is something so comforting about the beloved books of childhood. When the uncertainties of life assail us, they stand as healing verities, and we can return to them again and again. But only, of course, if someone helped us to find those books when we were very young.

I think books can be preparation as well as comfort. I remember quite well when we moved to Norfolk, taking our children from the only home they could remember living in and setting them down in an alien culture. In trying to explain her unhappiness to me, Mary, then ten years old, said: "If I'd just had some practice, I know I could do it. I just never had any practice moving."

Well, books are a kind of practice for life. Often people tell me they have given *Bridge to Terabithia* to a child who has suffered some terrible loss. When they do, I want to say, "Too late, too late." The time a child needs a book about life's dark passages is before he or she has had to experience them. We need practice with loss, rehearsal for grieving, just as we need preparation for decision making.

Jacob Bronowski speaks of the "plasticity of human behavior"[3] that allows enormous variation of action within our species. The same basic mental apparatus that allows for a Mozart will also produce an Einstein. Yet, for thousands of years, only a tiny remnant of humanity was allowed to fully develop those wonderfully varied capacities with which nature, or God if you please, had endowed them. There was an aristocracy of learning, and it was extremely limited. The rest of us—and since I seem to have been descended more from the poor and dispossessed than from the royal line—the rest of us were expected to know our place in society, regard it as divinely ordained, and act accordingly.

But something wonderful happened, at least, in Western civilization. The printing press was finally invented, and with it a new attitude toward learning began to emerge in the West. Bronowski calls this phenomenon, the "democracy of the intellect." Now there had been printing in China by A.D. 200 and movable type was invented in the tenth century, but because of the nature of the language, which requires up to forty thousand separate characters, movable type did not seem like a practical invention to the Chinese, and they soon abandoned it. But Western languages are blessed with an alphabet. In English the arrangement of the same twenty-six little characters will write *Frog and Toad* or *Romeo and Juliet*.

When in the middle of the fifteenth century movable type got reinvented by Europeans, everything was ripe for its immediate utilization. Between 1450 and 1500 more than six thousand separate works were printed. By 1500 there were 417 printers in the city of Venice alone. And those Italians weren't just printing Latin Bibles; they were printing the classics of Greece and Rome. Trouble was on the way. For wherever people can read freely and widely, they begin to think and to question, and there is nothing the established order dreads more than a thinking, questioning populace.

I have now completed twelve novels. It is of some interest to me that in every one of them there is an encounter with literature. In the first two novels, set in twelfth-century Japan, the arts of the Heian period, which flourished in the eleventh century, play a large role in the lives of my characters: music, poetry, story, even the making of pottery. In *The Master Puppeteer*, the great plays of Chikamatsu are the basis of my fictional puppet theater's repertory.

In 1973, with my ten-year-old daughter, Lin, in tow, I visited Japan to do research for the book. The public relations manager at the Osaka Bunraku theater made an appointment for me to meet the most respected scholar of the history of the puppet theater. Instead of coming into the city, Professor Yoshinaga invited us to visit him in his home some miles out from Osaka.

It was a typical Japanese country house with tatami rooms arranged around a small courtyard, where the last mandarin orange hung from a tree. Before he and I began to talk, the elderly scholar picked the orange and ceremoniously gave it to Lin. We were sitting on cushions on the mat floor of his study as we talked about the ancient theater. It was a rather messy room, with its sliding paper doors thrown wide open to the October sunshine.

Gradually, as he spoke, it became clear that in those stacks of old, worn books surrounding us on the tatami were first editions of the plays of Chikamatsu. It was like sitting in a room surrounded by First Folios of Shakespeare. A spark from the little charcoal heater—a leaky roof—a clumsy visitor tripping over a stack and shoving them out the open doorways into the dirt of the courtyard—a ten-year-old eating an orange and inadvertently dripping juice . . . I started to breathe funny.

I'm glad to say we got out of there several hours and a sukiyaki dinner later without any accidents to that trove of priceless manuscripts, but our host was utterly at ease among the clutter. They were his books, not some untouchable treasures.

Books are touchable treasures. That is what Leslie teaches Jesse Aarons. Even Gilly, who has made it a matter of honor not to make human friends, knows that books are friends, and the ice that has long encased her heart begins to melt on her first encounter with the warm liquid beauty of Wordsworth's poetry.

Our son David with the composer Steve Liebman has adapted *The*

Great Gilly Hopkins for the stage. It will premiere at Stage One in Louisville, Kentucky, this October, but my husband, John, and I went to Louisville last fall for the initial rehearsed reading of the play. Now I am somewhat familiar with this book. I had read David's script. I had already heard all the music that Steve had composed. But I was in no way prepared for my reaction to hearing the play presented by gifted actors in that simple public reading.

I began weeping about five lines in and only stopped in order to laugh and then go back to crying once more. The scene that I want to share with you is the one where Gilly first meets Wordsworth.

Trotter has asked Gilly to read aloud to her neighbor, who is old, blind, and black. Gilly's first reaction to Mr. Randolph has been offensively negative. But she can't resist showing off how well she reads.

"You want the Wordsworth one, Mr. Randolph?" Trotter asks. "Or do you have that by heart?"

"Both," he answers.

And then there begins a spoken duet with lines alternating between the belligerent child and the beautiful old man:

> "There was a time when meadow, grove, and stream,
> The earth, and every common sight,
>   To me did seem
>   Apparelled in celestial light,
> The glory and the freshness of a dream.
> It is not now as it hath been of yore;—
>   Turn wheresoe'er I may,
>   By night or day,
> The things which I have seen I now can see no more.
>
> "Our birth is but a sleep and a forgetting:
> The Soul that rises with us, our life's Star,

Hath had elsewhere its setting,
   And cometh from afar:
Not in entire forgetfulness,
And not in utter nakedness,
But trailing clouds of glory do we come
   From God, who is our home."

In the play the spoken duet turns at this point into a haunting melody as Gilly and Mr. Randolph sing together the final stanza:

"Thanks to the human heart by which we live,
Thanks to its tenderness, its joys, and fears,
To me the meanest flower that blows can give
Thoughts that do often lie too deep for tears."[4]

Steve Liebman is the composer that Stephanie Tolan and I worked with in the adaptations of *Bridge to Terabithia* and *The Tale of the Mandarin Ducks*, both of which have been premiered at Stage One. When you tell Steve you liked the play, he invariably replies: "You're *supposed* to say, 'I laughed, I cried, it changed my life.'"

Steve is only half teasing. That is what literature, that is what art is supposed to do—provide us with a shattering and gracious encounter—make us experience the spectrum of human emotion and somehow make us richer, more compassionate, wiser human beings in the process.

Certainly Louise Bradshaw's narrow life is opened up as she read Dickens and Scott and Shakespeare and Fenimore Cooper. Park got a glimpse of the father he never knew by reading the books the man had left behind; even Jimmy Jo is comforted when the librarian gives him *Ramona the Brave* and he realizes that there are other children who struggle to understand the unwritten code of school behavior, only to fail. Lyddie's life is transformed when her roommate reads *Oliver Twist* aloud to her.

From time to time people speak to me with surprise about the fact that my characters read. But I am the one who is more surprised to have it regarded as something unusual. Of course my characters read. Reading is a vital part of my life. My characters would seem less than human if books didn't enter their lives.

But I have also used the theme of learning how to read to say something about the process of becoming fully human, perhaps most pointedly in *Rebels of the Heavenly Kingdom. Rebels*, I think it is safe to say, is my least-read book. A number of people have asked me why I wrote it. The answer to that question is, simply, I had to write it. I could not help writing it. I think Frances Clarke Sayers would surely understand. Writing this book was for me a barely "controlled fury of desire to share [my] private revelation of life."[5] *Rebels* is also the book that jumped to mind when I read Dr. Bronowski's phrase "the democracy of the intellect." It is his contention that it is the printed word—it is books—that make this democracy possible. ✳

In a peculiar way we could say that Confucius, in 500 B.C., sought to establish such a democracy. He himself was born poor, but he was bright and ambitious, and by the time he was fifteen years old he had given himself to learning. His life's goal, which was never fulfilled except in romantic myth, was to become an ideal ruler of his people—a benevolent leader whose wisdom would be employed to enrich his people and educate them. No actual monarch or governor was ever daring enough to give Confucius a meaningful public office. How could a ruler who followed such a teacher's dictums hope to maintain his power over the populace? But Confucius's popularity as a teacher saved his life, because neither could any ruler dare to silence him.

Confucius's teaching about society, about the responsibility that each man owed to those below him, beside him, and above him in the social scale, this teaching, though never fully implemented, was the glue that held Chinese society together for nearly two thousand years.

His teaching is practical and flavored with humor. "I suppose," one of his critics said to him derisively, "if someone said there is a man in the well, the altruist would go after him." "Even an alturist would first make certain there really was a man down the well," Confucius replied.[6]

I can't claim that the teacher was a feminist, but, at least for the male population, he believed in the democracy of the intellect. And his ideal, though often honored more in the breach than in the observance, was that any boy with the intellect and moral strength to do so could rise from the lowest place in society to become a ruler of his people.

When I first began to read about the Taiping movement, which arose in China during the nineteenth century, I was struck with how their early proclamations sounded like a mixture of the best of Confucian teaching and the ideals of Christianity. For the Taiping not only valued all human life and declared the equality of all people under heaven, but they determined that every boy and every girl should be educated and that any child of either sex might rise to positions of leadership if he or she had the wit, the integrity, and the will. There was to be no foot-binding, no prostitution, no slavery, no stealing, no killing, no use of mind-altering drinks or drugs. Confucius's altruism and Jesus' commandments to love truly met in the Taiping's early teaching. "You should not kill one innocent person or do one unrighteous act, even though it be to acquire an empire," the heavenly king of the Taiping declared.

The Taiping's righteous ideals led to self-righteousness, corruption, and eventually to genocidal warfare. In the end they self-destructed, as do any people who fail to remember that righteous goals can only be reached by righteous means, but for a brief shining moment, they understood, even more fully than Confucius, the meaning of the democracy of the intellect.

Wang Lee, the peasant boy in my story who has joined the Taiping and learned to read and write, is kidnapped. The bandits who capture him disguise him as a girl and sell him to work in the kitchen of a wealthy household, where he is befriended by the one-eared cook and Precious Jade, the five-year-old daughter of the householder.

Though early in the story Wang Lee despises the big feet of the Taiping women, when precious Jade's feet are bound, he is horrified. The child can no longer run and play. She weeps constantly from the pain in her broken toes and arches.

One day when One Ear [the cook] was at the market, Wang Lee found her alone crying. And he carried her into the kitchen and put her on a stool at the table where he was working. "I'm going to teach you a new game," he said.

She looked up at him. The circles under her eyes were dark as bruises, and her face had grown as pinched as an old woman's.

"I'm going to teach you how to read and write," he whispered.

Her eyes flashed almost like before. "You can't teach me," she said. "You're nothing but a big-footed slave girl."

"Hush," he said. "It's a secret."

Then one day One Ear, the cook, comes in, thwacks Wang Lee in the rear with what proves to be the first reader in the traditional Confucian schoolboy's education. "It's not for free," the cook says. "You have to teach me, too."

And so Wang Lee taught them both, beginning with the first three-character sentence: "At birth men are by nature good."

If I'd been more alert when I wrote that last sentence, I would have translated Confucius more accurately. The word I have translated as "men" is, in Chinese and Japanese as well, the word for humanity, including both men and women.

In our own country we have tried with varying degrees of success to promote the democracy of the intellect. The public libraries of our great cities certainly have. As thousands of immigrants poured out of the steerage of the ships that brought them here to find squalid shelter in our slums, the libraries threw open their majestic doors and welcomed the poor, the huddled masses yearning to breathe free. The lady holding her lamp in the harbor may have been the symbol, but the librarian raising her date-due stamp was the true provider of liberty. I don't think it's merely a coincidence that the same politicians who despise immigrants think libraries are, by and large, superfluous. The democracy of the intellect has always threatened the narrow-visioned politician whose power depends on ignorance and prejudice and mistrust.

Why should there be libraries that are open long hours and welcome all manner and ages of people? Why do we need them? We *don't* need them unless we believe passionately in the democracy of the intellect—unless we cherish the long childhood of the human race as a time of preparation for wise decision making for the maturity of individuals as well as for the healing and illumination of the citizenry as a whole.

When we speak of the preparation of the young, we of course think of their schooling. The minute the word *education* is uttered, the cries of dismay go up. The horror stories about American education abound and I don't have the time nor the inclination to repeat them. But I must say, as a person who lived for four years in Japan, the holding up of the Japanese model as the ideal has always puzzled me. I felt vindicated when I heard on public radio the other day a report from Japan. It seems that Japanese business leaders had gathered to decry the state of education in Japan. Japanese education, they declared, is not producing graduates with the creative imagination that the twenty-first century will demand. And this from business leaders.

Jacob Bronowski has something to say on this subject as well. In one vital respect, he says, the ancient civilizations of Egypt, China, India, and Europe in the Middle Ages all failed. And this is how they failed: they limited "the freedom of the imagination of the young." Any civilization that does this becomes static and founders.

The Japanese businessmen who spoke up the other day are wise enough to recognize what happens when education is reduced to the memorization of answers for entrance exams. We have been a bit slower catching on. In our great drive to keep taxes in check, the first thing we do is cut funds for children and youth. And when we cut the school budget, the first to go is the art teacher, then the music teacher, and then the librarian. The imagination is a suspect commodity these days. The cry is "Back to the basics!" I've never been quite sure what that phrase meant, but I think it means that the creative imagination that the Japanese businessmen are saying is vital for the next century is for many of our citizens not merely a frill but a danger.

Those of us who write for the young, who seek to give "the best that is in us to the audience that lives by what it feeds upon" have been well warned. The challenges to books of power and imagination grow by the day. Write nice books, we are told. Write books that will make children virtuous. Avoid controversy. Don't write books that make children question authority or things as they are. The imagination is a fearsome, untamed quality. How can we keep our children in line if we let their imaginations run wild and free? Take children back to the day when two and two always equaled four—not into the mystical realms of theoretical physics. Take them back to Dick and Jane and Baby Sally. Beware fantasy and emotionally laden fiction. Look. Look. Look. Oh. Oh. Oh. Bland. Bland. Bland. Safe. Safe. Safe. Dead. Dead. Dead.

And so books of the imagination become suspect, their powerful summons a siren song against which we must stop the ears of our children. I can hear Frances Clarke Sayers thundering down from above.

"Of what are we afraid?" she cries. "Of words, of emotion, of experience? We are very tender, it seems to me, of the young, and tenderness is no preparation for a world half mad and savage. What children need to know is not how dairies and bakeries are run, not the organization of industry, but what spiritual disaster is at work in the world today."[7] She said those words back in 1937—the year of the great burning of books in Nazi Germany. I do not think she would alter them now, for the world is hardly less mad and savage today than it was sixty years ago, and if we are to survive as a civilization, our children must know what spiritual disaster is at work in the world today.

Yet despite the attempts through the ages of both the tyrannical and the timid, the riches of the imagination of the human race are still available to us. They are gathered and preserved in the printed word. We are still summoned by books to that wisdom, that strength, and that delight. We cannot surrender to those who fear the power of books—who know that a true democracy of the intellect threatens demagoguery, breaks open the narrowness of the spirit, and challenges the selfish interests of the privileged few.

I want to close with a story that seems to me to summarize all I have said today. It is a story of one of those moments of transition that Ms. Sayers points to in the title essay of her book—the moment "in the lives of perusers of books which turns them from desultory readers or nonreaders into those who become ineluctably summoned by books."[8]

This is a story about a child who once summoned by a book was never quite the same again. The child of the story is our daughter Lin. I mentioned her early on as the mother of those remarkable granddaughters. But Lin was not born into our family. She was born in

Hong Kong. When she was about three weeks old she was found on a street of that city by a policeman and taken to the orphanage where she spent her infancy. She came to us when she was a little more than two years old. Hers is a long, complicated, and presently very happy story, but I just want to focus on one aspect of her long childhood.

We began to read to her, of course, as soon as she came into our family. We talked to her, but she was slow to speak to us (although we could overhear her teaching her baby brother to speak behind their bedroom door), and, unlike her brother, she did not start reading before she began school. Still she began to read quite normally and happily when she entered first grade, and as far as I could tell was reading as well as most of her classmates until suddenly one day when she was eight years old she completely stopped. If I'd ask her to read to me, she'd begin to cry and say, "You know I can't read."

We tracked the problem down to the third-grade reading teacher who, for reasons I still do not understand, had convinced a number of children in the class that they did not know how to read. We tried to have Lin taken out of the class. We even (and in those days, we had no money for such) went to a child psychologist, who sent a written recommendation that Lin be taken out of the class. It would be far better, he said, for Lin not to have any reading instruction at all than for her to remain in that class. But bureaucracy being what it was and is, we were told that it would be impossible to remove our daughter from the class. So we said to Lin—"We know you can read. You know you can read. If Mrs. E. doesn't know it, that's her problem, not ours. We can't get you into another class, so try to be brave and we promise you, you'll never have to be in her class again."

Well, Lin got through the third grade. She had other fine teachers who cared for her and encouraged her. She made good grades and did well in school, but Mrs. E.'s legacy was that Lin never read anything that she wasn't absolutely required to. Even if I handed her a recipe to read aloud to me while I was preparing something, she'd take the book and pass it over to her brother.

This went on for seven years. I was still reading aloud to the children, and Lin seemed glad to come and listen, but she never, as far as I could see, voluntarily opened a book.

Then when she was a junior in high school, one of the required literature texts was J. D. Salinger's often challenged and banned *The Catcher in the Rye*. She began to read it not because she wanted to but because the teacher said she must. I can only describe the transformation in my child as a miracle, the change was so sudden and dramatic. A book had lit a fire inside her. You could see it blazing in her eyes.

She tried to explain to me what had happened. "Mom," she said. "It's the strangest thing. I can't get this book off my mind. I'm just living in it while I'm walking down the halls at school. It's like I've turned into another person. And I'm just *reading* a book." Suddenly she turned and looked at me as though she were seeing me for the first time. "What's it like for you, *writing* a book?"

"It's just like that," I said. "Just exactly like that."

This lecture was originally published in a limited edition by the UCLA Department of Library and Information Science in 1998. A revised version entitled "Asking the Question" was published in The New Advocate, Winter 2000 *(pp. 1–15).*

The Yearling and I

The green cloth binding is buckled and stained, showing the effects of a typhoon on the island of Shikoku in 1961, but the book itself is much older than that. On the flyleaf is a small sticker with my name, Katherine Womeldorf, and the Piedmont Avenue address where I lived from the time I was barely nine until I was just past twelve. I can't remember owning printed stickers with my name and address on them. They seem marvelously bourgeois. Yet there it is, fifty years later, firmly proclaiming my ownership of this book, which was, as I recall it, the first book that ever exclusively belonged to me. Certainly it was the first book I remember my mother giving to me.

There were five of us children and I was the middle child. We had books, because, poor as they were, my parents valued books and bought them for us when they could. But we shared them. The family name went on the flyleaf, not our personal names.

But somehow the year I was eleven going on twelve, my mother gave me this copy of *The Yearling*. The book had been published in

1938 and won the Pulitzer Prize the following year. No one in those days thought Marjorie Kinnan Rawlings had written a book for children.

I know that my conservative Presbyterian missionary mother had read it before she gave it to me. She would have remembered the jokes about the Almighty, the scenes where grown men and boys cavort about naked and are not ashamed. She would know that death hovered over its pages like a vulture over the Florida swamplands, and that when the characters invoked the Lord's name it was often not in prayer. She might well have known that Mrs. Rawlings herself was something of a scandalous woman who had left behind comfortable, civilized society and gone to live an unconventional life in the Florida wilds. She must have known all these things, yet sometime that year when I was just the age of Jody Baxter, my mother, returning from a trip where she had gone to speak to Presbyterian ladies about foreign missions, brought me the gift of this book that she knew I would love.

My mother was right. I did love *The Yearling*. It was so live with atmosphere, so rich in emotion, that all the other books I had loved until that time seemed to blanch in comparison. It never occurred to me to wonder about the author. If I'd even known, which I didn't, that she was a wealthy, educated journalist from up north, I wouldn't have thought to question how she could know so much about the hummock country of Florida or, indeed, so much about the heart of a rough and lonely child. I had no curiosity at all about the author. *The Yearling* didn't belong to Marjorie Kinnan Rawlings, it belonged to me. It was a world I had discovered. And I was Jody Baxter.

A year or so later we moved to a house which backed on woods, and for the first time in my life I had a puppy of my own that followed me everywhere. At thirteen, when other girls were beginning to experiment with lipstick and making eyes at boys, I was romping in the woods with my mongrel at my heels, feeling that we had become Jody and Flag now in fact and not just imagination.

I never discussed the book with other people. I feel sure that my seventh-grade teacher would have been shocked if she had known, not only that I had read it, but that my mother had given it to me. In reading class in those days we had textbooks called basal readers. The library at Calvin H. Wiley School was a good one, and the librarian one of my life's heroes, but reading books from the library was something teachers tolerated rather than encouraged. It was all right to read library books in one's spare time, and the occasional required book report took as much joy as possible from that enterprise, but reading books for pleasure mustn't be allowed to interfere with one's education.

I do remember Mother once pointing out the white tail in a picture of a deer. "I never see the white tail of a deer without thinking of Fodderwing," she said. And I remember being proud that she and I had a secret. We both knew strange, crookedy Fodderwing, who saw visions of the departed Spaniards and who could converse with wild critters. But I don't remember ever really talking about the book even with my mother.

I'm not sure I'd have known how to talk about it. The connection I felt with the story was so intense. How could I have expressed it in ordinary language? Although if I had met someone my own age who felt as passionately about the book as I did, wouldn't that have given us a special bond? But I didn't know a teacher like Mary Kitagawa in those days. None of my teachers would have given over precious school time for students to explore meaning in a story, much less dare to explore emotion or belief.

When I was sixteen, I met a girl who had grown up in Africa. The summer we became friends, Mary read aloud to me Alan Paton's *Cry, the Beloved Country*, rolling the beautiful Zulu words off her tongue like exotic music. In Paton's tragic story of his beloved South Africa, I saw for the first time what was happening all around me in the American South of the late 1940s. Reading a great novel is a conversion experience, we are never quite the same afterward.

Mary and I are still the closest of friends and still introducing each other to books we love. She taught me that books can provide a common language and enrich the best of friendships. So in a way, I'm sorry that I didn't have a friend to discuss *The Yearling* with—to watch with me, hushed, at the dance of the whooping cranes—to recoil in horror when Penny was struck by the rattler—to track old Slewfoot across the frozen swampland—to stand close to me when Jody put the muzzle against Flag's soft neck—and to weep with me for a friend and a childhood that were gone forever. But I didn't have anyone at twelve who I thought would understand those feelings, so I kept them to myself.

When the movie of *The Yearling* came along, I was in high school and more sophisticated than when I'd first read the book. I cried at the movie. I always cried at sad movies. Still, I couldn't help noticing that Gregory Peck was far too tall and handsome to play the wiry little Penny Baxter. I could talk about the movie and did, but it didn't occupy the same wild acreage in my heart that the book had claimed three years before.

Not until I reread the book fifty years later did I realize just how profound an effect it had had on me. Echoes from *The Yearling* reverberate through my own books. In *Come Sing, Jimmy Jo*, as if in answer to Hollywood casting, I have given James Johnson a father very much like Penny Baxter in size and wisdom. Jerry Lee loves his son just as Penny does, and he, as well as Penny, will, out of love, make the hard decisions that will appear harsh and unloving to his son.

I've had other surprises as I've reread *The Yearling*. If anyone had asked me where the theme for *Gilly Hopkins* had come from, I would have told her the story of my friendship with Barbara Thompson. Barbara and I were in high school together in a small West Virginia town. I moved to Charles Town in October of my junior year from a fine city high school in Richmond, Virginia. It was Barbara, cheerleader, homecoming queen, president of the junior class, who mysteriously reached out to me and liked me as I was—shy to the point of arrogance, intellectually starving, desperately lonely, with all my friends hundreds of miles away.

Barbara, like Mary whom I met the following summer, has remained a friend through the years. Our lives have gone in quite different directions. I married late and happily. She married her troubled high school sweetheart and is now divorced. In one of our all too infrequent visits since we were young, Barbara said something that haunted me until I was able to incorporate it into a book. "Kathy," (Barbara is one of a handful of people who can call me Kathy without making me cringe) "why don't we ever tell children that life is tough? We feed them all these fairy tales about happily ever after and then they feel cheated. We need to tell them early on that life is really hard."

When I began writing *The Great Gilly Hopkins* I named the town where Gilly finds unconditional love "Thompson Park" in Barbara's honor, and I put into the mouth of the most loving of all my characters, words which echo Barbara's concern.

Gilly was crying now. She couldn't help herself. "Trotter, it's all wrong. Nothing turned out the way it's supposed to."

"How you mean supposed to? Life ain't supposed to be nothing, 'cept maybe tough . . . Sometimes in this world things come easy, and you tend to lean back and say, 'Well, finally, happy ending. This is the way things is supposed to be.' Like life owed you good things . . . And there is lots of good things, baby . . . But you just fool yourself if you expect good things all the time. They ain't what's regular—don't nobody owe 'em to you."

"If life is so bad, how come you're so happy?"

"Did I say bad? I said it was tough. Nothing to make you happy like doing good on a tough job, now is there?"[1]

There are few among my friends that have done better on a tough job than Barbara or have been happier in the doing. You can understand, I think, why I thought *Gilly* was Barbara's gift to me. But when I reread *The Yearling* I was startled to find another seed for Trotter's philosophy in Penny Baxter's speech to Jody after Fawn's tragic death, Jody's flight, and his son's return. Perhaps I was able to hear Barbara's words as an adult because I had read Penny's words first when I was a child.

". . . You figgered I went back on you" [Penny says]. "Now there's a thing ever'man has got to know. Mebbe you know it a'ready. 'Twa'n't only me. 'Twa'n't only your yearlin' deer havin' to be destroyed. Boy, life goes back on you. . . . Ever' man wants life to be a fine thing, and a easy. 'Tis fine, boy, powerful fine, but 'tain't easy. Life knocks a man down and he gits up and it knocks him down agin . . . I wanted to spare you, long as I could. I wanted you to frolic with your yearlin'. I knowed the lonesomeness he eased for you. But ever' man's lonesome. What's he to do then? What's he to do when he gits knocked down? Why, take it for his share and go on."[2]

I'm sure those words were an enormous comfort to me at twelve, just as Barbara's words were a prod years later to share this comfort with other lonely and hard-pressed children.

In *Shadowlands*, C. S. Lewis's most troublesome student says to him, "We read to know that we are not alone." *The Yearling* let me know that I was not alone, and I am grateful that children have written me to say that reading *Gilly Hopkins* has tempered their loneliness.

Although the relationships among *Come Sing, Jimmy Jo* and *The Great Gilly Hopkins* and *The Yearling* were somewhat oblique, even hidden to me, I think I knew almost from the beginning that Jesse Aarons was a cousin to Jody Baxter. Their homes are hundreds of miles apart, but they are both lonely country boys. Jesse Aarons, Sr., is not Penny Baxter, but after Leslie's death when he comes to find Jess at the creek bank, his compassion for his grieving son stretches toward the love Penny daily displays toward his. Jess's father does not teach his son to hunt and farm, but he would envy Penny's opportunities to do so. Life has been hard for both men, but it has driven Jesse Aarons off the land, and his loss is immeasurable.

At the core of both books is friendship. It would be unjust to Leslie to compare her to Flag. Her friendship is one that opens up the world for Jesse, while there is always a hint of danger in Jody's love for a wild creature that cannot understand the constant struggle with starvation on Baxter's Island. But Leslie herself is a beautiful, untamed creature. She has the imagination to destroy monsters and to create new worlds. I think one reason many adults are uneasy with *Bridge to Terabithia* is just this untamed element, for imagination will not bend to neat rules and so threatens complacency and conformity.

Years ago when I was trying to learn how to write fiction, I made up a motto for myself that would run through my head like a mantra: *Something's got to happen. Someone's got to change.* In books for children, the someone who must change is, of course, the young protagonist. And the last lines of *The Yearling* still make me weep, even as I know, and knew when I was twelve, that the yearling Jody must grow to be a man.

. . . He did not believe he should ever again love anything, man or woman or his own child, as he had loved the yearling. He would be lonely all his life. But a man took it for his share and went on.

In the beginning of his sleep, he cried out, "Flag!"

It was not his own voice that called. It was a boy's voice. Somewhere beyond the sink-hole, past the magnolia, under the live oaks, a boy and a yearling ran side by side, and were gone forever.

In *Bridge to Terabithia* I see I could not quite dare that bleak a conclusion. Jess would have to take Leslie's death for his share and move on, but as he went, May Belle would tag along—May Belle the pest, the peeker, the exasperating voice of all his own inner doubts and fears. And though many readers young and old have argued the worthiness of May Belle, it is a measure of Jess's change that he at the end takes her into Terabithia. For if we were rewarded according to our worth in this life, where would most of us be?

"Whatcha doing, Jess?" May Belle had followed him down again as he had guessed she might.

"It's a secret, May Belle."

"Tell me."

"When I finish, OK?"

"I swear on the Bible I won't tell nobody. Not Billy Jean, not Joyce Ann, not Momma—" she was jerking her head back and forth in solemn emphasis.

"Oh, I don't know about Joyce Ann. You might want to tell Joyce Ann sometime."

"Tell Joyce Ann something that's a secret between you and me?" The idea seemed to horrify her.

"Yeah, I was just thinking about it."

Her face sagged. "Joyce Ann ain't nothing but a baby."

"Well, she wouldn't likely be a queen first off. You'd have to train her and stuff."

"Queen? Who gets to be queen?"

"I'll explain it when I finish, OK?"

And when he finished, he put flowers in her hair and led her across the bridge—the great bridge into Terabithia—which might look to someone with no magic in him like a few planks across a nearly dry gully.

"*Shhh,*" he said. "Look."

"Where?"

"Can't you see 'um?" he whispered. "All the Terabithians standing on tiptoe to see you."

"*Me?*"

"*Shhh,* yes. There's a rumor going around that the beautiful girl arriving today might be the queen they've been waiting for."[3]

My mother never knew what she gave when she gave her child a book. Neither will you as you give many books to all sorts and conditions of children. But I hope in this reflective history of one child and one book, you'll realize something of the riches you have at your disposal and will give them away, as my mother did, with perception and delight.

Metaphors to Live By

This speech was given in August 1993 as part of the Swords and Plowshares Conference held by the Children's Literature New England Summer Institute at Harvard University.

"And they shall beat their swords into plowshares and their spears into pruning-hooks: nation shall not lift up sword against nation, neither shall they learn war any more." (Isaiah 2:4)

Rabbi Joseph Weizenbaum tells a story that he says came out of Israel some years ago. It seems that Henry Kissinger, on finding himself suddenly unemployed, sent his résumé to the Israeli government. After all, he reasoned, he'd done a lot for Israel; they ought to reciprocate. So they looked in the file and found out there was only one available job—curator of the Tel Aviv zoo. To their surprise, Henry took the job, and they forgot about him. Suddenly, one day, someone woke up and realized that nothing had been heard from their inexperienced if overqualified curator for months, so they sent an inspector around to see how he was doing. The inspector went down to the zoo, and she saw that it was being perfectly cared for—if in a rather obsessive manner. The grounds were totally without litter. Every cage was scrubbed down to the bare concrete. The animals' coats were gleaming. Indeed, every blade of grass had been washed and blown-dry. The inspector marveled as she went from aviary to the apes—from the bears to the bandicoots. At last she came to the lion cage and found it surrounded by a huge crowd of people. The inspector pushed her way through the crowd to the front. There in the cage was the great maned lion, and lying next to him was a tiny white lamb. Henry himself was standing proudly in front of the cage. The inspector was overcome with awe. She took Kissinger to one side and said: "Henry, you have achieved the messianic dream: the lion and the lamb are lying down together. How did you accomplish that?"

"Very simple," Henry says. "Every morning a fresh lamb."

I don't think I know how many speeches related to the theme of peace I've made over the years. It is my experience that while the lions keep changing, there's never any shortage. But finding a lamb that can make it through the day seems harder every time.

Part of the problem, I think, is that we've lived by the wrong metaphors. One of my closest friends from Norfolk days, Kathryn Morton, wrote me a note last fall to thank me for sending her a copy of *The King's Equal*. And since Kathryn turns a simple thank-you note into a literary masterpiece, the thanks led into a meditation upon the metaphors we live by.

She told me about a panel she had recently moderated where the panelists talked about children and literature.

"The panelists," she said, "had read their Bettelheim and supported the violence and contention we are used to in children's rhymes and stories, as though it were a necessity like salt on food. . . . Personally I have always wondered if the nursery rhymes and the Grimm versions aren't the happenstance that we have gotten stuck with, rather than being paragons or paradigms. We are stuck with railroad tracks built to the width of the Roman roads, impractically narrow now. We are stuck with dangerous, badly designed, top-heavy yellow school buses, made new every year in the same anachronistic mold. I try to envision children raised not on jingles about manic farmers wielding carving knives intent on mutilating mice. Instead, what would it be like if they read more rhymes as wise and salutory as *Yertle the Turtle* for instance. . . ."

Then she goes on to talk about the power of language to shape us. "What if," she asks, "what if we didn't use as the basic metaphor of group activity, sports, which are ritualized warfare, but if we used the choir as the standard metaphor for group activities—then we wouldn't come up with idiocies like 'My country right or wrong,' we'd think: 'A good descant makes the music richer.' "

To return to the guiding metaphor of this conference—plowshares demand more of us than swords. The work of peace is infinitely more difficult than the waging of war. For one thing, we've had so little practice—not only little practice in peacemaking, but so little practice in imagining it.

If you look at the list of books you read for this institute, swords abound. We can imagine war. We (and I mean we) writers can write powerful, soul-wrenching books about it and its horrors. But when it comes to peace we are inarticulate. It's a truism that the snake has all the lines. That Lucifer is the hero we remember, not pale Adam. That without conflict we have no plot. But I think all that tells us is something tragic about ourselves. That when it comes to peace, our storied imaginations fail. We can't imagine what would be interesting enough about it to write a book.

If you learned history the way I did, it was: There was this great heroic war—names of generals, dates of battles, place and date where the peace treaty or armistice was signed. Then nothing happened for X number of years until, suddenly, there was another great war— names of generals, dates of battle, place and date of treaty. Then X number of years during which nothing happened, until, whew, just in time, another great war—

Growing up white in the South, there was, of course, only one really great war. That one always puzzled me as a child. How come if the

South had all the best generals and won all the big battles, we managed to lose the war? It was never adequately explained. I tried to remember something that happened between wars in my history book, and the only thing I could come up with was the invention of the cotton gin. So there must have been a tip of the hat to the industrial revolution in the schools I attended—but there again, in order to give it any importance at all, we had to call it a "revolution."

We don't know what to do with peace. It's like happily ever after at the end of the fairy tale. Nothing happens after that. Now all of us, married or not, know that "they got married" is not the end of the story. Nor is the end of a particular war a happily ever after. We can hardly wait to get on to the next war so something will be happening.

We don't know how to make peace. We stand looking at the great, hulking machinery of war and we are paralyzed. How do we begin to beat *that* into instruments of peace? It's easier to look for a new enemy to aim at than to figure out how we can transform our submarines into shelters for the homeless and our bombers into well-baby clinics.

When I reread the passage in Isaiah that was the theme for this conference, I suddenly realized that I had been reading it wrong all my life. I had read the passage as though it was talking about the end of things—the happily ever after—after which, as we all know, nothing happens. Whereas, the prophet is saying that it's only after the swords are beaten into plowshares that the real productive work of life begins.

I took a close look at a plowshare in May. I was engaged in the making of a video that was to prove once again that I was real and alive. I'm quite good at proving both points. In fact, I get more substantial every year. But this project was attempting a sort of cinema verité—or not very verité. I was to reenact some research that I had done in writing several of my books. This particular filming was done at the Shelburne Museum, where I had indeed gone to do research, but for cinematic purposes, I was re-creating a conversation with a member of the staff there that had never taken place, since I'd never even met Garet Livermore until after *Lyddie* was published. But the director thought a mid-nineteenth-century New England plow would make a good picture, so she had me asking Garet just how the plow would be used.

As Garet explained to me the angle at which I should hold the shafts, my mind jumped forward to tonight. Plows, I thought, demand much more of the user than swords. For one thing, you couldn't use this plow by yourself. You needed a partner—a horse or ox or a strong family member to pull while another strong member held up the shafts and directed the point of the plowshare through the rocky New England soil. On particularly rough fields, you might need a third partner—a family member to walk by the head of the beast and guide it as it strained to pull the plow through the unfriendly soil. Now the writer who wrote these words in the book of Isaiah lived in an agricultural community. He knew that plowing was hard work. He never said recycle your swords into mobiles or sculptures or belt buckles, he said beat your swords into plowshares—something that will make you work like a beast of burden but that will in the long run produce food for your family and your community. The same goes for spears. The only thing you do with a spear is skewer someone on it. But have you ever tried to trim a fruit tree? We've got a couple of old apple trees in our yard, so I've seen it done. It's hard work, potentially dangerous work, which is why I talked my husband out of doing it a second time. I got very nervous watching him climb that ladder and lean way out to lop off those dead or superflous branches. But you have to do this if you want to make those trees produce—to be in the truest sense fruitful.

We haven't figured out, most of us, that peace is really hard work. We'd thought it was the happy ending. Remember the crumbling of the Berlin Wall? Before we'd really had a chance to celebrate we were confronted with neo-Nazism. Remember Yeltsin heroic on the top of that tank? Before we could pop the champagne cork we were confronted with a society that simply disintegrated before our eyes. And what shall we say of Bosnia and Liberia and Cambodia and Somalia and Iraq and Sudan and Northern Ireland?

Finian O'Shea, an Irish teacher, sent me a book of poems written by children from Northern Ireland.

This one by a six-year-old:

> St. Patrick, I know you help us in very many ways
> But now comes the time to help us in these days
> The fighting starts in Belfast
> And works its way to Dublin
> I'm afraid it's not snakes
> It's fighting that's our problem.

And this by a sixteen-year-old:

> They talk, the older folks,
> And paint a rosy past.
> Oh! I am tired of hearing
> How things were in Belfast.
>
> They talk and tell me stories
> Of the good times they once had
> And the more they talk about it all
> The more it makes me sad.
>
> For I cannot remember
> A childhood free from strife,
> To me the bombs and bullets
> Are just a way of life.

So I have just one question
To ask our violent men.
What about my wasted childhood,
Can you bring it back again?[1]

Libby Hofstetler at the Lion and the Lamb Peace Arts Center sent me these words, which accompanied children's artwork from Serbia:

"Yesterday my friend cried. He survived the hell. His mother, father, and his brother died in the war. Isn't it enough to stop that dirty war!"

"We want that our childhood spend in peace! Don't worry, be happy! I ask you: Why we, children, must live in war? Return me my smile, please. Stop's the war. He is guilty for everything."

And from this nine-year-old: "Have you a childrens? I don't want the war. I am sorry. . . . We are the children. Listen to us because we are not guilty for this war."

As I was writing down these words from children caught up in war, I remembered a Lenten anthem we used to sing: "Listen to the lambs, all a-crying—" And suddenly the joke I told at the beginning of the speech turned very grim. The children of the world are the fresh lambs we supply every morning, noon, and night.

But what can we do? I don't know about you, but sometimes I feel that I'm just standing on the edge of the abyss wringing my hands.

When I was in Finland briefly in 1987, the tour guide was telling us about the Finnish language, which no one in the world except Finns speaks. I may not remember this correctly, but my recollection is that in the Finnish language there are ninety-seven words to describe various degrees of drunkenness. Well, since then I've learned another Finnish word that we don't have a proper English translation for. The word is *sisu* and means, I'm told, a sort of spiritual toughness.

Ah, I thought, that is what we lack, both the word and the quality. When it comes to making peace, we're a bunch of sissies. We have no degree of spiritual toughness. It takes *sisu* to beat swords into plowshares and more *sisu* to guide and pull the plows.

So where do we begin? Well, there is only one place we can begin, and that is where we are. Let me amend that. There is only one place for me to begin, and that is here in this room tonight.

I must look inside myself and discover the instruments of destruction that must be beaten into the instruments that work for life.

So I look inside and find—not despair exactly—but a hardening crust of cynicism. Surely not me? I, the great spy for hope? I looked up the word *cynicism* in the dictionary just to prove myself not guilty, and this is what I found: "cynic—a sneering faultfinder; one who doubts or denies the goodness of human motives, and who often displays his attitude by sneers, sarcasm, etc."

Well, okay. So I doubt and deny the goodness of human motives. All we Calvinists do. We're realists, after all. Okay, so sometimes I've been caught sneering at certain former presidents, not to speak of vice presidents and current members of Congress and even certain benighted writers of so-called children's books. And maybe a few sarcastic words concerning those who seek to ban my beautiful books from the schools and libraries of this country have managed to slip through my clenched teeth. Is that cynicism? Surely not.

And then I remembered a story that I should never, ever allow myself to forget. Some of you have heard this story before, but I'm not going to let you forget it, either.

It was the spring of 1975. We watched the television with growing horror as the years of fighting in Southeast Asia came down to Vietnamese clinging in vain to the ladders of escaping American helicopters and then on to the killing fields of Cambodia. And the children—always the suffering children. Some of them were snatched up out of the debacle and dumped parentless and bewildered into refugee camps.

Our own four children watched in horror. Their immediate, unanimous reaction was that we should adopt as many of these children as we could pack into our seven-room house. Now I would like to say that I was thrilled by my children's concern. Actually I was appalled. I was barely managing as the mother of four normal, happy, healthy children. Besides, I was in the middle of writing a book that was tearing me to pieces. Where was I supposed to summon up the sheer animal energy needed to feed and clean up after, not to speak of the psychic energy that would be demanded to care for and nurture, this small army of refugee children that my own four felt sure their mother would welcome with open arms?

Well, we compromised. We offered to be a temporary foster home for two Cambodian brothers who arrived with a group of children without parents or papers at Dulles airport in May. We bought bunk beds to turn the boys' room into a dormitory, and I began cooking rice three times a day. For all my failings, I thought smugly, at least these boys have come to a home where the mother knows how to cook rice properly.

Well, I do know how to cook rice. That was never a problem. But rice was one of the few things that wasn't a problem. The days stretched into weeks and the weeks into nearly two months, and, although there were some exceptional incidents, on a day-to-day basis, my foster parent's lot was not a happy one.

What is the matter? I asked myself. Yes, the boys have problems, real problems, but I certainly had expected that. Yes, my own children are having difficulties accommodating, but come on, now, that was only to be expected. And then I realized that the real fault lay not in any of the children, homemade, adopted, or foster. The real fault lay in me. Whenever a problem arose, I was saying, "Well, we can't really deal with that. They're only going to be here a few days, weeks, months." Or "Thank heavens, they're only going to be here a few days, weeks, months." And what I was doing was treating two human beings as though they were disposable.

Looking back, I'm not sure what I could or should have done differently, but I am sure that I should have thought differently. Because if anything is true, it is true that no human being is disposable. That every crime committed, every injustice permitted, every war that is waged goes back to this cynical assumption by one person or group of persons that another person or group of persons is disposable.

It is a cynicism I must constantly search out in my own heart and mind. But just to search it out is not enough. Guilt and despair do not make peace. The sword and the spear must be utilized, they must be beaten into something that will be productive for life. So what can I make of this cynicism of mine? Perhaps it can be beaten into a pruning hook. The person who wields a pruning hook must be a realist. She must see what is harming growth and productivity and not be afraid to trim where needed, but the end result is life, not destruction. The spear of cynicism becomes a pruning hook—an instrument of imaginative judgment.

I've been reading a book about children's war play entitled *Who's Calling the Shots?* In it the authors, Diane Levine and Nancy Carlsson-Paige, make the point that while it is almost impossible to stop children playing war, adults can help children turn war play into a productive, imaginative activity. The problem with war toys, they say, especially those hawked in half-hour commercials on children's TV programs, is that they lead to imitative violence rather than imaginative play. I think these women are on to something. They never say to parents—stop all war games; rather, they show how those games may help a child evolve beyond aggression. So while most of us are sneering cynically at Saturday-morning cartoons, produced by cynical toy merchants who consider money valuable and children disposable, these writers are showing parents who have to live in the real world how to beat cynicism into imaginative play that will help rather than harm their children. I would be interested in other people's reactions to this book. I was impressed.

Okay, what else is down there in that murky psyche? Well, there's envy. Oh, surely not. Who could I be envious of? Hah! I'm not naming names tonight, some of them are sitting here tonight a bit close for comfort, but if you think for one moment that I am envy free you haven't read *Jacob Have I Loved*. It would be nice to think that writing that book cured me of that particular sin, but the best I can say is that it made me confront it rather baldly. Suffice it to say, I recognize and continue to recognize the sword of envy. Envy cuts both ways. The sharpest edge cuts toward the envious one. A. S. Byatt, writing in *The New York Times Book Review,* in its series on the seven deadly sins, quotes the Wisdom of Solomon: "Through envy of the devil came death into the world." Of course, this is the theme of *Paradise Lost,* Lucifer's envy, which brings Adam and Eve to sin. It is envy that causes Cain to kill his brother, Abel. It is envy that blinds and hobbles Louise, which prods Iago and twists Uriah Heep.

There is a terrible corrosive quality to envy, all the more so, as Byatt reminds us, because there is a kinship between envy and justice. The small child cries out, "It's not fair!" demanding that the universe be just. But as most of us remember telling our outraged children, "Life is not fair." It is not the nature of the created world to be just. The only creature who expects or demands justice is the one created in the image of God. For better and oftentimes for worse, the work of justice has been entrusted to human beings.

My friend Kathryn Morton tells of a Jewish prayer in which you say, "What is it for us to do? It is for us to heal the world." This prayer, called the *tikkun olam,* comes from the mystical aspect of the Jewish tradition. "The story," says Kathryn, "is that there was an original great light and it was divided and spread and cast all asunder and it is for each of us (who has a part of the light inside themselves) to gather more, to gather the light back together, and when the light is all re-united, it will be the coming of the Messiah—heaven on earth. I'm not much into mysticism," Kathryn says, "but I think it's a wonderful metaphor . . . it's a metaphor I can live by."[2]

So part of the work of peace is gathering of light or, to go back to our original metaphor, the beating of the sword of envy into the plow-share of justice. It's not just doing what comes naturally. It demands a whole new way of looking at ourselves and our fellows. We must turn from the childish demand for fairness for ourselves and turn toward the vision of justice for everyone.

At St. Michael's four summers ago, many of you heard Tom Feel-ings give one of the most powerful speeches I have ever heard one of my colleagues give. In that speech Tom quoted President Carter in a statement that I have gone over and over in my head since I first heard it.

" 'There is still an element of racism that is inherent in perhaps all of us,' President Carter said. 'I try not to be a racist and wouldn't call myself a racist, but I have feelings that border on it. And that is em-barrassing to me sometimes. When the TV screens were filled with little Ethiopian and Sudanese children walking along with distended bellies and dying in the arms of their dying mothers, it's hard for me to believe that one of these children in the eyes of God is as impor-tant as Amy, my daughter.'

" 'How many of these little black kids does it take to equal one Amy? Fifteen . . . twenty . . . ten . . . five . . . I think the answer is one. But it's hard for me to believe this. I think all of us to some degree are guilty of an insensitivity to the needs and ideas of others . . .' "

In the arithmetic of justice, my friends, one must always equal one.

Perhaps the most troubling phrase to come out of the Gulf War was the oft-repeated sentence of our leaders: "Thank God, there was so little loss of life." And yet we know that 100,000 men, women, and children died in that war. A woman in Ohio has made a mural with 100,000 faces on it. It takes a long time, my friends, to walk past 100,000 faces.

As Barbara Harrison reminded you earlier this week, the sword and plowshares metaphor occurs more than once in the Bible. The prophet Micah uses it to portray the messianic ideal, but he adds a verse that I find significant. Let me read again Micah's addition to the now familiar words of swords and plowshares:

> But they shall sit every man under his vine and under his fig tree, and none shall make them afraid; for the mouth of the Lord of hosts has spoken.
>
> For all the peoples walk each in the name of its god, but we will walk in the name of the Lord our God for ever and ever.[3]

Justice for the Hebrew prophets meant not only turning the instruments of war into the tools necessary for productive life, but making sure that all persons have their own productive space—where they can live and work totally without threat. They can even worship any gods they choose. "And none shall make them afraid." So let me say as an aside something that should never be thought of as an aside— that the messianic vision is totally inclusive. No one is disposable. Everyone's individual home and work and for that matter religion is respected. Wow, if we could only plant that vision in Cambodia and Northern Ireland and the Middle East and the United States.

Well, we only have one place we can begin and that is with ourselves tonight in this room. But to do this we need to beat our own cynicism, our own envy, and yes our own fears into instruments of life.

Thomas Jefferson has a tattered reputation in our day. Much has been made of his maintaining a black mistress and speaking out for freedom while remaining a slave owner. Which leads to the accusation of hypocrisy—which, as all us righteous people know, is the worst crime anyone could be accused of.

In the book *Thomas Jefferson: An Intimate History*, the author, Fawn Brodie, writes:

> When Jefferson wrote that all men were created equal and entitled to life, liberty, and the pursuit of happiness, he was enunciating an ideal as if it were a reality. This was one of Jefferson's special qualities as a revolutionary statesman: that he could define the visionary future as if it were the living present. . . . There was no contradiction when he said, "It is so," and meant, "It will be so." It was not the melancholy of his great burdens but the vision of what could be that held him. He would not let faith in his own destiny be destroyed by what was . . .[4]

As I read these words I remembered the prophet Jeremiah, who had prophesied the destruction of his nation while being scorned as a fool and imprisoned as a traitor. Then, finally, the worst of his prophecies were about to come true; the city was about to fall, and he was in jail for uttering treason. Instead of saying, "I told you so," Jeremiah sent his assistant, Baruch, out to buy a piece of land. Yes, the land would be overrun by the enemy; yes, the city would be destroyed and the inhabitants would be taken away to live as exiles in Babylon. But Jeremiah had the deeds to his property put into an earthenware vessel "that they may last for a long time. For thus says the Lord of hosts, the

God of Israel: Houses and fields and vineyards shall again be bought in this land."[5]

Perhaps some of you have seen the *Time* magazine issue of July 26. In it is a group of pictures that had been taken on black market film and sent out of Sarajevo through enemy lines. The pictures were taken by a Bosnian photographer determined to document for the world the suffering of his people. They are pictures of utter desolation and despair—with one startling exception. Two hospital beds have been pushed together. On the beds are a young man and a young woman, their arms entwined. There is a bouquet on her bed and a large sign hung at the foot of each bed. Her sign reads: "Just" and his reads: "Married." The caption beneath the picture says: "Eternal Optimism: A couple who both lost legs to Serbian shells bet on the future."

This is not eternal optimism. In the self-declared "city without hope," this is hope worthy of a Jefferson or a Jeremiah.

In closing, I want to share a swords and plowshares story from my own family history. Among old letters, I found some which my father as a young man had written home from France during World War I. He returned with one leg and gas in his lungs, but that's another story. As a student, my father became a part of the volunteer ambulance corps, recruited from American colleges and universities to serve with the French army. Perhaps you remember another of those young men—Ernest Hemingway.

The letter is dated July 28, 1918, and tells of the Second Battle of the Marne. My father was twenty-four years old, driving a Model T Ford ambulance, fondly nicknamed a Tin Lizzy.

Just a part of the letter:

> . . . The souvenir gatherers should be here. They could find anything from a [German] tank to cartridges and the like.

I have seen so many helmets, etc., that I would like to get to a place where there are no souvenirs. You have seen the pictures of the forests, how they are torn and ruined; well those are no exaggerations. I saw this afternoon one tree between three and four feet in diameter cut off. And the smaller trees are lying in a tangled heap everywhere. Now and then there will be a shell that did not explode in a tree, while some of the trees are so full of shrapnel and bullets that they are well loaded.

We are well. Our headquarters are in a small town where it was impossible to find enough of a good roof left to keep the cooking stove dry. So you see we must sleep in our cars or in dugouts, which are very damp, especially after several rainy days that we have had. Such is life in a place that wherever you and your "Lizzy" keep together you are at home. You never worry about getting back, you are always there.

And then, almost as an afterthought, he adds these words:

"The wheat, what is left, is very fine indeed, if it could be harvested."

The letter ends there, but not the story. A friend in my father's ambulance division, the only Yankee to be placed among the Washington and Lee University volunteers, tells in his memoirs what happened a few days later.

There was a lull in the fighting, and my father came to him. "See that field of wheat?" he asked. "There's only an old couple living on that farm. There's no one left strong enough to bring in a crop of that size. It would be a shame to let it go to waste."

So the two of them, Virginia farm boy and Wisconsin schoolteacher, borrowed scythes and harvested the field of ripe grain before the next battle could destroy it.

This, as my friend Kathryn Morton would say, is a metaphor I can live by.

This speech appears in the collection of Children's Literature New England pre-sentations, Origins of Story: On Writing for Children, *edited by Barbara Harrison and Gregory Maguire (New York: Margaret K. McElderry Books, 1999).*

Hope and Happy Endings

I am very glad to be here today. I am honored to be the thirtieth recipient of this distinguished award, especially when I read the names that have preceded mine. Today is one of those occasions when I wish my grandmother Goetchius were still alive. Grandmother would be amazed to know that I turned out something other than trifling. She used to make sweeping pronouncements that all of her children and grandchildren were "*far* above the average," but when it came down to specific children—perhaps I should say, this specific child—she despaired daily.

There was a time when I would come home from school with a book in my hand, push open the front door, and without removing my overcoat fall prone upon the living room floor, where I lay reading until suppertime. I remember one particular afternoon, my mother was quietly sweeping the rug around me. My infuriated grandmother tolerated this scene as long as she could, then came and stood over my inert body and announced to my mother in a voice tremulous with disappointment, "I'm afraid Katherine is a lover of luxury."

Usually I couldn't hear anything when I was reading, but I remember hearing that judgment and swelling up with self-righteous indignation. I was reading A *Tale of Two Cities*, for Pete's sake, Dickens—a classic. Anybody else's grandmother would be proud to have such an intellectual grandchild, thought I. But I didn't say it. We didn't argue with my grandmother. I had graduated from a church college, earned a master's degree in English Bible, become a missionary, and married a Presbyterian minister before she died, but by the time I started straightening out, she was having to be introduced to me every time we met, so I don't think she ever gave me any credit.

Actually if she were alive and in her right mind today, she'd be a hundred and twenty-one and probably fretting that this lovely medal was being presented to me in New York City by Roman Catholics. I grew up among people for whom there was something sinister, if not slightly scandalous, about consorting with Yankees and/or Catholics. The Goetchius family of Georgia traced their Calvinist roots to the Netherlands of the sixteenth century.

There's a rather bizarre legend about that first Protestant Goetchius. He was examined, condemned, and beheaded during the Inquisition. This in itself was pretty heavy stuff for me to listen to as a child, but Aunt Helen, who was telling me the story, couldn't leave it at that. "And after the ax fell," she told me, "your ancestor rose to his feet and walked three steps before he dropped dead. That," she said, "proves that a Goetchius cannot be easily defeated."

What it proved to me at twelve was that I should take my Aunt Helen's stories with a grain of salt. She was, after all, sort of the black sheep of the family—the only one of us who smoked cigarettes, played cards, and recanted the faith to live out her life as an Episcopalian.

There is another reason it is probably fortunate that my grandmother didn't live to see this day. She was a foremost proponent of the "Be sweet, my child, and let who will be clever" Southern school of raising female children. I'm sure she would have felt that for me to see my name included in the list of winners of this award would be perilous for my soul. My mother would have handled the threat with more equanimity. After I was awarded a Newbery Medal on the heels of a National Book Award, friends and family asked my mother in alarm: "What will happen to Katherine? What will all this notoriety do to her?" My mother replied, "You don't need to worry about Katherine. She has *plenty* to keep her humble."

I'm keeping in mind all those things today as you are honoring the body of my work. I love that phrase "body of work." Actually, to be honest, I love my books. All of them. It is similar to the way I feel about my four grown children. There they are, all different, none perfect, but I look at them—bright, funny, beautiful, loving people—and I'm very grateful to have had a part in their lives. Similarly, I look at the books and they are all different, none perfect, but I reread them with affection and a sort of surprised admiration. Knowing myself as well as I do, I am always a bit amazed that I could have written them, and grateful—believe me, very grateful.

I tell myself it's all right if my books are not universally loved and admired, but of course I don't mean that, not in my heart of hearts. I want everyone to love them as I do, faults and all. Which makes this award especially welcome. It says to me that you love them all—not just one of them. But the truth of the matter is there are people who are not as kind as the Catholic Library Association—those who fail to love my books—and I have to learn to deal with that or find another line of work.

One of my coping mechanisms over the years has involved the designing of an imaginary book jacket—the jacket for the one-volume complete works of Katherine Paterson. I don't know yet what will be on the front, but the back will consist of blurbs from reviews and articles. You know those stock paperback blurbs: "Believable and moving . . ." "So-and-so is a breathtakingly brilliant writer." "You emerge from this marvelous novel as if from a dream, the mind on fire. . . ."

No writer I know believes those blurbs—especially the ones that have three dots preceding or following the adjectives. It is nice to have compliments in a review that make for good blurbs on your paperback, but those are not what a writer remembers. The reviews that stick tighter than a burr are the negative ones. Those are the ones that you need to learn how to deal with. So I am going to put them, or some of the choicest ones, on my dream jacket. Let me give you a sampling: "Gilly Hopkins is a robot constructed for the purpose of instructing the young." "Pompous, pretentious, and one wonders indeed why it was ever published." ". . . exceedingly irksome." ". . . a clutter of clichéd metaphors . . ." "[dot dot dot] trivial [dot dot dot]." "Sara Louise's bright new beginning moves with astonishing haste to a final dead end."

That one really smarts. Particularly, I think, because I get a lot of questions about the endings of my books. Not long ago a child asked me, "Why are your endings all so sad?" I was a bit thrown. I know sad things happen in my books, but I certainly don't perceive of them as all having sad endings. I was forced to take another look at the body of my work, or at least at the endings of my novels, and I must confess that none of them has what might be conventionally called a happy ending. But does that make them sad? Or, as one troubled mother complained to me when speaking of *Gilly Hopkins,* "totally without hope"?

Surely not. I couldn't write a book "totally without hope." I wouldn't know how. "But what do you mean by hope?" Sarah Smedman, a children's literature scholar and a nun, asked me that question last fall, and I have been mulling it over ever since. Have you noticed that about questions? The really good ones can never be answered on the spot. The better the question, the longer it will take to answer.

Which makes me wonder why we expect children immediately to raise their hands and spout forth instant wisdom. Perhaps it is because we are realistic about the quality of our questions.

Anyhow, the question Sarah asked me was perfectly legitimate. What did I mean by hope? I have from time to time made sweeping pronouncements about hope as it has to do with fiction, particularly children's fiction. Sarah had every right to think, therefore, that I had already carefully thought through my own definition of the word *hope*.

I was somewhat embarrassed to hear myself defining in negatives—what I didn't mean by hope, certainly as I thought of hope in my books. I didn't mean wishful thinking. I didn't mean happily ever after, or even conventional happy endings. Certainly in the scope of a juvenile novel I didn't mean hope of heaven or the Second Coming. So what did I mean?

When some readers—especially adult readers, in my experience— define hope in children's books, they do seem to mean wishful thinking. One critic asks:

> Must Paterson's capable, imaginative protagonist-narrator in *Jacob Have I Loved*, Sara Louise Bradshaw, be forced, in the name of historical accuracy, into the same kind of quietistic and blatantly antifeminist womanhood as her mother before her? Why must we witness "Wheeze" Bradshaw cheerfully trading her hopes of medical school for marriage to a widowed farmer in an Appalachian community no less isolated by the mountains than Rass Island was by the sea, while her gifted but pusillanimous twin sister, Caroline, having stolen Wheeze's old friend Call Purnell for her husband, pursues wealth and fame as an opera singer in New York? Could Paterson provide no more equitable conclusion than this to her

often powerful tale of sibling jealousy and rage—for the sake
not only of her narrator's aspirations but those of her teenaged
female readers as well?[1]

My temptation here is to start yelling at the critic. What did you want
for an ending? I want to say. Would you have been satisfied if Louise
had ended up a feminist radiologist in Baltimore? Would that have
made her worthy in your eyes? Or, Screebies! Can't you see that
Louise is more a doctor than any M.D. you or I are ever likely to
meet, limited as our doctors are to specialties and technology and
frightened as they are by lawsuits? This woman is out there really doing it. She doesn't need a diploma on the wall to prove to her patients
that she's qualified. She proves that every day in actual practice. And
what's this about her mother? What have you got against women who
make the conscious choice to be homemakers? This woman had a fine
husband who loved her. She raised two terrific daughters. Which reminds me. Wherever did you get the idea that Caroline was pusillan-
imous? Don't you know better than to take as gospel the adolescent
Louise's description of her sister? The whole portrait is done in green,
for heaven's sake!

You'll be relieved to know that I haven't even written a letter to
the editor of that scholarly journal. I've just quietly seethed that an
intelligent scholar should so malign these people that I care for so
deeply.

And as for those teenage female readers for whom he is concerned, none of them has ever complained to me about my antifemi-
nism or indeed despised the ending that so many adult critics love to
hate. I think we are dealing here with a fundamental disagreement
between the young reader and the adult teacher, parent, or critic.
Children do not go to novels looking for role models. They may go for
adventure, for escape, for laughter, or for more serious concerns—to

understand themselves, to understand others, to rehearse the experiences that someday they may live out in the flesh. But they don't go for role models. When they go to a serious novel they expect to find truth, and everyone knows that role models are ideals, not realities. They want hope rooted in reality, not wishful thinking.

The child who asked about my sad endings was asking for something different. I think she was expressing a wistful yearning we all share for happily ever after, and I am the last person to denigrate happily ever after. There is a stage in a child's development when his basic psychic diet should consist of large servings of fairy tales.

We owe Bruno Bettelheim a great debt. Most of us have known in our guts that we needed fairy tales, but Bettelheim has articulated the important role they play in children's lives. Children, he reminds us, think in sweeping extremes: "I'll never learn how to tie my shoes." "It'll kill me if I eat this squash." "I'm always going to hate Susie." "Mom, you're the most beautiful woman in the world!"—There's one four-year-old's sweeping declaration I hated to let go. "No one will ever like me ever again." "I hate you! I hate you! I hate you! I hope you die and never come back here again!" The child's fears and feelings are enormous and unrealistic, and thus he needs hopes that are enormous and unrealistic.

Nothing less than happily ever after will satisfy children who see themselves helpless and hedged in by huge and powerful persons. And so the fairy tale becomes a great source of comfort for them. By the time a child is reading fairy tales, she knows the difference between fantasy and reality. But the fairy tale gives the child hope. You are a nobody now, poor little Cinderella, but just you wait. You will show them all someday. It won't be easy, but you will grow up. You have a wicked stepmother who will try to stop you, but you also have a fairy godmother who will come to your aid. You must discipline yourself, obey the limitations that her magic lays upon you, and then someday, your prince will come and you will truly be somebody.

The hope that the fairy tale provides is a limited hope. It is, according to Bettelheim, simply the hope that the child will grow up. Realistic stories can't give a child this same hope, Bettelheim says, because "his unrealistic fears require unrealistic hopes. By comparison with the child's wishes, realistic and limited promises are experienced as deep disappointment, not as consolation. But they are all that a relatively realistic story can offer."[2]

I have to admit that I think there is a great deal of truth in this view of both realistic fiction and fairy stories. And I say this as I remember that my youngest read *Cinderella* over and over again. I know perfectly well who the wicked stepmother was, and I hope like mad that the fairy godmother is the same person in this scenario. But if I say that Bettelheim is right, then don't I have to stop writing? Even if I made a switch to fairy tales, they couldn't be the old ones, the ones buried in our primitive psyches, the ones that have the power to move a child from his infantile fears and fixations toward the relative integration and self-empowerment of adulthood.

It is no use to pretend that I read *The Uses of Enchantment* before I began writing realistic fiction for children, figured out the fallacy in Bettelheim's argument, and then proceeded to write my own books on the basis of a well-thought-out philosophy. In the first place, I started writing my first novel in 1968, and *The Uses of Enchantment* wasn't published until after I had written five of my now nine novels. Even after I had read it, and found myself in essential agreement with its premises, I went right ahead and wrote the same old thing for four more novels.

I do, you see, what most writers do. I write what I can. And I never think about what I'm doing until afterward. I philosophize when questions come after the book is published. Someone asks:

"Why did you do such and such?" and I wonder, "Why *did* I do such and such?" and I begin to write a speech that essentially speculates on why I did something that at the time was done totally subconsciously. This is one of those speeches.

Last month our public television station broadcast the film musical *Oliver! Oliver Twist* is a good example of *peripeteia,* or reversal of fortune, which is as popular a theme in fairy tales as it is in Greek drama, and a favorite plot with Dickens. Oliver starts out as a foundling in an orphanage and ends up as the heir to the kindly Mr. Brownlow. Dickens loves to make things work out happily in the end. Sometimes, as in *Nicholas Nickleby*, he makes us positively dizzy as he whirls about tying up all the loose ends and making all the good guys delirious with newfound joy.

I first saw the film *Oliver!* years ago, so I'd frankly forgotten exactly how it ended. I remembered, of course, Nancy's tragic sacrifice and Bill Sykes's horrible end. I even remembered that wonderful non-Dickensian duet that sends our beloved rogues, Fagin and the Artful Dodger, skipping out of town together to work their villainy elsewhere.

But I'd forgotten the actual ending. What would the writer do with this devastated child, who has seen his beloved Nancy savagely murdered and then been taken hostage by the killer, dragged through the slums of London, only to end up high above the narrow street on a rotting scaffold that is rocking back and forth, back and forth, as the heavy body of Bill Sykes swings below in a grotesque parody of a public hanging?

Dickens himself has no trouble turning Oliver's trauma into an almost fairy-tale happy ending. Of course it takes three chapters and twenty-eight closely printed pages to do it, but as always, Dickens manages to tie every stray thread into a splendiferous macramé of justice and joy. The evil are punished, the good are bountifully rewarded, and those in the middle repent and reap such benefits as befit their middling estate. I've often wished that Dickens could have had Virginia Buckley for an editor. The ending of *Oliver Twist* is a dramatic example of what travesties can befall a good writer with a bad editor, or, as I darkly suspect, no editor at all.

But would the writer of a modern musical handle the ending any better? Would he insist on a reprise of "Who Will Buy?" with all of London singing lustily while clicking their heels in dazzling sunlight—which would come as a blinding surprise to anyone who has ever lived in the actual gray and drizzly city?

No. The writer of the film turned away from both the excesses of Dickens and the conventions of the musical comedy form. As you may remember, the carriage draws up in front of Mr. Brownlow's house, Mr. Brownlow and an exhausted Oliver get out and walk up the front steps. The kindly housekeeper comes out to greet them and, without a word spoken, much less sung, Oliver puts his arms around her and weeps.

What a lovely ending. I wish Dickens could have seen it. No singing, no dancing, no words. Any of them would have diminished Oliver's pain. We know from the way Mr. Brownlow puts his arm lightly across the boy's shoulder as they walk up the steps, and the way the housekeeper's warm arms enfold him, that Oliver will be cared for. But his pain is not trivialized, much less erased. He will grow up to be a wise and compassionate gentleman, but deep in his heart, he will bear the hunger of the workhouse and the grief of Jacob's Island to his grave.

This, I maintain, is a proper ending. Perhaps I should amend that. It is a proper ending for me. It is not, strictly speaking, a happy ending. It is certainly not happily ever after. But it is a positive demonstration of what I mean when I speak of hope in stories for children.

In order to make this clearer, I want to take you back to the Bible—to the call of Moses. You remember that God first speaks to

Moses from a burning bush on the mountainside. The reason Moses is wandering around that mountain in the first place is that he's a fugitive from justice. He killed a man and then had to run before the law got him. He's living in the desert, most likely under an assumed name, working as a shepherd for his father-in-law, when God speaks to him out of a burning bush and tells him to do something totally crazy: Go back to Egypt, where your picture is on the post-office wanted posters, go straight to Pharaoh's palace and tell him you've come to organize the free labor he has slaving away on those treasure cities he's building. Pharaoh's workers are going to stage a permanent walkout, because I've chosen you to march this unruly mob across the trackless desert to the country your ancestors left four hundred years ago, which is now inhabited by fierce nations that live in walled cities.

Moses is understandably reluctant. He offers a number of objections to this plan. Nothing much has been heard from God for the last four hundred years. God isn't exactly in the forefront of everybody's mind these days. If Moses starts talking to the average Israelite about God, the fellow's likely to reply, "God who?" So Moses says, "If I come to the people of Israel and say to them, 'The God of your fathers has sent me to you,' and they ask me, 'What is his name?' what shall I say to them?"[3]

All of us know enough about ancient thought to know the power of the name. If the people of Israel know God's true name, they will in a sense have power over God. But at this point in the story, something wonderful happens. God does indeed give Moses a name, but it proves to be unpronounceable and a verb to boot. God says, "I AM WHO I AM. . . . Say this to the people of Israel, 'I AM has sent me to you.' . . . this is my name for ever, and thus I am to be remembered throughout all generations."[4] Here is a God of the present time—of the world as it is and also the God of what will be. Nothing will ever be the same again. Being human, we will have to pronounce something to take the place of the name of this reality. We will assign nouns and pronouns, but we won't have hold of God thereby. The One whose true name is a verb is the One in whom we live and move and have our being. It is he who has hold of us. The story also assures us that the One who is and will be hears the cries of those in distress and acts to deliver them.

As a spiritual descendant of Moses, and of the prophets and apostles who followed him, I have to think of hope in this context. We are not really optimists as the common definition goes, because we, like Moses, must be absolute realists about the world in which we find ourselves. And this world looked at squarely does not allow optimism to flourish. Hope for us cannot simply be wishful thinking, nor can it be only the desire to grow up to and take control of our own lives. Hope is a yearning rooted in reality that pulls us toward the radical biblical vision of the world remade.

Those of us who worship a God whose name is an unpronounceable verb that can be translated as both "I am" and "I will be," we know that what is reality for us at this moment is not the sum total of truth. We are always being pulled toward an ultimate vision of a world where truth and justice and peace do prevail in a time when the knowledge of God will cover the earth as the waters cover the sea. It is a scene that finds humanity living in harmony with nature, and all nations beating their swords into plowshares and walking together in the light of God's glory. Now there's a happy ending for you—the only purely happy ending I know of. The Book of Revelation calls it a beginning, but that's another story.

Paul tells us all creation is standing on tiptoe waiting for the ushering in of this vision. Or, we could say, the pull of that vision draws all creation toward itself. And the movement from where we are today on this dark and shadowed planet to that cosmic burst of glory— that movement is the hope by which we live.

If we think of hope in this way, there is no way that we can tack it on the end of a story like pinning the tail on the donkey. A story for children should at least have a happy ending, some say, as though happy endings are an adequate definition of hope—as though a story for children, as distinct from a story told to adults, is incomplete without a bit of cheer pasted to the end.

So what counts as an ending in a story for children by a writer who lives by hope? In the middle of writing my latest book, *Park's Quest*, I found myself once again engaged in a search for the lost parent. I was horrified. What's with you? I asked myself. Why are you always looking for a lost parent? You had two perfectly good parents of your own who loved you and did the best they could for you under often difficult circumstances. Why this constant theme of searching or yearning for the absent parent?

I think I know at last the answer to that question. I'm not sure, as I'm never sure about these things, but I think the fact that this theme keeps coming up in my books reveals a longing—not so much for my own parents—but a yearning for the One whose name is unpronounceable but whom Jesus taught us to call Father.

So the hope of my books is the hope of yearning. It is always incomplete, as all true hope must be. It is always in tension, rooted in this fallen earth but growing, yearning, stretching toward the new creation. I am sure that it does not satisfy children in the sense that Cinderella or Jack the Giant Killer will satisfy them. I know children need and deserve the kind of satisfaction they may get only from the old fairy tales. For children who are still hungry for happily ever after, my endings will be invariably disappointing. Children need all kinds of stories. Other people will write the stories they can write, and I will write the stories I can write.

When I write realistic novels, I will be true (as best I am able) to what is. But I am, as Zechariah says, a prisoner of hope. My stories will lean toward hope as a sunflower toward the sun. The roots will be firmly in the world as I know it, but the face will turn inevitably toward the peaceable kingdom, the heavenly city, the loving parent watching and waiting for the prodigal's return. Because, by the grace of God, that is truth for me and all who share this hope.

Come to think of it, and I must confess, I didn't think of it when I was writing the book, Parkington Waddell Broughton the Fifth is a kind of prisoner to hope. He sets out on a quest to find his father, who was killed in Vietnam. Neither Park nor most of my readers will know that as he pursues his quest he is living out the medieval legend of Parzival the Grail knight. In the legend as Wolfram von Eschenbach tells it,[5] the Grail knight is brought by enchantment to the castle of the Grail king. The king is suffering from a wound that will not heal, and he will only be healed on the day that the Grail knight appears and asks the question.

The young Parzival, however, is the prototype of the innocent fool. He has no idea that he is the Grail knight. When he finds himself in the mysterious castle of the Grail, he's not about to ask any questions, because he has been told by those wiser than he that a man who keeps asking questions appears to be even more of a fool than he is.

So he does not ask the question. The king is not healed. And Parzival is thrown out of the castle on his ear. In his subsequent wanderings our innocent fool becomes sadder and, if not wiser, certainly less gullible, and increasingly world-weary. Try as he will he cannot find his way back to the Grail castle. He refuses to return to Camelot, convinced that he is no longer worthy to take his seat at the Round Table.

Brought back from despair by a wise hermit, Parzival comes a second time to the Grail castle, and this time he asks the suffering king the question. "Dear Uncle," Parzival asks, "what aileth thee?" And hearing these compassionate words, the king is healed.

Thus God brings both Parzival and the wounded king to wholeness. But Wolfram, like Dickens, is not content. Teller of romances that he is, he not only proceeds to restore Parzival to his kingdom and to his beloved queen, he also baptizes all in need of baptism, marries all who need marrying, and gets them "lovely children." It is truly happily ever after for Parzival and all his kin.

Park Broughton, in my story, is also an innocent fool and a bumbling knight with no notion of what his real quest is. If you read both stories, you will see that *Park's Quest* shares many elements of Wolfram's tale—the mother who tries to keep her son from the quest, the shooting of the bird, the battle with the stranger who turns out to be a brother, the king with a wound that will not heal, the failure of the knight to ask the compassionate question, and the consequences of his failure. But I did not take the happily-ever-after ending of the old romance. I tried to give it a proper ending.

And, as you tell the children, if you want to know how it comes out you'll have to read the book yourself. Actually, I thought of reading the last two pages to you, but my husband talked me out of it. And he is right. If it is indeed a proper ending, it belongs flesh, bone, and sinew to the rest of the story. If I cut it off, it will lose its life.

So to demonstrate to Sarah Smedman and to you all what I mean by hope in my books, I want to go back to a novel I wrote more than ten years ago, to a story that I think many of you already know. A book that has been called both a "story of redemption" and a story "totally without hope."

Gilly and her grandmother have gone to meet Courtney. In five minutes, or in less than two pages, her mother manages to bring Gilly's lifetime dreams crashing to the ground. Gilly flees—first to the bathroom and then to the telephone to call Trotter and tell her she's coming home because nothing has turned out the way it's supposed to. Whereupon Trotter explains to her that happy endings are a lie, and that life "ain't supposed to be nothing, 'cept maybe tough."[6]

> "If life is so bad [Gilly asks], how come you're so happy?"
> "Did I say bad? I said it was tough. Nothing to make you happy like doing good on a tough job, now is there?"

"Trotter, stop preaching at me. I want to come home."

"You're home, baby. Your grandma is home."

"I want to be with you and William Ernest and Mr. Randolph."

"And leave her all alone? Could you do that?"

"Dammit, Trotter. Don't try to make a stinking Christian out of me."

"I wouldn't try to make nothing out of you." There was a quiet at the other end of the line. "Me and William Ernest and Mr. Randolph kinda like you the way you are."

"Go to hell, Trotter," Gilly said softly.

A sigh. "Well, I don't know about that. I had planned on settling permanently somewheres else."

"Trotter"—she couldn't push the word hard enough to keep the squeak out—"I love you."

"I know, baby. I love you, too."

She put the phone gently on the hook and went back into the bathroom. There she blew her nose on toilet tissue and washed her face.

By the time she got back to an impatient Courtney and a stricken Nonnie, she had herself well under control.

"Sorry to make you wait," Gilly said. "I'm ready to go home now." No clouds of glory, perhaps, but Trotter would be proud.[7]

No happily ever after, not really a happy ending, certainly not the heavenly city, but an ending rooted in this earth and leaning in the direction of the New Jerusalem. Not perfect, but I do love it. A proper ending—at least a proper ending for me, just one more in a long line of prisoners of hope.

The Story of My Lives

The title I had chosen for my remarks was "The Story of My Lives." I took a look at the title and decided that perhaps I should propose an alternative that sounds less like a description of a personality disorder. So I do have an alternate title. I got this one from a note card that lives in my desk drawer. The card has a three-panel illustration. At the top lies a zonked-out whale with Xs where his eyes should be. Below is the same whale with his eyes popped in amazement as a voice coming from its mouth declares: "Incredible as it seems . . ." In panel three the sentence is completed by a person who is climbing out of the whale's mouth: ". . . my life is based on a true story."[1]

Well, incredible as it seems, my life is based on a true story. Sometimes it is incredible even to me. In February I spent two weeks in England. I could spend all my allotted time telling you about that trip—tea with Rosemary Sutcliff, twice; long, relaxed visits with Jan Mark, Clive King, John Rowe Townsend, Jill Paton Walsh; and lunch with Philippa Pearce right across the street from Tom's Midnight Garden, which you'll be happy to know still exists. I guess the incredibility of my life truly hit me the day I sat sipping a glass of Madeira, which in itself seemed something of an exotic experience.

My dear friends Jean Little, Jill Paton Walsh, and John Rowe Townsend were there. And so was the ninety-five-year-old Lucy Boston, because the room in which we were sipping the Madeira was the dining room of the 850-year-old house most of us recognize by the name Green Knowe.

Well, as one of my friends said recently, "Katherine has given up name-dropping and moved on to place-dropping." Indeed, but can't you sympathize? There I was with those people in that setting—me! I was like the man in *The New Yorker* cartoon who sits at the telephone before his huge office window overlooking the Manhattan skyline, and he is saying, "And, Mama, would you call Miss Simpson, my third-grade teacher, and tell *her* I made it to the top?"[2]

I think it is my fourth-grade teacher I wish I could contact. The one who counted my spelling words wrong whenever I used the Palmer method of penmanship that had been forced on me in my previous school instead of the Locker method she adhered to.

The fourth grade was a time of almost unmitigated terror and humiliation for me. I recognize now that some of my best writing had its seeds in that awful year. But I can't remember once saying to myself at nine, "Buck up, old girl, someday you're going to make a mint out of this misery."

But there are two people whom I remember with great fondness from that horrible year. One was the librarian of Calvin H. Wiley School who, I'm afraid, died long before I could let her know what she meant to me. And there was Eugene Hammett, the other weird kid in the fourth grade.

There was a difference between me and Eugene. I was weird by no choice of my own. My parents had been missionaries in China, and we'd just fled from the war there. I spoke English as my friends in Shanghai had, with something of a British accent. I could hardly afford to buy lunch, much less clothes, so from time to time my classmates would recognize on my back something they had earlier donated to charity. On December 7, the Japanese attacked Pearl Harbor, and because it was known that I had come from that part of the world, there were dark hints that I might be one of *them*.

Eugene, on the other hand, was weird by choice—or mostly by choice: I guess he didn't choose his looks. He was a perfectly round little boy who wore full-moon steel-rimmed glasses long before John Lennon made them acceptable, and sported a half-inch blond brush cut. My only ambition in the fourth grade was to become somehow less weird. Eugene's declared ambition was to become a ballet dancer. In North Carolina in 1941, little boys—even well-built or skinny little boys—did not want to be ballet dancers when they grew up.

Now, sometimes outcasts despise even each other, but Eugene and I did not. We were friends for the rest of fourth grade and all of fifth, sixth, and seventh grades. During my public school career, Calvin H. Wiley was the only school I went to for two years running, and by the time Eugene and I were in the seventh grade, I had fulfilled my modest ambition. I was no longer regarded as particularly weird. Eugene, having more integrity, continued to march, or should I say dance, to a different drummer.

I moved the summer after seventh grade. I grew up at last and had a full, rich life in which people loved me and didn't call me names, at least not to my face. But from time to time over the years I would think of Eugene and worry about him. Whatever could have happened to my chubby little friend whose burning desire in life was to become a ballet dancer?

Decades pass. There are a lot of scene changes. We are living in Norfolk, Virginia, and our son David has become, at seventeen, a serious actor. But in order to get the parts he wants, he realizes he needs to take dancing lessons. There is, however, a problem. Even in 1983, boys in Norfolk, Virginia, do not generally aspire to become ballet dancers. He asks me to find out about lessons he can take without the rest of the soccer team knowing about it.

My friend Kathryn Morton's daughter takes ballet, so I say to Kathryn, "David needs to take ballet lessons, but he's not eager for all his buddies to know about it. Do you have any recommendations?"

"Well," says Kathryn, "if he's really serious, Gene Hammett at Tidewater Ballet is really the best teacher anywhere around. You may think he's strange but—"

"W-w-w-wait a minute," I say. "Gene who?"

"Hammett," she says. "He sends dancers to the Joffrey and New York City Ballet and Alvin Ailey every year. He's especially good with young black dancers. Terribly hard on any kid that he thinks has talent, but he'd give his life for them."

"Gene who?" I say again.

"Hammett," she says. "You may have seen him around town. He's huge and wears great flowing caftans. He does look a bit weird, but he's a wonderful teacher."

"You don't happen to know where he came from?"

"Well, he came here from New York."

"New York? He wasn't a dancer?"

"Oh, yes. He was quite good in his time. You wouldn't know it by looking at him now, but he was a fine dancer twenty, thirty years ago."

"You wouldn't happen to know where he grew up?"

"Oh, I don't know," she says. "North Carolina somewhere, I think."

"Next time you see him, would you ask him if he remembers anyone named Katherine Womeldorf from Calvin H. Wiley School?"

Some days later the phone rings. "Katherine?" an unfamiliar male voice begins. "This is Gene Hammett."

"Eugene! Do you remember me?"

"I even remember a joke you told me in the fourth grade. I asked you why if you were born in China you weren't Chinese. And you said; 'If a cat's born in a garage, does it make it an automobile?' "

"Yep," I say, recognizing one of our family defensive lines. "And what about you? You danced in New York and now you're a famous teacher of ballet. It's hard to imagine. You were a little round boy when I knew you."

He laughs. "Well," he says, "now I'm a big round man."

I have since seen Eugene, and he *is* a big round man. But I have also seen pictures of him leaping like Baryshnikov from the boards of a New York stage, thin and muscled and bearing no resemblance whatsoever to the chubby, bespectacled boy in my mind's eye. And even if I missed knowing him when he was slim and gorgeous and at the height of his career, I wouldn't give anything for knowing that it happened as he had determined it would back there when we were both weird little nine-year-olds at Calvin H. Wiley School.

Yes, incredible as it seems, my life is based on a true story, but rarely does it have such a satisfying plotline. That's the trouble with life. It tends to be deficient when it comes to offering up adequate plots. I'm sure that's why I resist writing an autobiography. As hard as it is for me to come up with a decent plot, I'm fascinated by a good one, and life, even my incredible one, offers so few well-rounded stories like the one about Gene Hammett. Thus, in a real sense, I am constantly writing autobiography, but I have to turn it into fiction in order to give it credibility. "She lived to tell the tale," we say. Because what we applaud is not simply survival but the ability to step back, or beyond survival, to organizing the experience—to imaging—to telling the tale.

If you are observant, you will have noticed that in both my proposed title and my alternate, the word *story* is singular. The singular was a deliberate choice, based on literary research and not on a deficiency of grammar. It comes from having read *The Hero with a Thou-sand Faces.*

In this book Joseph Campbell reduces the multitude of the world's myths, legends, and folktales to a single story—that of the hero who ventures forth from the ordinary world into a realm of wonders. There he is met by a supernatural guide who aids him as he confronts and de-feats fabulous forces and returns a victor, able to bestow boons on his fellows. I think somewhere in the backs of our minds, we writers agree. We may write many books, but there is a common thread. It may not fit Campbell's formula exactly, but we cannot deny the kinship.

When I was in England, my British editor asked me what I was working on. She did it very delicately, which made me think that as she asked she was hoping against hope that I was not doing another of those dadgum historical novels that she, being a loyal sort of editor, would probably go ahead and print and then have trouble selling. And I heard myself answering, "Oh, you know, Chris, it's the same old thing I always do."

Which, come to think of it, is not a very clever way to advertise your nearly finished book to a publisher you hope will love it. But ac-tually, when pressed, it is hard to put into a sentence or two exactly what that "same old thing" is. So I asked myself, as someone who goes to great pains to set her stories in different countries at different peri-ods of history, and who resists all pressures to write a sequel, What on earth did I mean by "the same old thing"?

Well, if you promise not to write a dissertation on it, I'll let you in on what, as of this moment, I think it might mean. I went to church twice on Ash Wednesday and as a reward for my unusual diligence, I was given what may be a key to the story of my fictional lives.

We were discussing the feast liturgy of ancient Israel and read what has long been a favorite line of mine from the Book of Deu-teronomy. I guess I should put the line in context.

At the feast of the first fruits, the worshiper is to take a basket of the first of all his fruits and give it to the priest. The priest sets down the basket at the altar, and then the worshiper is to say:

> A wandering Aramean was my father; and he went down into Egypt and sojourned there, few in number; and there he became a nation, great, mighty, and populous. And the Egyptians treated us harshly, and afflicted us, and laid upon us hard bondage. Then we cried to the Lord the God of our fathers, and the Lord heard our voice, and saw our affliction, our toil, and our oppression; and the Lord brought us out of Egypt with a mighty hand and an outstretched arm, with great terror, with signs and wonders; and he brought us into this place and gave us this land, a land flowing with milk and honey. And behold, now I bring the first of the fruit of the ground, which thou, O Lord, hast given me.[3]

As I study this passage, it seems to echo Joseph Campbell's archetypal story—but the language, the feel of the words themselves, does something to my insides. "A wandering Aramean was my father." Do you realize how much effort is expended by characters in my books looking for the wandering father and, occasionally, the mother? And if the child knows just where his or her parents are, geographically speaking, it is the child who is wandering, either physically or spiritually. And the wandering, whether it be the parent's or the child's, takes the child of my story into some sort of bondage.

James Johnson fits very nicely into this scheme I'm proposing. He is not only a wanderer—witness the song he loves, "I'm Just a Poor Wayfaring Stranger"—but both of his fathers and his mother are wayfarers. He travels down to Tidewater and into the bondage of the General Douglas MacArthur Elementary School. There, with the aid of a supernatural helper, he overcomes the foes within and without and wins the victory that enables him to give his gift to his fellows.

Oh, you're wondering about that supernatural helper? I didn't know he had one, either, but it occurred to me to look up the meaning of the name *Eleazer*—long after I had given James's friend that name. Sometimes we write more truly than we know. The name *Eleazer* means "God has helped."

If the helpers of the heroes of my other stories have less blatantly supernatural names, everyone has at least one helper. Muna has the swordsmith, Takiko has the Empress, Jiro has Kinshi, Gilly has Trotter, Louise has the Captain, Wang Lee has Mei Lin and Chu—and Shen, whom he betrays. Jesse has Leslie, who is the quintessential helper, but who—like all the helpers in my books—is in fact mortal, which means that Jesse's father and Mrs. Myers must come to his aid before the battle is done.

But as a novelist, it is the mortal that matters to me. My stories, like all stories, may be ultimately descended from the story of the princely hero with a thousand faces, but their father is a wandering Aramean.

That means that the battles my fictional lives must confront are not against fabulous forces. There's not, alas, a dragon in the entire body of my work. It's not that I wouldn't like to write about dragons. It's that I don't know how. Maybe someday I'll figure out how, but at the moment fantasy is to my writing what downhill skiing is to my athletic life—strictly a spectator sport.

I'm always interested when people say to me, "Why don't you write fantasy?" Or, "Why don't you write mystery stories?" Or, "What we need for you to write are plays that children can perform in school." As though the only reason I have never done what they're suggesting is that no one had been wise enough to present the idea to me before, and I myself had not been clever enough to think of it.

The reason, in case you're interested, that I don't do a lot of things is not that I haven't considered them, but that the gift I have been given is a limited one.

It is, however, a gift that I am very grateful for and that I seek to employ as responsibly as I am able. I don't get to write about the god-like heroes. I get to write about the wandering Arameans. I get to write about real people who must confront the messy battles of the world as we know it.

Last year in Minnesota a group of parents asked their district board of education to ban *The Great Gilly Hopkins* on the basis of what they saw as its anti-Christian bias, its profanity, and its "pervasive vulgarity."

"It isn't a question of censorship or no censorship but a question of where we're going to draw the line," said one of the protesters. "God," he continued, "does have a standard, and we all have to answer to him."

Now, when I wrote *Gilly Hopkins*, it occurred to me to wonder if my secular publishing house would reject it because it seemed to me so blatant a rewriting of the parable of the Prodigal Son.

In Maine more recently, a teacher was called before a school board to defend her use of *Bridge to Terabithia* in her fifth-grade classroom. The book was being attacked not only for its profanity but for the hint of sexual feelings that the boy has for his teacher and for the references to magic and praying to spirits.

I want you to know that I do not take these complaints lightly. I do not put words or scenes into books just to make life harder for teachers and librarians. I am trying to tell a true story about real people. The fact that I call myself a Christian and see my work as a calling from God does not make people who wish to ban my books very happy. Nor could I succeed in explaining to them my belief that if I tried to write books according to their guidelines, I would be untrue to the gift that God has given me.

Flannery O'Connor, who was a devout Catholic as well as a fine writer, expresses this conviction better than I can. She says, "Fiction is about everything human and we are made out of dust, and if you scorn getting yourself dusty, then you shouldn't write fiction. It isn't grand enough for you."[4]

A wandering Aramean was my father. In Deuteronomy the wanderer is not named, but we can tell from the context that he is Jacob. Not father Abraham or noble, gentle Isaac, but Jacob the trickster, the cheat, the cowardly runaway. Now, I have a love-hate relationship with Jacob. Didn't I write a whole book from Esau's point of view? I always thought Esau had a dirty deal. He was the victim of his brother Jacob's trickery and the cheated witness to his good fortune.

When I named my book *Jacob Have I Loved*, I was sure that my publisher would make me change the title. Even today perfectly sensible people will ask me why I called the book *Jacob Have I Loved* when there isn't a character named Jacob in the entire book. One thing you learn pretty quickly in this business is how little people know about the Bible. I can't begin to count the number of times in 1980 that I was asked the question "What is the title of your new book?" And when I replied, "*Jacob Have I Loved*," exactly one person responded, "But Esau have I hated."[5]

Perhaps the fault was my own. Maybe I chose to tell the wrong story. From reading both Joseph Campbell and the Bible, it is obvious that Jacob is the hero whose story must be told. Esau is more an obstacle to be overcome than a character in his own right.

It was certainly not my original intention that anybody identify Sara Louise Bradshaw with Jacob. She was quite obviously intended to be Esau, the cheated elder twin. And yet, deep inside ourselves exists the image of the twins—two parts of one whole. The light and the dark. Jacob looks into a darkened mirror and sees Esau. Sara Louise looks into a bright mirror and sees Caroline. In order to be whole, Jacob must make peace with Esau, Sara Louise must make peace with

Caroline. In life both the light and dark exist in each of us; each of us is our own twin. So finally Sara Louise, in order to be a whole person, must come to love Caroline, so that she can love both the Jacob and the Esau within herself.

Which brings us to the greatly lamented final chapters of *Jacob Have I Loved*. How many critics have fussed and fumed and cried and demanded a bit too late that they be vastly expanded or simply lopped off. In the book's defense I should like to state that as of this date no young reader has ever complained to me about those chapters. This unhappiness with the ending is distinctly a postadolescent phenomenon. The fact that I refuse to call this criticism of the ending adult or mature may suggest where my bias in this matter lies.

But now that I have become enlightened and know what my books are all about, I have decided to tackle the problem of the ending one more time.

Looking at it freshly, I see that Louise, the Esau, is indeed the wandering Aramean. The Arameans were nobodies as far as the real world of Egypt and Assyria and Babylon, and later Greece and Rome, were concerned. They conquered no empires, built no pyramids. For centuries they served as the whipping boy of civilization—the "no people," as Peter says. But Louise takes it a step further. Not only does she believe she is nobody, she thinks it's all God's fault. He didn't choose her. He chose her sister instead. So she will choose deliberately not to choose God. She is wandering not as Israel wandered—toward the promised land—but away from it. And where is God while all this is going on?

Oh, but, as I have often claimed, the author has no right to tell a reader how to read her book. It is the privilege of the reader to discover what a book means for his or her particular life. The book either speaks for itself to the reader, or it fails to speak.

But, just in case, just in case it spoke and somebody out there wasn't listening, will you remember that the hero's supernatural helper may take many forms—the fairy godmother, the crone, the dwarf, perhaps even a baby. Will you consider that if Louise had not delivered Essie's twins she might never have told her story? She might not even have known her story.

Hours later, walking home, my boots crunching on the snow, I bent my head backward to drink in the crystal stars. And clearly, as though the voice came from just behind me, I heard a melody so sweet and pure that I had to hold myself to keep from shattering:

I wonder as I wander out under the sky . . . [6]

The hero must leave home, confront fabulous dangers, and return the victor to grant boons to his fellows. Or a wandering nobody must go out from bondage through the wilderness and by the grace of God become truly someone who can give back something of what she has been given.

That—incredible as it may seem—is the story of my lives.

FROM **THE WRITER** ~
APRIL 1987

People I Have Known

"How do you build your characters?" It's a familiar question to those
of us who write fiction, and, I suspect, one of the most uncomfortable.
When someone asks me about "building characters," I'm tempted to
remind them that characters are people, not models you put together
with an erector set. You don't "build" people, you get to know them.

All human beings are born on a certain day in a particular place
and from two parents. These are all givens. When I am beginning a
book, the central character is little more than an uneasy feeling in the
pit of my stomach. I spend a long time trying to understand who this
person is—where he or she was born, when, and from whom.

When I was trying to start *Jacob Have I Loved*, I knew the protagonist was a girl of about fourteen, who was eaten up with jealousy for
a brother or sister. That was all I had to go on in the beginning.
When I discovered, quite by accident that she lived on a tiny island
in the middle of the Chesapeake Bay, I was well on my way to getting
to know her.

(Incidentally, anyone who has written fiction knows that such revelatory accidents are a way of life for writers. This one involved a Christmas gift book about the Chesapeake Bay, which I happened to read because I was desperate for reading material on the twenty-ninth of December. Time after time, writers stumble blindly upon the very secrets that will serve to unlock the story they are currently struggling with.)

Anyhow, as I discovered, life on a Chesapeake Bay island is different from life anywhere else in America. On Tangier and Smith (the islands upon which I modeled my imaginary island of Rass), there are families that have lived on the same narrow bits of land since well before the Revolutionary War. The men of the island earn their living crabbing in the warmer months and oystering in the colder. For island people, all of life is organized about the water that surrounds them and even today cuts them off from the rest of our country. The speech of the people is unlike that of those in nearby Maryland or Virginia. Scholars think it may resemble the Elizabethan speech of colonial America. The islands were converted to Methodism in the eighteenth century and remain strongly religious communities. I could go on, but you can see how being born and spending her formative years on such an island would affect the growth of Louise Bradshaw. She could be molded by her adaptation to her environment or by her rebellion against it. Either way, the place is of vital significance to the person she is and will become.

When a character is born is another revealing point. You can see this in life. My husband and I were born at the height of the Depression. Our older boy was born soon after Kennedy was assassinated. Our younger daughter was born the year both Martin Luther King Jr. and Robert Kennedy were killed. When I am trying to get to know a character, I always ask what was happening in the world when this person was born and what effect these events might have had on his life.

Usually, I determine the date of birth of all of my central characters, not just the protagonist. This was crucial to the story in my novel *Come Sing, Jimmy Jo*. James was born in 1973, and his mother was born in 1959. "But that means . . . !" Yes, it means that Keri Su was fourteen when James was born. If I know that, I can begin to understand some of the problems that have always existed between them—why almost from birth James has looked to his grandma for mothering rather than his mother.

This leads directly to the question of parentage. When I first began writing *Jimmy Jo*, I assumed that Keri Su was James's mother, and Jerry Lee was his father. The fact that Jerry Lee was ten years older than his wife explained to some extent why he was the more responsible parent of the two. After all, he was already a grown-up when the boy was born.

But the better I got to know this family, the more I realized that there was something there that they weren't telling. Gradually, I got a picture of Keri Su, a thirteen-year-old girl from the West Virginia hills. The mountain boyfriend who has made her pregnant has run away and joined the navy to escape the wrath of the girl's hard-drinking father. Now all of the father's anger is directed toward his daughter. She runs away with nowhere to run and happens into a tiny mountain town where the Johnson Family Singers are performing at one of the local churches. The girl loves music, and she hangs around until the Johnsons, especially Grandma and Jerry Lee, realize the extent of her desperation and take her under their wings. She is a good-looking, spunky kid with a powerful singing voice, and Jerry Lee, with a mixture of admiration and pity and affection, marries her. James, the child that is born so soon afterward, is a Johnson heart and soul, made so by the love of Jerry Lee and Grandma, who share with him the special love they have for each other.

What happens, then, to the rest of the family members? There is brother Earl, who was a young adolescent when Keri Su joined the family. He has always resented Jerry Lee, who is older, wiser, nicer, and, as Earl sees it, much their mother's favorite. Now his brother has married a girl Earl's own age, a girl who, under different circumstances, he might have liked to take out himself. Earl is jealous of the position Keri Su immediately achieves in the family and at the same time is attracted to her despite himself.

And what about Grandpa? He seems to take his wife for granted, but perhaps he, too, feels a wistful twinge when he sees how she dotes on Jerry Lee and on the fatherless child that their son has totally accepted as his own. Doesn't blood count for something? Grandpa wonders. Like most mountain men, he puts a lot of stock in good blood. He likes the boy and all, but it's not as if James were really his grandson.

So far nothing I've said is actually in the book. It is all in the background to the story—the life these people lived before they entered the pages of this particular book. But I have to know all of these things about the characters or run the risk that my characters will be as separate and inanimate as Barbie and Ken. If you let *living* people into a story, they will move each other. If you put in *constructed* characters, you'll have to do the moving yourself. The reader won't be fooled. He'll be able to tell which is which.

When it comes to deciding what about these people will actually be revealed on the printed page, I am guided, of course, by the story I want to tell, but also, quite particularly, by point of view. *Jacob Have I Loved* is written in the first person. The only point of view the reader is given is that of Louise, who is so jealous of her sister that she is blind to the affection that her parents, Call, the Captain, and even her sister have for her. Now, I am not Louise. I can see what she cannot, and it breaks my heart to realize how much her mother loves her and to know how little Louise can understand or trust that love.

A wise reader will be aware of the narrowness of Louise's vision, but since I write principally for children and young people, I know that many of my readers will assume that Louise's badly skewed view is the correct view. I suppose I could have written the book differently to give Louise's mother and even sister Caroline a sporting chance, but then the power of Louise's jealousy would have been diminished. It would have been a different, and, I believe, weaker story.

Again, in *Come Sing, Jimmy Jo*, the story is told wholly from James's viewpoint. He's never been told about his origins, but that doesn't mean he doesn't feel the uneasiness of the other family members when the past is referred to.

Often children will ask me about the parents in my books. "Why are they so mean?" is a question I've gotten more than a few times about Jesse Aaron's parents in the book *Bridge to Terabithia*. I use the occasion to try to help young readers understand point of view. All the parents in my stories are seen from their children's point of view, and it has been my experience that children are very seldom fair in their judgments of their parents. I hope I've sent all my questioners home to take another, more objective look not only at my book, but at their own parents, most of whom, I dare say, are like the parents in *Bridge to Terabithia*, doing the best they can under trying circumstances.

Characters are like people in another way. Some of them are very easy to get to know, others more difficult. Maime Trotter, the foster mother in *The Great Gilly Hopkins*, simply arrived one day full grown. She was so powerfully herself that the other characters in the book came to life responding to her immense loving energy. Gilly, who had spent her time before the book began cynically manipulating the people about her, had to learn how to reckon with a force greater than her own anger.

The actual appearance of one of the most important characters in *The Great Gilly Hopkins* takes up less than two pages of the text. She is Gilly's mother—the unwed flower child who gave Gilly up to foster care years before the book opens. Yet what she actually is and what Gilly dreams she is (two different things, as you might suspect) combine to help shape the troubled and troubling child, whom we first meet in the backseat of the social worker's car on the way to yet another foster home.

There is, finally, something mysterious about the life of one's characters. In my secret heart, I almost believe that one of these days I'll meet Jesse Aarons walking toward me on a downtown street. I'll recognize him at once, although he will have grown to manhood, and I'll ask him what he's been doing in the years since he built that bridge across Lark Creek.

On second thought, I probably won't ask. I'll smile and he'll nod, but I won't pry. Years ago he let me eavesdrop on his soul, but that time is past. He is entitled to his privacy now. Still, I can't help wondering.

SIMMONS COLLEGE CENTER FOR
THE STUDY OF CHILDREN'S LITERATURE ~
JULY 1983

Do I Dare Disturb the Universe?

My grandmother was a formidable Victorian whom I feared more than I loved, and it is a matter of interest to me that I remember so many things she said when I spent so much of my childhood trying hard not to listen to her. Although I never recall her forgiving me anything, I recall with surprise and perhaps envy that she was often tolerant of strangers and near strangers whose behavior seemed unacceptable to me. Rude waitresses or testy shopgirls could always count on my grandmother's compassion. Even arrogance in the great and snobbery in the less-than-great would earn my grandmother's coverall phrase of understanding. I was not to be offended by these seemingly obnoxious people because, according to my grandmother, their behavior was "simply a form of timidity."

Why she did not extend her understanding to me, I did not know—I, who was truly timid and would have loved to have it be the excuse for all my unlovely behavior. But in my grandmother's eyes, the rest of the world was timid; I was unregenerate.

Now whether I was and/or am unregenerate is not within my province to judge, but I can surely decide whether I am timid or not. Am I subject to fear? Easily alarmed? Timorous? Shy? Yes to all of the above. If only my grandmother could have recognized it—a near-classic case.

It was, therefore, with fear, alarm, and timorousness that I sidled up to the title of this lecture: "Do I Dare Disturb the Universe?" Certainly not. I hardly dared disturb my springer spaniel. But, then, I had a sneaking suspicion that I was looking at quite a different universe from the one Prufrock was referring to. The universe that confronted me was no sleeping spaniel. It was a universe already greatly disturbed. What could I do, puny creature that I was, that would make a perceptible stir in such a whirlwind? Better, I thought, to gather my children about me, double-lock the doors, bolt the windows, and huddle together against the elements. The trouble with this metaphor is that I knew full well that my husband and probably my children would be out there somewhere battling the storm. I have never figured out just how Chicken Little managed to get herself married to the Man of La Mancha, but there you are. While John and those I truly admire are out there where the wind blows hardest, I am in my little study typing out a story for the young. Perhaps writing a book is a form of timidity.

The irony, of course, is that try as I may, I cannot escape the universe. And in the end, the books I write must mirror it in all its terror as well as grandeur. I am condemned to write what I see, and so the books that might have been a hiding place turn into something quite different.

> To live [says Ibsen] is to battle with troll folk
> In the vault of heart and head.
> To write is man's self-judgment,
> As Doom shall judge the dead.[1]

I have often joked that writing is cheaper than psychotherapy. But there is truth in the flippancy. Writing *is* a form of self-judgment, and so, in my books, I must battle the giants I shrink from. "There's no hiding place down here," as the old spiritual says.

From 1981 to the spring of 1983 I went about the country making speeches as I am tonight. Almost invariably during this time span someone would say, "I'm so glad you've stopped writing those historical novels." And, of course, the person had no way of knowing that lying on my desk at that minute, waiting for me to return, was the most ambitious historical novel I had ever attempted. Why? Why, when I had achieved a measure of success writing about twentieth-century America, would I go back to writing about the Orient and not even the modern Orient? There are a number of answers to that question, some of which I do not know, but I think I do know some of the reasons. The first is that history is a pair of powerful eyeglasses with which to look at life. We cannot look directly at reality because our eyesight is too poor, and our hearts are too faint.

When I heard the news of Martin Luther King Jr.'s death, one of the first things I did was go to the music store and buy a recording of Brahms's Requiem. The only one they had was sung in German, but that hasn't mattered over the years, for the music has helped me face death over and over again. I do not mean to say that the Requiem has become for me a kind of medicine—in case of pain take two choruses and a solo—neither would I say to anyone who is bereaved, "All you have to do is put on Brahms and put up your feet." Art is never a quick cure, and it is not necessarily a comfort. But art is a means of seeing truth that cannot be observed directly, and historical fiction at its best gives us two routes to truth—the route, or eyeglasses, of history and the route, or spectacles, of art. A double whammy, if you please.

Jill Paton Walsh once said something that has been a great help to me as I think about historical fiction. She said that if you want to know what a certain period of history was like, you don't go back and read the contemporary fiction that was written in that period but the historical fiction that was written in that period. Now why should such a statement be true? Because the writer is wrestling with the giants of her own time by means of the giants in history. Or, to go back to our spectacles image, she is using history to enable her to bring the present into focus.

I was born in China and lived there for nearly eight years, but I had not felt either anxious or ready to write about my native land until after I finished *Jacob Have I Loved*. What is there in the psyche that prevents you from writing something for years, and then suddenly, without any warning, tells you that the time is ripe? I don't know. I only know that one day I had no desire to write about China, and the next day I did.

But what did I want to say about China? I was sure I didn't want to write about my childhood there. A historical novel was the obvious choice. But what period of history? Recorded history in China goes back four thousand years. I began reading a brief, general history of China, trying on the one hand to stuff four thousand years into my head and on the other, to choose from those millennia a tiny segment. I had come nearly to the end of the volume when a two-paragraph description of the Taiping Rebellion of the nineteenth century hit me between the eyes.

I suppose I must have heard of the Taiping before, but I had no memory of it. Here were a group of people in China who in 1850 were talking about the equality of men and women before God. Here were people who were saying that to harm or kill a fellow creature was against God's law. They were opposed to any sort of oppression—foot-binding, prostitution, multiple marriages, the buying and selling of human beings for any purpose. They did not kill, steal, use alcohol or opium, or bow to any graven images. Moreover, they believed that every child, regardless of sex or parentage, had a right to an education—all this at a time when in America we were still arguing whether or not God meant us to hold slaves. I was fascinated by these people. Where had they gotten their high ideals and what had become of them? And I was led into the tragic story of what happens when persons of high ideals take them into a holy crusade to save the world.

Now it is entirely possible that this short epoch in Chinese history does not speak to you about what is troubling your life, but it shouted at me. And a writer who is constantly engaged in self-judgment must write about what impinges on her own life, not try to guess what will be important to the general population a year or two or three in the future when the book will finally be published. So I embarked on a study of the Taiping, which could not, of course, begin in 1850 but had to begin at least with Confucius in about 500 B.C. It had to include the whole philosophy of history that began with him —the idea that Shang Ti, or the High God of Heaven, gave to the emperor of China a Divine Mandate, enabling him to rule over the Chinese people. In turn the emperor must rule justly, placing the needs of the people above his own needs and desires. When an emperor betrayed this heavenly trust, there would be a series of natural disasters revealing Heaven's withdrawal of the Divine Mandate. This was a signal to the peasants, the poor and the oppressed, that Heaven no longer demanded their obedience to the present emperor— they were given the right, perhaps the obligation, to overthrow the unjust rule and establish a new dynasty, which would now receive the Divine Mandate.

It was in this spirit that the Taiping arose to overthrow the despised Manchu Empire. In the early days of the movement, it was really a religious movement—a preaching to the oppressed of dignity and self-worth under God. But like almost any idealistic human movement, the impulse to spread their message was very strong. One of their early and basic declarations was: "You should not kill one innocent person or do one unrighteous act, even though it be to acquire an empire." So when they launched the campaign to conquer China, which, of course, entailed the killing of many innocent people and the committing of untold unrighteous acts, some justification of this behavior had to be made. The simplest justification was to regard their enemies as nonhuman and therefore outside the province of the care of the High God. Chinese had always regarded non-Chinese as less than human. The Taiping followed this pattern. The Manchu, or whoever supported or sided with the Manchu, were less than human—demons, in fact. One cannot be faulted for ridding the world of demons. They are by definition enemies of God, and whoever would honor God must hate his enemies. Or so the reasoning goes.

I am sure I do not have to fill in for you the consequences of such thinking. History is full of it. Every person, as well as every nation, seeks to dehumanize the adversary. We kill the nameless foe and discover later, as Oedipus did, that we are members of the same family.

Now this is a terrible truth, and in a historical novel this truth will be illustrated in terrifying and agonizing events. The writer cannot simply say, "Isn't this kind of thinking awful?" She must portray this awfulness. Along about January 1982, at the point in the story where Wang Lee is turning from a reluctant recruit into a flaming zealot, I decided I couldn't stand it any longer. I simply could not finish this book. It took me a few days longer to broach the subject to my husband. After all, by this time I had been working on this book since early 1980, and I had spent three expensive weeks in China in the fall of 1981 while he kept everything going at home. We already had one child in college and a second entering in September. We needed this book. But finally I decided there was no help for it. Facts, however painful, must be faced. I was never going to finish this book. I broke it as gently as possible, but the bitter truth could no longer be withheld. I was never, ever going to be able to finish this book. "Oh," he said. "So you've reached *that* stage."

Needless to say, I went back to my typewriter. The book would be finished. "Two pages a day," I ordered myself. "You do not get up from this chair until you have produced two pages." Now, some days those margins were mighty wide, but mostly it worked. For several weeks, it was two extremely malnourished pages a day, then a bit more, until finally, toward the end of May, I had a draft.

By now you're already asking yourself the next, most logical question. Okay, you had to write this book, but what right do you have to inflict it upon the young? How do you dare disturb their universe with this disturbing tale of war and betrayal?

I have to ask myself that question all the time. As a matter of fact, within days of the publication of *Rebels of the Heavenly Kingdom* there was an article titled "Where Have All the Children Gone?" in our local paper.[2] The author, Marie Winn, lamented the fact that parents no longer seek to protect their children from the world. She pleaded for a restoration of the boundaries between childhood and maturity— a reassertion on the part of adults that they know what is best for children—a willingness on the part of adults to spare children experiences that are too burdensome for them.

As I thought about Ms. Winn's article, I felt some glaring omissions. She never mentioned books or, indeed, art of any sort. She never considered—at least not in the scope of this article—that art might have a role in children's lives. Bruno Bettelheim is one of the experts she accused of robbing parents of their self-confidence, but she didn't mention *The Uses of Enchantment* or its thesis that the hearing and reading of fairy tales might provide hope for the troubled and questioning child.

I think there are points in Ms. Winn's article that we adults need to consider. There is a fine line between allowing a child to know what is happening in the family and the world and simply laying one's own emotional baggage upon the child's narrow shoulders. But I think, whatever the cause, we must recognize the burden that most of our children already bear. It's significant, I think, that Ms. Winn's article, which was supposedly about children in the United States, was only about a tiny minority of our children—those who are born in middle- or upper-class white families. And even these children are frightened by forces beyond the fondest parents' control.

"Kids already know [about the nuclear threat]," a fourteen-year-old has said. "I think it's more terrifying not to talk about it. Mystery is the worst thing possible. Being left alone to deal with it—that's much more frightening."

So while my writing begins as self-judgment, it is also for children and young people who do not live in the paradise of childhood but in the same disturbed universe that I find myself in—children who do not want to be left alone to deal with the terrors they live with every day. I cannot write for myself, or these children, books that pretend that we live in another, more placid universe. It simply will not work for any of us.

Recently a woman challenged me to admit that my books were not really for children. "I read them," she said, "and I was stunned. The intensity of them is overwhelming. I don't believe a child could understand what they are about." But that very week a teacher had shared a book report with me, written by her class troublemaker. The report was on *The Great Gilly Hopkins*. Without a shred of either shame or modesty, I will share with you the last two sentences of the book report. "This book is a miracle," the boy said. "Mrs. Paterson knows exactly how children feel."

Now, of course, I don't know exactly how children feel. No one knows exactly how someone else feels. But I do know how I feel, and I try to stay true to those feelings.

And so, as disturbed and discouraged and as near to despair as I feel when I confront the universe as it appears to me, I do not give up hope either as a person or as a writer (as though one could divide oneself up between form and function). My primary task is not to disturb a complacent universe or to decry a chaotic one. My task is to see through the disturbance to the unity so marvelously built into the Creation—to somehow find my way through the cacophony of reality to the harmony of truth. I have said elsewhere that my task is to write the best, the truest story I know how to write. Someone may find these two statements contradictory. I do not.

When I remember the books I loved as a child, three stand out in a particular way. The first is *The Secret Garden*. *The Secret Garden* is exactly the kind of book Ms. Winn would like children to read. It is a book that gives the harmony of Eden to the child reader. I adored that book when I was eight or nine. Of course, by that time I had been through bombings and had twice fled from war. I was living as an exile in a land that was foreign to me—a land that was supposed to be my homeland, but as Jean Fritz showed so well in *Homesick*, America is never quite home to the expatriate child. Mary, in *The Secret Garden*, was also an expatriate child. Perhaps this was one reason I loved the book so much, but it can't be the whole reason, because my own children loved it, too, and they hadn't just fled from war-torn China. No, I think the reason so many of us have loved that book is precisely because we are homesick for a garden we have never visited. We long for a music we have never really heard.

The second book is related to the first. It begins in a sort of Eden. This book is *The Yearling*. I'm sure I loved it when I was eleven for some of the same reasons I had loved *The Secret Garden* two years or so before. The wonderful harmony between child and beast is a reminder of Eden. But Flag dies; the harmony is destroyed. Jody must become a man and take on the responsibilities of a man. I wept over his loss, and I knew he had lost far more than a pet or even a companion. He had lost the garden, and it could not be regained. I never thought to write Miss Rawlings a letter. It never occurred to me to take her to task for killing Flag. I knew deep down that it had to happen. I was already wise by the time I was eleven. There was no way my parents could have protected me from the world as it is. I had already seen too much. What I needed was not an outer guard but an inner strength. I needed to know that one could endure the loss of Paradise. "That's what we were put on the earth to do," says Margaret Drabble, "to endeavor in the face of the impossible." This is what reading *The Yearling* helped me to do—to endeavor in the face of the impossible.

The third book I read when I was sixteen. If you read only the first two paragraphs of this book you will think you are back in Eden.

> There is a lovely road that runs from Ixopo into the hills. These hills are grass-covered and rolling, and they are lovely beyond any singing of it. The road climbs seven miles into them, to Carisbrooke; and from there, if there is no mist, you look down on one of the fairest valleys of Africa. . . .
>
> The grass is rich and matted, you cannot see the soil. It holds the rain and the mist, and they seep into the ground, feeding the streams in every kloof. It is well-tended, and not too many cattle feed upon it; not too many fires burn it, laying bare the soil. Stand unshod upon it, for the ground is holy, being even as it came from the Creator. Keep it, guard it, care for it, for it keeps men, guards men, cares for men. Destroy it and man is destroyed.[3]

The book, of course, is Alan Paton's *Cry, the Beloved Country*. South Africa is Paradise. South Africa is Hell. The difference depends not just upon the color of your skin, but it begins there. There are many children in that land whom no loving parent can protect.

Cry, the Beloved Country was a pivotal book for me. On reading it I had to face myself in a way I never had before. I could not pretend innocence or try to throw blame elsewhere. I knew when I had finished this book that I had met the enemy and it was myself.

A novel, as Eudora Welty reminds us, "says what people are like. It doesn't know how to describe what they are *not* like, and it would waste its time if it told us what we ought to be like, since we already know that, don't we? But we may not know nearly so well what we are as when a novel of power reveals this to us. For the first time we may, as we read, see ourselves in our own situation, in some curious way reflected. By whatever way the novelist accomplishes it—there are many ways—truth is borne in on us in all its great weight and angelic lightness, and accepted as home truth."[4]

There are adults who would rather teenagers not come face-to-face with such agonizing home truths. But I have never been sorry that I met my shadow when I was sixteen. I'd had earlier glimpses—my grandmother certainly tried to help me see—but this was different and I knew it. This was my own truth, something that no one else could discover for me or pressure me to discover for myself. And who would have suspected that this particular book would have had such an effect on me? Certainly, no librarian, no teacher, not even my grandmother would ever have given it to me to help me see my own situation reflected. What character in the book would an American teenage girl identify with? The old black priest? The white landowner? The murdered activist? His condemned killer? And yet it was this book more than any other that enabled me to discover myself. I was shattered by my discovery, but the very devastation made a kind of healing and growth possible. A great book can do this for a reader. It can give us hope as it judges us. It gives us a place to stand even as it casts us out of Eden.

When I look at the books I have written, the first thing that I see is the outcast child searching for a place to stand. But the next thing that I see is the promise of such a place. Terabithia is the most obvious return to Eden in my books. Eden is, it seems to me, the metaphor for the universe in perfect harmony.

It is no accident of an ignorant storyteller that the temptation in the Garden of Paradise is the temptation to eat the fruit of the tree of knowledge of good and evil. When Eve tells the serpent that God has forbidden the man and woman to eat of this tree, lest they die, the serpent says: "Ye shall not surely die: For God doth know that in the day ye eat thereof, then your eyes shall be opened, and ye shall be as gods, knowing good and evil."[5] And, ironically, the tree did make the woman and man as gods. They were no longer content to play their parts in the perfect harmony of the created universe. They now stood outside of Eden. They had not known that judgment of one creature by another would rip apart the seamless garment of Creation. By choosing to be as gods, they chose apartness and dissolution and ultimately death—not the natural return of that which is of the earth to the earth—but death that is poisoned by fear. By stepping out of their place to approve of or condemn or evaluate the worth of their fellow creatures, they destroyed the harmony God intended and put all of Creation in jeopardy. We have been homesick for Eden ever since.

Perhaps this is why, against all our experience with the world, we still deep down inside crave a happy ending—a return to innocence and joy. Perhaps this is why so often we try to convince ourselves that though Eden is lost to us, surely our children are still in the Garden. But the deed has been done—not only in that mythical Paradise but throughout human history. There's no hiding place down here. There's no going back to a place of perfect harmony and innocence. As persons we chose and every day choose again to eat the fruit. We cannot do otherwise. That is the way the world is. Our condemnation is our distinction. We are as gods. We must judge between good and evil now. We have become disturbers of the universe, but with fear and trembling, knowing that we must first judge our own hearts.

When one of our sons was at Dartmouth I had a chance to hear Dr. John Kemeny speak. For those of you who know computers, I do not have to explain who Dr. Kemeny is, but for the rest of us lesser mortals, Dr. Kemeny is one of the pioneers in this whole field. With his colleagues at Dartmouth, he invented BASIC, which is the language most people in the world use when talking to a computer. He and his Dartmouth undergraduates were the first to effect time-sharing on a computer. In the question and answer period after Dr. Kemeny's talk, someone asked him if there was anything a computer would not be able eventually to do. Dr. Kemeny replied that there were two tasks for which the human brain was perfectly suited that he did not believe any computer would ever be able to accomplish. And if somehow computers were able to do these things, he hoped that no one would ever use them in these ways. The areas where the human mind must always hold sway, according to Dr. Kemeny, are the area of creativity and the area of value judgments.

I believe Dr. Kemeny is right. Both creativity and judgment belong to humanity, and although I look upon creativity as a gift and judgment as a burden, I cannot turn either over to a machine or an organization or even to another human being. When we make value or moral judgments, we *do* further disturb the already disturbed universe, we cannot escape it. But happily, in creative endeavors, we can to some degree connect with nature and with one another. In art we can recover something of the harmony of the universe. We can become reconcilers as well as judges.

Judgment will divide and disturb the already disturbed universe. It must, and we must not like Prufrock hang back cowardly when the words must be spoken, the judgment made. But something of Eden remains with us. We can still create—we can still find harmony and connection through works of the imagination. That these works in themselves will disturb and judge is true, of course. But for them to be art and not merely propaganda they must have that deep connective quality that links soul to soul.

We must remember, however, that the balance is never a neat one. The material of the novelist is neither simply judgment nor reconciliation nor even a judicious combination of the two. The material of the novelist is human experience, in which nothing is ever neatly sorted out. It's more like watching the window of the washing machine. Now the blue jeans flap into view, now the towel, now the blouse. Mercy, will the jeans turn the blouse blue? And everyone knows that when you open the door, one of every pair of socks that went in will have mysteriously vanished.

Few things make me feel as helpless as the critic who demands that it all be sorted out, that I be consistent, that the message be clear and the characters exemplary—the ending happy. That's not what I'm about. There is a basic morality to what I say and an ultimate hope, but these are, as Eudora Welty says, "deep down; they are the rock on which the whole structure of more than that novel rests."[6] Morality and hope will be in my book because the only human experience I've had is my own. But, believe me, they will be mixed up with lots of other laundry, and a few socks will always come up missing.

There is a story that Karl Barth, the greatest of this century's Protestant theologians, told on himself. Barth was a great lover of Mozart and used to begin his day playing Mozart on the phonograph to clear his mind and prepare him to go to work writing his *Dogmatics*. But Barth was always troubled that Mozart in his own lifetime had despised Protestantism. One night, Barth relates, he had a dream, and in his dream he was appointed to examine Mozart in theology. Since Barth loved Mozart's music, if not his theology, he sought to make his examination as favorable as he could. But when the time came for Mozart to reply—to defend himself—Mozart remained absolutely silent.

Here we have an example of the artist as both disturber and reconciler. Please note that Mozart's art needed no justification. The music said all that could be said, and both Barth and the Mozart of his dream knew it. Mozart connected with Barth at a level far below that of the rational argument that was Barth's accustomed language, but he also disturbed Barth. Perhaps in seeking to reconcile, the artist always disturbs as well. Eden is no longer our natural habitat. We can never simply go back. Even the Bible acknowledges this, for the final scene set after the end of the world does not take place in a garden but in a city. And cities are the products of judgment as much as they are the product of creativity.

In closing, I'd like to share a story that was given to me by the poet and author Stanley Kiesel. It seems to me to show the artist as disturber and reconciler in a rather wonderful way. "I work as a writer in the Minneapolis public schools," Mr. Kiesel said, "and one day I walked into an upper elementary classroom in which the teacher had told me no writing ever went on. She also warned me about Tony, the troublemaker who sat in the back row. True, he was. He made noises. Interesting noises. One of them sounded like my old hand lawn mower in Los Angeles. I asked him to come up and be my old lawn mower in Los Angeles. He was quite happy about this. Actually, he did it with éclat, mowing up and down the aisles. Other kids volunteered their machinelike noises and we had a fine time. This led easily into talking about machines and imagining ourselves and others as machines. The last twenty minutes I asked them to write down their machine fantasies. This is what Tony wrote: 'My dad broke down two years ago. First, he lost his hubcaps then he got no brakes. His gas tank started leaking so he run out of gas a lot. Then serious stuff goes on like flat tires and motor conking out. Mom and I revved him up every once in a while. But no good happening. He's just a piece of junk gone somewhere we don't know. But I miss him sometimes and I'm going to be a car fixer when I'm eighteen.' "

For Tony there is no hiding place, no Eden. We cannot protect him from this disturbing universe, but he—both the disturbed and the disturbing—can be a fixer, an artist, a reconciler. So, perhaps, can we.

NOTE: *An abridged version of this speech appeared in* The Horn Book *magazine, September / October 1984, pp. 640–651.*

Ideas

The writer of an article about Dr. Seuss reported that at the end of an interview Theodore Geiss congratulated him for not asking the one question that people invariably ask. When the writer asked him what that one question might be, Dr. Seuss replied, "Where do you get your ideas?" "Well, all right," said the reporter. "Where *do* you get your ideas?" "I'm glad you asked that," Dr. Seuss said, and pulled out a printed card. On the card was spelled out the secret that the world pants for. It seems that on the stroke of midnight at the full moon of the summer solstice, Dr. Seuss makes an annual pilgrimage into the desert, where an ancient Native American hermit and wise man has his abode. That old Indian, Dr. Seuss declared, is the source of all his ideas. But where the old Indian gets *his* ideas, he has no notion.

Where do you get your ideas? I suppose the people who ask this question are expecting a rational, one-sentence reply. What they get from me is a rather stupid stare. Unlike the good doctor, I have no earthly notion of how to answer this question. My impulse is to retort rudely, "Where do you get *your* ideas?" I've never met anyone devoid of ideas. Of course, a lot of ideas are bad or dumb. Indeed, a lot of *my* ideas are bad or dumb, but I try not to publish those. What is the questioner asking for? Does he want geography, history, philosophy? Is he asking for a chart of my inner space with a star at the spot where ideas come from?

It occurred to me in the middle of all these ravings that I might be doing what the mother of the old story did when her Johnny asked where he came from. She took a deep breath and spent fifteen minutes initiating her six-year-old into the mysteries of human birth. At the end of which Johnny said, "Well, I was just wondering. Billy said he came from Philadelphia."

There are, after all, some answers to the question Where do you get your ideas? that are not lost in the nether regions of my subconscious. I can remember, for example, a lot of things that led to the writing of *The Great Gilly Hopkins*. It began initially because I wanted to write a funny story. No, there was something even before that. It occurred in the spring of 1975 while I was hard at work on *Bridge to Terabithia*. Events on the other side of the world were invading my peaceful living room every night. Vietnam fell and then Cambodia. My children were watching the films of the homeless children and saying, "Can't we help? Don't we have room for some more children?" And I was saying, "I can't take care of more than four children. We can't possibly afford another child." But finally I agreed with the family's feeling that if we couldn't adopt any more, we could certainly provide temporary foster care. Since we had been certified as genuine okay parents by the local Lutheran Social Service when we adopted Mary, we were asked to take in two Cambodian boys for two weeks. That didn't seem so hard. We bought a bunk bed so we could turn the boys' bedroom into a dormitory, and I started cooking rice three times a day, thinking how lucky these boys were to come into the home of a woman who knew how to cook rice properly. Well, it wasn't as easy as cooking rice. The two weeks stretched into two more weeks and then two more and two more. The honeymoon period, when everyone was on his or her best behavior, was all too quickly over. I learned a lot about children, about being a foster parent, and about myself that, given the choice, I'd just as soon not have learned. I had always thought of myself as a B– or at the least a C+ mother, and here I was flunking.

I had to ask myself why. And I found the answer in my attitude. When I first met each of our four children, either in the delivery room or at the airport, I knew this child was mine—that there was no backing out for either of us. No matter what happened, for better or worse, in sickness or in health, as long as we both lived, we would belong to each other as parent and child. This sort of absolute conviction does something to a relationship, and both you and the child know it. When problems arise, you know there's no escape, so you work them out. But with foster children, there's no such conviction. I would find myself thinking, I can't really deal with that. They'll be here such a short time. Or, Thank heavens this is only temporary! And what I was doing was regarding another human being as a disposable commodity. Now, I am quite aware of the fact that there is nothing funny about this attitude. I am also aware of the thousands of foster children in this country who have to live out their lives in a world that regards them as disposable, and it took me quite a while to realize that the funny book I wanted to write was buried in this tragic idea.

It was the summer after the boys left us for their adoptive homes that I started to read *The Lord of the Rings*. My apartment mate in 1961 had been a Tolkien fan, and she had wanted me to read the books back then. But I had been too busy studying theology to take on three fat volumes of fiction, so I had put it off until, suddenly, it had become a cultic act to read Tolkien, and I have never been one to join a cult. Finally, that July, exhausted from writing *Bridge* and trying to be a foster mother, I took the books to Lake George and began to read.

I remember vividly the day I came to the end of *The Return of the King*. Sam, as you will remember, has gone to Grey Havens to see Frodo off on the mysterious ship that will carry him away forever.

"Then Frodo kissed Merry and Pippin, and last of all Sam, and went aboard; and the sails were drawn up, and the wind blew, and slowly the ship slipped away down the long grey firth; and the light of the glass of Galadriel that Frodo bore glimmered and was lost." Tolkien then relates how the three companions return home in silence, until they part and Sam at last "came back up the hill as day was ending once more. And he went on, and there was yellow light, and fire within; and the evening meal was ready and he was expected. And Rose drew him in, and set him in his chair, and put little Elanor upon his lap.

"He drew a deep breath. 'Well, I'm back,' he said."[1]

I looked up from Sam's last words, startled to find myself in a bathing suit, sitting on a towel, shivering in the sun, with people about me chatting, and children running and splashing into the water, calling out to one another. Where was I? It took me several minutes to reorient myself, until I was no longer in Middle Earth but had made the long, long journey home.

Someday, I told myself, someday, I'm going to write a book, and the central character is going to be a girl named Galadriel. Eventually, my young heroine became Galadriel Hopkins, for a reason that only surfaced this past year. Waiting in an autograph line was a distinguished-looking man with a volume of poetry protruding from his jacket pocket: *The Collected Poems of Gerard Manley Hopkins*. Instantly I knew where Gilly had gotten her last name. Gerard Manley, like his namesake Gilly, lives in the deepest places of my soul.

Anyhow, for months I carried her about with me—Galadriel Hopkins—my child without a story.

I don't know how long I would have borne this child around unfleshed, but we have at our house one inexorable deadline. It is called Christmas Eve. Somehow, years ago, I began writing a story for my husband to read at the Christmas Eve service, and before I knew it, it had become a tradition. Every year I say, How can I possibly write another story? There are only so many themes attached to Christmas, and I've already done them all—several times. But somehow, each year, I manage one more, swearing it will be the last.

The events of the spring were still in my mind and on my conscience, and the Christmas story for 1975 was about an elderly man who takes in two foster children for Christmas. The old man is full of love and generosity, but something terrible happens. The recipients of his compassion *are not grateful.* If you have read "Maggie's Gift," you know already that once I had written it, I knew exactly who Galadriel Hopkins was. She was a foster child, born to a flower child who had read all of Tolkien, but who was still too much of a child herself to care for a real live child of her own. Not a funny subject—but there you are—these were the ideas that came together for the funny book I wanted to write.

Whenever I repeat a word often enough, I realize how dimly I understand its meaning. What exactly is an idea? I try to define it, and the image that pops into mind is the comic-book balloon with the lightbulb inside. You can't talk to teachers and librarians in comic-book images, so I went, magnifying glass in hand, to my *Compact Edition of the Oxford English Dictionary.* It was like telling Johnny where he came from. Even in print that you have to read with a magnifying glass, the word *idea* consumes sixteen and a half inches. The esteemed editors take us back to the Greek origins—where *idea* is the general or ideal form, the archetype, as opposed to the individual form. I kept searching for what I thought an idea was, and came upon it eventually, buried in the fourth inch. And I quote: "In weakened sense: a conception or notion of something to be done or carried out; an intention, plan of action."

It's sad to think that when I use the word *idea* I am using it in the weakened sense, but there you are. I do, however, have one advantage over some people. If a definition doesn't satisfy me in English, I can look it up in Japanese. And in Japanese, the word is *i*, which is made up of two characters—the character for *sound* and the character for *heart*—so an idea is something that makes a sound in the heart (the heart in Japanese, as in Hebrew, being the seat of intelligence as well as the seat of feeling).

Isn't that a wonderful picture? There is something lying deep within you that suddenly one day without warning sets off an alarm, rings, sounds, waking up your heart.

Now what does all this have to do with writing fiction? A great deal, it seems to me. Because I believe that in writing fiction, I must be released from the concept of idea as ideal form or archetype, I must be released from the concept of idea as notion or plan of action, and I must cling to those ideas for fiction that are truly sounds from my heart.

If you are observant, you have noted that, like any good Presbyterian preacher, I have just handed you the three-point outline of my sermon. It seems to me, you see, that a great deal of our problem with fiction, especially fiction for children, stems from the fact that we don't know what fiction is. I will proceed, therefore, to tell you, captive audience that you are, what I believe fiction to be.

A novel, first of all, deals only indirectly with ideal forms or archetypes. Myths and fairy tales deal directly with archetypes, and there is a very real place for them, especially as they help children to map the dark regions of their souls, to face and conquer their inner dragons. We cannot, we must not, deprive children of these powerful images. With-out them, not only do art and literature lose their power, but the soul itself stands ravaged and windowless like a vandalized cathedral.

But a novel, while it has its roots in the ancient stories, is not the same thing. It is much more humble, perhaps the least lofty of all the arts. In fiction, you see, our medium is not the archetypal forms but human experience, which is truth at a very earthly level. If we are told in Genesis 1 that God created us male and female in God's own image, in the very next chapter, we are told that we were created from the dust of the earth. Now, most of us high-minded people who want to write fiction are very happy with the idea of Genesis 1, but we get most uncomfortable when we turn from the august and the abstract and find ourselves in the mud by the creek bank. It is not simply the behavior of real live people or even the language of real live children that we shy away from. It is the fact that in fiction, the writer does not dress up grand ideas in human form, she *starts* with the human be-ing—who may very well have torn cuticles and BO but who, at best, is a mortal creature that tastes, smells, hears, touches, sees, and some-where down the line begins to conceptualize and believe. A person in a novel can certainly *have* ideas, but if the idea has the person, we are not looking at truth but at propaganda.

I have been very aware of this first misunderstanding of fiction in the varied responses I've gotten to *The Great Gilly Hopkins*. I got a ter-rifying letter from a teacher telling me how much she liked the book because, she said, Gilly is such a wonderful role model for today's children. Well, I don't know about you, but I don't want for my chil-dren a role model who lies, steals, takes advantage of the handi-capped, bullies the weak, acts out her racial bigotry in a particularly tasteless fashion, and regularly takes the name of the Lord in vain. I do not personally approve of any of these forms of behavior. I am not, in *Gilly*, trying to tell anyone how I think children *ought* to behave. I am trying to tell the story of a lost child who is angry with the world that regards her as disposable and who is fighting it with every available weapon—fair or foul.

And when, on the other hand, I am accused of writing less than the ideal book, when I am taken to task for Gilly's cursing—never, alas, for all her other sins, just her cursing—when I am asked the painful question "Couldn't the book have been just as effective without profanity?" I have to say, "No, I do not see how it could have been." We all know that a child who lies, steals, bullies, and acts out her racial bigotry with vicious ferocity—we all know that this child does not say "fiddlesticks" when frustrated. If Gilly is to be believed, her mouth must reflect the lost child within. Of course, if the book had faithfully reproduced the language of the Gillys some of us know all too well, the weight of obscenity would have totally unbalanced the story. Such, you see, is the power of words, and the writer must be aware of this power and walk gently.

Which brings us to the second definition of *idea* and the second point I want to make about fiction—that is, fiction as notion or plan of action. I am quite aware that I have been accused of writing didactic books that try to foist lessons and values on unsuspecting little minds (which would mean that I have violated my own guidelines by erring in the direction of the ideal rather than the true), but I have also been accused (in reviews of the very same book) of this second sin—that of being too practical and down to earth—of writing so-called problem fiction. Now, what is problem fiction and what is the problem with it?

Let me use one of my own books to illustrate. Sara Louise Bradshaw has this big problem. She is jealous of her gorgeous, talented sister. So the plan of action—the plot, if you please—of this book is to solve Sara Louise's problem. The first thing most of us ever learned about writing fiction is that conflict is at its very heart. If there is no problem, there is no story. So what am I fussing about? I am fussing about what my dictionary calls the weakened sense—the reduction of human life to a series of problems that can, with insight and a bit of doing, be solved.

The first time I was told that *Bridge to Terabithia* was "on our death list," I was a bit shaken up. There follows, you see, the feeling that if a child has a problem, a book that deals with that problem can be given to the child and the problem will be cured. As Jill Paton Walsh points out, only children's books are used this way. "One does not," she says, "rush to give *Anna Karenina* to friends who are committing adultery, or minister to distressed old age with copies of *King Lear*."[2] Still, if we look at life as a series of problems needing solving, it is hard not to offer nicely packaged, portable solutions, preferably paperback. I know. No one has given out more copies of *Ramona the Brave* to first graders in distress than I have. . . .

I had wanted to write the story that became *Jacob Have I Loved* for a long time, because I knew how important the relationships between sisters or between sister and brother are, but before that idea—that notion—that problem—could become a book, at least two things had to happen. The idea had to be incarnate in a person—it had to cease being general and abstract and become individual in a child who lived in a specific place at a specific time. The book had to be researched every bit as carefully as a novel set in twelfth-century Japan. But, more important, the book had to come from the sounds within my deepest heart. I could not cheat and I could not hurry.

Someone—I think it was Goethe—once said, "The beginning and end of all literary activity is the reproduction of the world that surrounds me by means of the world that is in me. . . ."

Now, of course it is the height of arrogance to suppose that the world that is in me has any significance for you—much less for children whose experience of the world is necessarily limited. How can I ask them to see their own nuclear-threatened world through, for example, a rebellion of Chinese peasants in the middle of the nine-teenth century? And yet I do, because the world that is in me is the only world I have by which to grasp the world outside, and, as I write fiction, it is the chart by which I must steer. I must never forget how limited my own experience is and how partial my vision of truth must be, but nonetheless, it is the only vision I have right now, and I must be as faithful to it as I can.

The work reveals the creator—and as our universe in its vastness, its orderliness, its exquisite detail, tells us something of the One who made it, so a work of fiction, for better or worse, will reveal the writer. There is always for me a horrible moment just before a new novel is published when I wonder if I can stand being stripped naked still an-other time. Someone said to me recently that she had read my books and now wanted to really get to know *me*. I didn't say it aloud. Con-vention keeps me quiet once in a while. But inside myself I was say-ing—Lady, you already know me far better than you have any right to. It is not that Wang Lee's or Gilly Hopkins's or Louise Bradshaw's life is a retelling of my own. Of course not. But feelings reveal more than facts. And a writer can never know about a character's feelings what is not somewhere mirrored in her own.

The poet Rilke describes what must happen. "For the sake of a single verse," he says, ". . . one must be able to think back to roads in unknown regions . . . to days of childhood that are still unexplained. . . . And still it is not yet enough to have memories. One must forget them and one must have great patience to wait until they come again. For it is not yet the memories themselves, not till they have turned to blood within us, to glance and gesture, nameless and no longer to be distinguished from ourselves—not till then can it happen that in a most rare hour the first word of a verse arises in their midst and goes forth from them."[3]

The memories must turn to blood within us before the images, ideas, the sounds of the heart can come forth.

A seventh grader in California asked me, "What do you want the reader to achieve by reading *Bridge to Terabithia?*" And I said to him, "Look, my job is to write the best book I know how to write. Your job is to decide what you're to achieve by reading it." A book is a cooperative venture. The writer can write a story down, but the book will never be complete until a reader of whatever age takes that book and brings to it his own story. I realize tonight, as I realize every time I speak, that I am addressing an audience that includes many of my coauthors.

So please don't ask me where I get my ideas as if I were some creature foreign to you who drinks at an alien watering trough. Don't ask me where I get my ideas as though you have no part, no responsibility, in bringing what you read to life. Frances Clarke Sayers speaks of the "shattering and gracious encounter that art affords." It is only when the deepest sound going forth from my heart meets the deepest sound coming forth from yours—it is only in this encounter that the true music begins.

Sounds in the Heart

Several years ago I read an article about writing for children in which the writer said that her qualification for writing for children lay in her photographic memory. She had never forgotten anything that had happened to her as a child, and therefore she could write meaningfully for children. I have typically forgotten who the writer was and where the article appeared, and the only reason I remember the statement at all is that it made me resolve all over again not to read any more articles on the qualifications to be a writer for children.

Indeed, as I was writing *Jacob Have I Loved*, I was carrying on a running quarrel with Louise Bradshaw. I wanted to write the book in the third person because I knew perfectly well that no one—well, no one I knew—could remember her past in the kind of detail that Louise was pretending to. I was very nervous about this, since I know I have a poor memory for specific events. When I am called upon to tell about something from my past, I find myself wondering in mid-story how much of what I seem to be remembering actually occurred.

Gilly Hopkins would probably say that I lie a lot, but I assure you that I do not lie intentionally. I seem, however, incapable of separating the bare facts from my constantly enlarging perception of those facts. It is part of what makes me a writer of fiction, for a writer of fiction is never content with mere fact; she must somehow find a pattern, a meaning in events.

Of course, this is what Louise Bradshaw has done from the vantage point of age. She has scooped out a hunk of her youth and molded it into a story. The difference between writing a story and simply relating past events is that a story, in order to be acceptable, must have shape and meaning. It is the old idea that art is the bringing of order out of chaos, and it is interesting to me how much I crave that order. Recently, I read Elizabeth Hardwick's *Sleepless Nights*. On the front of the jacket it is called a novel. On the back, it is called "subtle, beautiful, extraordinary, haunting, daring, miraculous, and almost perfect." For a change, I have little argument with the back of the book. It may very well be subtle, beautiful, extraordinary, haunting, daring, miraculous, and almost perfect. But it ain't no novel. At least it is not what I would ever call a novel. Perhaps there is order in the book, but if there is, it is far too subtle for me. I find no shape to the memories set down in this book, and I put it down deeply dissatisfied.

I believe it is the job of the novelist to shape human experience so that a reader might be able to find not only order but meaning in the story. It also seems to me that the way a writer shapes human experience depends to a great extent on her history—all those forces, most of which she had nothing to do with, that made her what she is. In speaking of those forces, we are speaking of our human heritage, our particular family history, and our individual past experience. These are the memories that we call up consciously or unconsciously as we write.

Among the many Chinese and Japanese ideographs for our word *idea* is one that combines the character for *sound* with the character for *heart*—the heart being the seat of the intelligence as well as of emotion. Thus, an idea is something that makes a sound in the heart. Now, if you want to change *idea* into a verb that means "to remember," you do so by adding an extra symbol for *heart*. In preparing to talk of the relation of memory to writing, I tried to ask myself as objectively as I could: What are the sounds that I hear in my deepest heart? What causes me to shape human experience in the way that I do?

If I tell you that I was born in China of Southern Presbyterian missionary parents, I have already given away the three chief clues to my tribal memory.

Let me start at the end and work backward through the description. Missionary parents. I have discovered as I have gone out into the world that most people do not regard missionary work as a respectable occupation. And I'm sure that many of us "mish kids" would argue whether having been born one was a plus or minus for the living of this life. There is no way to escape a certain peculiarity of personality. But all that comes later. For the most basic and most lasting gift of this parentage was a total identification with the children of Israel. The stories of the Bible were read to us not to make us good but to tell us who we were. It seems a bit strange to me, as I look back, that my feeling of kinship was not with the early Christian church but with the Hebrew people. In fact, it was years later, after considerable study of Paul's Epistles, that I had to come to the conclusion that *Gentile* after all was not a dirty word.

It is still hard for me to accept as fact that my blood ancestors were Gentiles and were until fairly recently painting themselves blue and running around naked. My real ancestors left Ur of the Chaldees with Abraham and wandered in the wilderness with Moses. Add to this strong biblical heritage its interpretation by Calvin, Knox, and the Westminster divines, and you have got one sure foundation beneath your feet. Again, it was amazing to me to learn that to most people Calvinism seems more like the foundation that ladies of my mother's generation used to wear—squeezing all the breath out of you and poking into you every step you took. This, of course, was not my experience. For if the Bible told me who I was, my Presbyterian tradition told me why I was.

"What is the chief end of man?" the Westminster catechism asks in its very first question; and we could all answer before we could read: "Man's chief end is to glorify God and enjoy him forever." Again, many people outside this tradition have a very different view of the Calvinist position. They think of it more like a slogan that was on a T-shirt our son John used to own. This one had four monkeys: Hear No Evil, See No Evil, Speak No Evil, Have No Fun. Other people contend to the contrary that Presbyterians see nothing but evil—from original sin to total depravity—dragging guilt through the world as Marley's ghost dragged his chains. Still others can't understand why Presbyterians, who profess to believe in divine predestination in which everything depends on God, spend their lives working as if everything depended on them. I haven't the time, and you haven't the patience for me to pursue this line of thought in much more detail, but I bring it up because I am trying to discover what this heritage has to do with what I write.

The other day someone was telling me of an article he had read about a recent discovery of galaxies ten billion light-years from Earth, and it reminded me of something a former theology professor of mine said last year. He had just survived a heart attack and bypass surgery. "People are always asking me if I believe in the next world. Why," he said, "I can hardly believe in this one."

Those of us, you see, who were raised in this tradition know how puny we are. It is not our ability to understand or believe or remember that ultimately matters. That will come and go. But the truth we have drunk in with our mother's milk is that the one who flung the stars in their courses does not forget his children. A friend asked me how I dared to go into Louise's loss of faith. Wasn't I afraid that I would lose my own along the way? But I know that I am always carrying about within myself faith and unfaith, obedience and rebellion, trust and fear. When I write with the eyes of hope, it is not my own ability to believe that I am writing about but the biblical affirmation that God is faithful—justice and righteousness will prevail. In the words of one of my spiritual fathers, the Roman Catholic priest and poet Gerard Manley Hopkins: "Because the Holy Ghost over the bent / World broods with warm breast and with ah! bright wings."[1]

I am also a child of another heritage that will seem strange to most of you. Let me illustrate. A man I met at a party had just taken his son to Gettysburg and had found out a fascinating detail of history there. He learned, while at the site of Pickett's Charge, that the Union officer who had repulsed the charge and therefore saved the day and perhaps the Union was George Custer. "So, you see," he said, "Custer did have his moment of glory."

Now, this story did not have the effect he intended. The teller did not realize that I had been raised on the story of my grandfather's two older brothers who died in the War Between the States. (We even called the war by a different name where I came from.) One of these brothers was a cavalry officer under Pickett and was mortally wounded in that desperate, heroic charge. (Here again, those with a different heritage might call it suicidal or insane.)

There is a very romantic (once more from our point of view) story connected with my uncle's death. As he lay dying, a young Union chaplain came to him and asked if there was anything he could do. My uncle asked him to unpin the Confederate flags and cut two brass buttons from his uniform and send them to his father and his sweet-heart in Georgia. He was able to tell the chaplain his name—Goetchius—but he died before he could give the chaplain his address. For years the chaplain carried the flags and buttons in his pocket, un-able to forget the dying man's request but unable to fulfill it. Twenty years later, he was traveling on a ferryboat in Georgia and heard one of the black ferrymen address an elderly passenger as Marse Goetchius. He approached the man and asked him if he had had a relative who took part in Pickett's Charge. The man was my great-grandfather, whose son had been listed as missing in action all those years. Together he and the chaplain traveled to Pennsylvania. They located the trench grave because the corn grew taller and greener along it, and—as I was told as a child—they identified my uncle's body by his dental work. My great-grandfather took his son's remains home to Georgia. My mother remembered my uncle's sweetheart, who was, of course, no longer young when my mother knew her. She always reminded my mother and her sisters that she should have been their aunt. She never married and, I was told, treasured those two brass buttons until she died.

Now it doesn't matter that I know it would have been tragic if our nation had become two nations, one slave and one free. It doesn't matter that I think that the holding of slaves is an abomination be-fore God and that to regard any other human being as inferior to one-self is a grievous sin. Somehow, there is still something in me that sees the glory in my uncle's death and not in Custer's triumph. The image of the saintly, larger-than-life Robert E. Lee in defeat will forever seem more magnificent than that of Ulysses S. What's-his-name in victory.

One of the things I was told as a child never to forget, and haven't, is that I have been kissed by Maude Henderson. (In my own defense, I should like to have it in the record that I spent an enormous effort in my childhood wriggling out from under kisses. Missionary children are fair game for any maudlin matron.) The significance of this particular kiss, however, is that when Maude Henderson was a little girl, her father, one of the landed Virginia gentry, was a close friend of Robert E. Lee's and a fellow vestryman in the Episcopal church in Lexington. The general used to give little Maude rides on his horse. (I was sure that meant Traveller, but I have no proof for those of you who prefer your history straight.) Coming home together from a vestry meeting one evening, the general stopped by the Hendersons' house to speak to his friend's wife, and as he was leaving, he stooped and gave little Maude a kiss. Then he went home, sat down at his own supper table, and slipped into unconsciousness. Miss Maude explained to us that the general's widow had told her that she must always remember that although many people had kissed the general before he died, she was the last person on earth whom *he* had kissed. And my brother and sisters and I were to remember that she in turn had kissed us. This would be even sappier than it sounds (if that is possible), except that Maude Henderson is one of the genuine heroes of my life. But more about her later.

I want to make one probably obvious point about this part of my heritage, which is that since 1865 we white Southerners have been suckers for a losing cause. Struggle dashed to defeat by inexorable might is somehow more glorious than mere success. I, for example, cannot escape the notion that those seven years when I was writing doggedly and publishing nothing were far more honorable than the years since. This heritage explains, of course, why I was drawn to the Heike Clan rather than to the Genji when I read Japanese history. And then, too, the Japanese tend to romanticize the person who struggles but is in the end brought down.

This brings me to the third sound in my heart—the music of the East. Among my earliest memories are those of a Chinese woman who lived very close to us. When I was four years old, it was my habit every day to walk to Mrs. Loo's house precisely at her lunchtime. One day as I was going out on my usual jaunt, my mother said to me in what I'm sure she thought was a joking manner, "If you keep on eating so much Chinese food, you might turn into a little Chinese girl." Her remark bothered me. I didn't really want to give up the parents I had. But it didn't bother me enough to keep me from going to Mrs. Loo's for lunch. Today, I still discover that when I am happy and want to celebrate, I will cook Japanese food; but when I hit bottom and need all the comfort life can afford, it is Chinese food that I crave. This is a very physical heritage of smell and sight and touch, because these are my earliest impressions.

Chinese was my first language, although I quickly became bilingual. When I was five, we were refugeed to the United States for the first time, and even though we returned to China the following year, only my father got back to our home in Huai'an. The rest of us lived among foreigners, so my fluency in Chinese disappeared. I have forgotten Chinese almost entirely, but I believe and hope it is still there, bred into my bones along with steamed pork dumplings.

I spend a lot of time trying to explain to people that China and Japan are two different countries with different languages, histories, and cultures, although I cannot but feel that those early years in China prepared me in a unique way to live in Japan.

My father was raised a farmer in the Shenandoah Valley of Virginia. His people never owned slaves, although they were farming the valley before the Revolutionary War. They were a combination of German peasant and Scotch-Irish rock, fiercely independent, glorying in God and in their own strong backs. My father went from Washington and Lee University to join the French as an ambulance driver before the United States entered World War I. He left his right leg in France and brought home a Croix de Guerre and a dose of toxic gas.

He was, I believe, as ideally suited as any Westerner to go to China. He was intelligent, hardworking, almost fearless, absolutely stoical, and amazingly humble, with the same wonderful sense of humor found in many Chinese. Not only was he capable of learning the language and enduring the hardships of his chosen life, but also he was incapable of seeing himself in the role of Great White Deliverer.

We lived, unlike most foreigners of that era, in a Chinese house in a school complex where all of our neighbors were Chinese. My father's coworker and closest friend was the first son of a first son, a well-born man, and a recognized scholar. He chose to become a Christian pastor. He and my father traveled together, riding donkeys from village to village, sleeping on the straw in flea-ridden pigsties because they were the best accommodations some friendly farmers could offer. Where there was famine—as there too often was—they went with food, and where there was plague or disease, they went with medicine. Mr. Lee disappeared in the first Communist purges in 1949, and my father grieved for him until he died.

What this meant for me was that when I went to Japan many years later, I had, through no virtue of my own, an attitude toward the Orient that most Westerners, especially the Americans I met there, seemed to lack. I knew that I had come to a civilization far older than my own, to a language that after a lifetime of study I would still be just beginning to grasp, to a people whose sense of beauty I could only hope to appreciate but never to duplicate.

Against these convictions, there was, of course, a fear. The only Japanese I had known as a child were enemy soldiers. What made it possible for me to go to Japan at all was a close friend I had in graduate school, a Japanese woman pastor who persuaded me that despite the war I would find a home in Japan if I would give the Japanese people a chance. And she was right. In the course of four years I was set fully free from my deep, childish hatred. I truly loved Japan, and one of the most heartwarming compliments I ever received came from a Japanese man I worked with who said to me one day that someone had told him that I had been born in China. Was that true? I assured him it was. "I knew it," he said. "I've always known there was something Oriental about you."

How, then, has this affected how and what I write? The setting of my first three novels is the most obvious result. But there are other things, some of which I can identify and some which I cannot. One thing living in Japan did for me was to make me feel that what is left out of a work of art is as important as, if not more important than, what is put in. (As Virginia Buckley, my editor, will testify, I tend from time to time to eliminate to the point of obscurity, but the principle is a good one.) I am also a great lover of form. As a writer, I seek freedom within a form. I rather doubt that I am capable of truly experimental art. And form for me has something to do with the order woven into the universe.

A friend of mine who had lived in Japan for a number of years was preparing to return to the States, and at her farewell party a young student said to her, "You must tell them the truth about us." "What do you want me to say?" she asked. "Tell them that we have four seasons," he replied. Now, if you know anything about the Japanese, you know that this is not an idle request. The sound that rings deepest in the Japanese heart is not Sony or Mitsubishi or even Honda, but spring, summer, fall, or winter. Every time I change the season in a novel, I remember that I have lived in this rhythm. I have known the glory of spring as seen in the cherry blossoms, which so quickly fade and fall to the earth; reminding us that life, too, is fleeting but that the seasons continue, the earth turns, and an order greater than our single lives prevails.

As I was trying somehow to pull together this talk, it came to revolve, to my surprise, around Maude Henderson, the woman who as a little girl had been kissed by Robert E. Lee. The reason I knew Maude Henderson was not because she came from Lexington, Virginia, where my father's people have lived for more than two hundred years. Her family was wealthy and Episcopalian; mine was solvent and Presbyterian. Maude Henderson and my parents became friends in Shanghai. Miss Maude left her elegant Virginia home to become a deaconess in the Episcopal Church. She went out to China at about the turn of the century, and there, in the poorest section of Shanghai, she opened a home for abandoned baby girls. She was their mother in every way and stayed in that home for forty-nine years. Her teeth fell out, as did most of her hair. When Japanese soldiers pillaging the city appeared at her door, demanding her girls, she stood there, all of five feet tall, and would not move. They would have to kill her first, she said. They didn't kill her. Even after December 1941, when they were arresting all Americans and determined that she must be arrested, they made it house arrest—her own house, with her current generation of girls.

In 1949 she was forced out of China, and for the first time in fifty years she came back to Virginia. We were living in West Virginia at the time, and she got on a bus and came to see us. My mother was a wonderful cook, and Miss Maude loved every bite. "I've only got one tooth left," she told us, "but it's all right. The doctor says it's my sweet one." She had then only the barest suggestion of white hair under her deaconess's cap, and her face looked exactly as though it had been shriveled like a dried apple, but from deep among the wrinkles, her blue eyes shone with humor and delight. I find in Maude Henderson the convergence of all my heritages. I will never forget her. And the fact that she kissed me will sound and resound in my deepest heart.

In May of 2000 I was able to go back to my hometown of Huai'an, which I had left when I was not quite five years old. There I was able to meet with two elderly people who had been close to my parents. One was a pastor who had been a young man then. "I called your father Wong Ta ta, Big Brother Wong. I was the one who found the boat for him when he had to flee. So many years have passed. So much has happened," he said, and then he began to cry. About that time an elderly woman came bouncing in. "We lived behind the same gate!" she cried. "My father and your father were best friends. They did everything together!" I couldn't believe I was seeing Mr. Li's daughter. "When did your father die?" I asked, believing, as my father had, that Mr. Li had died in 1949. "In 1979," she answered. I asked her to write her name, and when the interpreter wrote out it out in Pinyin, I saw that it was indeed Mr. Li's daughter who, as a teenager, had played with us younger children. Mr. Li had not died in prison or on a work farm but had returned to his family to live out his years. But in those years China was still closed to us, and my father never knew his friend had survived. His daughter remembered us all. "I saw you and I thought your mother had come," she said. I could not have asked for a more joyful homecoming.

Newbery Medal Acceptance Speech
for <u>Jacob Have I Loved</u>

I was thrilled, honored, gratified, not to say shocked to learn that *Jacob Have I Loved* was to be given the 1981 Newbery Medal. But there was a problem. "What shall I say in San Francisco?" I cried out to my husband. "I don't know what to say." He proposed: "Thank you." Yes, but what next? A writer I know suggested that it was time I said to the American Library Association: "We have got to stop meeting like this." I was sorely tempted, but these speeches tend to get preserved, and who wants to appear flippant to posterity? I complained to another friend that everything I thought of sounded either coy or dumb, and she replied: "Well, I don't think you need to worry about coy. It's just not your style to be coy." It took me several seconds to get it. Call Purnell would have caught on sooner. Into the midst of all this inner turmoil there came one cool, clear voice. It had a distinct Chesapeake Bay island ring to it. "Oh, my blessed. Wouldn't you know? Here I bring up a prize catch and the fool's fixing to ruin it for me."

So with Sara Louise Bradshaw prodding me at the end of her skiff pole, I was made to turn from the frazzled writer to the book. How could I forget that it is books that are being honored, books for children? And who could be happier than I to join in the sixtieth anniversary of such a celebration?

Those who know me best will testify that I am far more of a reader than I am a writer. If you understand that, you will understand something of what it means to me to be sharing this occasion with Jane Langton and Madeleine L'Engle, writers whose extraordinary vision lighted many of those dark days when I was still struggling to write fiction that someone would find worth publishing. And Arnold Lobel. There we are—my children Lin, John, David, Mary, and I—all crowded onto one bed, five heads poked together over the pictures, warming ourselves on Arnold's beloved Frog and Toad, delighting in them and in each other. In those days before I had ever met any real writers, much less become one, the books of these three were among those wonderful works that were enriching my life and the lives of our children. If Arnold will allow me to steal a phrase, it is a moment of true happiness to find myself in this distinguished company. And, speech or no speech, I am very grateful to the members of the Newbery Committee, as well as all of you in the Association for Library Service to Children, who have made this possible.

Thank you, John Paterson, for your love and patience and unswerving conviction that I can, too, write another book. Thank you, Lin, John, David, and Mary, for all the joy you bring us, as well as your total lack of reverence, which keeps me anchored to the real world of gallon milk jugs and swimming meets and socks that never match.

Thank you, Harper & Row. Thank you, Crowell. You know how I love you all. Pat Allen, thank you for liking my peculiar title and insisting that it stay on the book. And my editor, Virginia Buckley. What more can I say to you, Virginia? Surely you know that any honor that comes to a book we have done together is more than half yours. And Gene Namovicz. One book will never repay you for all the wear and tear of friendship, but it was all I had. Thank you for liking it even before it had a gold seal. I'm glad your name is in it. And, finally, the Womeldorfs. Thank you, each one. I am proud as well as grateful that we have belonged to one another.

But this speech must be concerned not with me and my myriad debts but with a book. One of you asked me three years ago what I wanted to do next, and I, seeing not the glamour of an awards ceremony but the pile of mess upon my desk back home, said: "All I want to do is write a publishable book." At the time my aim seemed far in excess of my grasp. Lauren Wohl and Bill Morris at Harper would call me, passing on invitations to speak, and I would whine: "Oh, Lauren, oh, Bill, please. I've got this book I want to write." That sounds pretty convincing for a few months, but when more than two years go by and there is no tangible evidence that any such book exists, someone might begin to think of the tailors who toiled night and day on a magnificent new wardrobe for a certain emperor. But neither Lauren nor Bill ever pried, or even raised an eyebrow. There were times when I suspected that they had more faith in this invisible book of mine than I did.

At one point, near desperation, I said to Virginia Buckley: "If I ever finish this book, Virginia, I'm going to mail it to your home address in a plain brown wrapper. And you must promise me that if it is no good you will not only refuse to publish it, you will never tell another soul that it exists." Virginia, being a gracious person as well as a great editor, did not even point out whose integrity was being impugned by such a demand. She took all my melodrama with a simple nod and one stipulation. "Just don't put a pseudonym on it," she said. I didn't have the nerve to tell her I'd seriously considered it.

Then there were those of you who would ask most politely the perfectly logical question "What are you working on now?" only to receive a snarl or a disconsolate mutter in reply. Well, this is it. This is that book that I would not talk about for so long even with my husband or my editor or my closest friends, the book that took me months to begin and that I often wondered if I could ever finish. This is *Jacob*, whom I have loved off and on for years.

Whenever I speak, one of the questions sure to be asked during the question-and-answer time is: "How long does it take to write a book?" as though books, like elephants or kittens, had a regular and therefore predictable gestation period. Often I will begin my reply by asking, "Which book?" trying to indicate that each book is different and has its own unique history. There is, however, one answer that would be true in every case, but whenever I try to put it in words I find myself swimming in pomposity. The correct answer, you see, is this: It has taken all my life to write this book. Maybe longer.

The conflict at the core of *Jacob Have I Loved* began east of Eden, in the earliest stories of my heritage. Cain was jealous of his brother, and, we are told, "Cain rose up against Abel his brother and slew him." If, in our Freudian orientation, we speak of the basic conflict as that between parent and child, the Bible, which is the earth from which I spring, is much more concerned with the relationships among brothers and sisters. "A friend loveth at all times," says the writer of Proverbs, "but a brother is born for adversity." They never taught us the second half of that verse in Sunday school.

The fairy tales, too, are full of the youngest brother or sister who must surpass his supposedly more clever elders or outwit the wicked ones. In *The Uses of Enchantment* Bruno Bettelheim suggests that a great deal of the apparent rivalry between brothers and sisters in fairy tales is in actuality an Oedipal conflict, since the usual number of brothers or sisters is three. In the stories of two brothers or sisters, Bettelheim suggests that the story is about the divided self, which must be integrated before maturity can be attained. Although both of these explanations make sense, I do not think that we can avoid the most obvious meaning of the stories, which is that among children who grow up together in a family there run depths of feeling that will permeate their souls for both good and ill as long as they live.

I was the middle child of five, swivel position, the youngest of the three older children and the oldest of the three younger. Although I can remember distinctly occasions when I determined that someday I would show my older brother and sister a thing or two, and I have no recollection that my two younger sisters were plotting to do me in, still the stories in which the younger by meanness or magic or heavenly intervention bested the elder always bothered me. They simply weren't fair. The divine powers, whether the Hebrew God or the European fairy, always weighted the contest. And although the civilized Calvinist part of my nature spoke in quiet tones about the mystery of divine election, there was a primitive, beastly part, a Caliban, that roared out against such monstrous injustice. Novels, I have learned, tend to come out of the struggle with the untamed beast.

It was the fall of 1977. *The Great Gilly Hopkins* was at the printers, the hoopla following the National Book Award for *The Master Puppeteer* was over, and I had finished the curriculum unit on the Shang and Chou dynasties of ancient China. I could no longer put it off. I must face the beast in its den, or, what was worse, that stack of blank paper beside my typewriter.

How do you begin a book? People always want to know how you begin. If only I knew. Think of all the agonizing days and weeks I could have spared myself, not to mention my long-suffering family. They know better than to ask me about my work when I'm trying to start all over again. My replies are never gracious. There must be a better way. My way is to write whatever I can, hoping against hope that, with all the priming, the pump will begin to flow once more.

Here is a sample from those dry, dry days in the fall of 1977:

Her name is Rachel Ellison but I don't know yet where she lives. It might be in the city or in the country. It might even be Japan. It seems important to know what her parents do. How does religion come into the story? Will Rachel be burdened by guilt as well as everything else? Will her relationship to God play counterpoint to her relationship to her brother? I said brother but perhaps after all it has to be a sister. I'm avoiding sister because it comes too close to home. Am I contemplating a book I can't write? The feelings start boiling up every time I begin to think about it. All raw feeling. No story. There has to be a story. There has to be a setting. There has to be something more than boiling anger. Why am I angry? . . . Where is the key that turns this into a book? Jacob and Esau. Cain and Abel. Rachel and Leah. Prodigal and elder brother. Joseph and his brothers. The sons of David. Lord, make my brother give me the portion of the inheritance that comes to me. Maybe Rachel's brother is an adopted Southeast Asian war orphan. Sister.

Excitement to pity to rage to hatred to some kind of accommodation. Step one: Go to the library and find out everything possible about Southeast Asian orphans. . . .

And I was off on a wild-goose chase that lasted for days.

All November and December were spent in pursuit of similar geese. How long this would have gone on I have no way of knowing, but Christmas came and with it a gift of grace. It was not even intended as a gift for me. My sister Helen gave our son John a copy of William Warner's *Beautiful Swimmers: Watermen, Crabs, and the Chesapeake Bay*. I began reading it during those low after-Christmas days, and by the time the new year dawned I had a place to set my story, the Chesapeake Bay, less than an hour from my front door.

In the Bay there are many islands, most of which are not inhabited. Two of these islands, Smith and Tangier, are separated by miles of water from the rest of America. Even now, with television, telephones, and, in the case of Tangier, an airstrip, they seem a world apart. My story was going to be chiefly about a young adolescent who felt terribly isolated. Of course, all fourteen-year-olds who are not social clones feel isolated, but what better way to show this isolation than an island? Rass (the name for my island squirted up from my subconscious and has yet to reveal its source or meaning), Rass would be none of the actual islands, but something like all of them.

Now I began going to the library as well as to the Bay to find out everything I could about the Chesapeake. At the same time I began setting down on scraps of paper and three-by-five cards ideas as they would occur, things that might happen in the story.

What about a grandmother or other live-in relative who spouts pietisms? She may be one who brings up "Jacob have I loved . . ." theme.

Old man gets off ferry. He left thirty years before and has come back. Takes shack at farthest end of island to live as recluse.

Make the kid sentimental—moons over tombstone—tries to convert friend who is boy to sentimentality.

These are bound with the same sturdy rubber band that holds notes taken from reading and observation.

pain of being stung in the eye by jellyfish

how peelers are separated
    2 wks. to go—snots, greens, white sign crabs
    1 wk—pink sign
    hrs to go before busting—rank, red sign

reactions to thunderstorms
    chopped down mast
    climbing up it swinging hatchet at the almighty—daring
     God to meet him halfway—

cats around garbage dump scavenging. Big cats.

wintering birds on Smith
"Oh, my blessed, what a noise."

There is another large pack of four-by-six cards, but I think all those notes were collected much later. I think so, not that I ever seem capable of dating, but the cards are ones I remember buying at Gray's Pharmacy in Norfolk. So between the first batch of cards and the second, there came the January 1978 announcement of a Newbery Medal, the acceptance, the knowledge that after thirteen years in Takoma Park we would be moving, the discovery of my mother's terminal cancer, the choice of *Gilly* as the Newbery Honor Book, the move to Norfolk, Mother's death, and a National Book Award. That is not everything that happened in our lives between the fall of 1977 and the spring of 1979, but it may give you some idea why poor *Jacob* was languishing.

But even as I present to you these impeccable excuses, I know in my heart that the reason I nearly despaired of finishing this book was

more the internal storms it stirred up than those that came from without. I was trying to write a story that made my stomach churn every
time I sat down at the typewriter. "Love is strong as death," says the
writer of the Song of Songs, "jealousy is cruel as the grave." I did not
want ever again to walk the dark path into that cruelty.

Yet even while I was having trouble going back into my young
self, I was being drawn more and more into the world of the book. I
knew that in Rass I was trying to create a facsimile of the Bay islands,
but my feeling as I worked was not so much that of a creator as that of
an explorer. Here was a hidden world that it was my task to discover.
If I failed, this world would remain forever unknown.

I do not mean by this that I thought I had a monopoly on the
Chesapeake Bay. Not long after I had begun work on my book, James
Michener's massive *Chesapeake* was published. I read it with dread,
fearing that he might have preempted me, might have discovered my
world. But he hadn't. He couldn't have. The Chesapeake world I was
exploring was mine alone. No other living soul had access to it unless
I could somehow reveal it in *Jacob*. I think I have finally learned that
no one can steal your novel from you. No matter how closely his material may come to yours, he can only write his story, and you, yours—
the intricate design of an individual life upon some portion of the
outside world. I knew, for better or worse, that if I did not write *Jacob*,
it would never be written.

I say my world, my story, but it hardly ever felt like mine. For one
thing, it refused to obey my rules. I have always sworn that I would
never write a book in the first person. It is too limiting, too egotisti-
cal. And yet, the book refused any voice but Louise's. "Oh, well," I
said to myself, "I'd better get it down any way I can in the first draft.
In the next draft I can write it properly."

At some point I wrote a very peculiar note to myself. Not content
with writing a book in the first person, I apparently was thinking of

writing it as three first-person stories—one for Louise, one for Caro-line, and one for Call. "Perhaps," I added, "end with a fourth section which goes back to Sara Louise and ties the story together."

Heavens above. I think the only reason this book ever got written is that I would regularly lose all my notes. I must remember that next time. Take all the notes you wish, but do not fail to lose them once you start.

By now it was the fall of 1979. I was piling page upon page, revi-sion upon revision, until finally my husband made a strong suggestion that it was time to get the manuscript out of the house and to Virginia Buckley. I think he felt that if drastic steps were not taken soon, he would be living with *Jacob* in an eternal triangle. He was right. I had become so entangled in the story that I did not know if it was worth further effort, if it would ever be a publishable book. So I sent it.

Virginia got it on Friday and called me on Sunday. "I love it," she said. I knew that she did not mean it was perfect. I knew there were months of intensive rewriting ahead, but you cannot imagine the joy with which I heard those words. I know very well that I am capable of writing a bad book, but I have never, in my right mind, believed that Virginia would publish one. She loved *Jacob,* and, as I began the painstaking revisions, I came to love it, too—until, though I never managed to bring it to perfection, I felt that it was the best that I could do. My child had grown up and must, at long last, be let go.

An earnest young reporter asked me: "What are you trying to do when you write for children?" "I'm trying to write as well as I possibly can," I answered. He thought I hadn't understood his question. "No, no," he said. "What I mean is, what is your philosophy of writing for children? Isn't there some moral you want to get across to them? Aren't there some values you wish to instill in your young readers?" "I'm trying," I said, "to write for my readers the best story, the truest story of which I am capable." He gave up on me and changed the subject, frustrated and annoyed. He seemed to share the view of many intelligent, well-educated, well-meaning people that, while adult literature may aim to be art, the object of children's books is to whip the little rascals into shape.

But you and I know better. We know that those of us who write for children are called, not to do something to a child, but to be someone for a child. "Art," in Frances Clarke Sayers's wonderfully passionate definition, is "a controlled fury of desire to share one's private revelation of life." And she the librarian summons us who are writers to the service of art—to give the best that is in us to "the audience that lives by what it feeds upon."

Among my notes I found this one written while I was stalled one day during August of 1979. I can date it because it is written on Gene Namovicz's electric typewriter and is full of stray *l*'s and *k*'s.

There is another sibling rivalry in the story of Jacob. It is, of course, the story of Leah and Rachel. "Jacob have I loved—" Poor Leah, the homely elder sister. Married in trickery to the man passionately in love with her younger sister. She goes to his bed and must lie there and bear his seeing who she is. Watch his face as the truth of his father-in-law's treachery dawns. His disappointment. How does he react? What does he say? Even if, and it is hard to believe he might have been, even if in his own disappointment he remembers her pain and tries to be tactful and kind, that very kindness would be next to unbearable, if Leah loves him at all. Esau's grief is nothing compared to Leah's. She must watch her husband go joyfully to her sister and joylessly come to her. But God does give her many sons. That would be a comfort if we did not know that Rachel, who only has two sons, is the mother of Joseph—that younger brother of all younger brothers. This puts a new dimension into the phrase, "Jacob have I loved . . ." It is a woman speaking now, a wronged and grieving woman, not God. The loving is not here a matter of divine election but of the eternal weight of women who have neither the beauty of Rachel nor the cleverness of Rebekkah. What shall we do for the Leahs?

The only thing I can do for the Leahs, the Esaus, and the Louises is to give them now, while they are young, the best, the truest story of which I am capable. I have learned, for all my failings and limitations, that when I am willing to give myself away in a book, readers will respond by giving themselves away as well, and the book that I labored over so long becomes in our mutual giving something far richer and more powerful than I could have ever imagined. I thank you, and I thank God that I have been allowed to take part in this miracle once again.

And now, if you will excuse me, I have this book I want to write.

FROM **THE WRITER** ~
DECEMBER 1980

Creativity Limited
Novels for Young People Today

I had been writing fiction for years with hardly anyone noticing when, suddenly, a book of mine won a National Book Award and overnight I seemed to have opinions worth consulting. "Dear Mrs. Paterson," one correspondent asked, "do you think civilization as we know it will survive the twentieth century?" "Dear Mr. So-and-so," I replied, "I don't know at four o'clock what I'll be having for supper at six, a matter which is almost entirely under my control."

Most questions were less cosmic and more relevant, like the one asked me by an editor friend at the end of a business call. "Oh, by the way," she said, "while I've got you on the phone, what is your theory of creativity?" She wanted a quotation for an article she was writing. What she got was several minutes of stammering at the prime day-time rate.

In order not to be caught like that again, I began to read articles and books about creativity. Incidentally, the word *creativity* doesn't even appear in my *Oxford English Dictionary*, 1971 edition. Aside from the fact that the word didn't exist until quite recently, the chief thing I learned about creativity is that students of human behavior seem to know very little about what it is. Psychiatrists writing about it were either reduced to poetry or else they sought to explain it as some kind of neurosis. The one point that seemed to make sense to me out of my research was a point Rollo May makes in *The Courage to Create*. That is—there is no such thing as unlimited creativity. It is within limits, often very narrow limits, that a creative work comes into being.

I am as concerned about freedom as the next American, but freedom is quite different from the lack of limitations. Let me illustrate. Very often people ask me, "How do you find time to write?" The first time I remember being asked this question it was by a woman who worked a forty-hour week outside her home. I was puzzled. "How do *you* find time to work?" I asked, feeling her life was far more complex than mine. But she didn't see it as the same thing at all. Instead she began to list what she saw as my limitations. You have four lively children. Your husband is a church pastor. You have three PTAs, choir, church activities, et cetera, et cetera. At last I realized that the questioner was assuming that my husband's work and my children's activities were limitations that enslaved me, whereas I felt that they were the very boundaries that gave form to my life.

You'll remember that Boris Pasternak had a great dread of being deported. He felt that, if he were forced out of Russia, he would no longer be able to write. Russia was for him a necessary limitation. "Don't you wish," I am asked, "don't you wish you could just sail away alone to a Caribbean isle and write all day?" Never. "What? No, never?" Well, hardly ever. The more perceptive question came from a critic who knows my work almost better than I do. "Your writing is so bound up with your children," she said. "What are you going to do when they all grow up?" For a moment I had a hint of the panic Pasternak must have felt when threatened with deportation. But only for a moment. I've lived long enough to know that in this world there is rarely a shortage on limitations. There'll be plenty more when I need them.

Now life is often a parable for art. Many of the same people who worry that I don't have time to write are bothered by my choice of form. "Don't you feel constricted writing for children?" they'll ask. William, don't you find fourteen tightly rhymed lines an absolute prison? Ah, Pablo, if you could just yank that picture off that lousy scrap of canvas! You get the point. Form is not a bar to free expression, but the boundaries within which writers and artists freely choose to work.

"You choose an art form," says C. S. Lewis, in one of his most quoted sentences, "because it is the best form for something you have to say." It seems to me, therefore, more than a little silly to complain that your freedom has been restricted by the form you chose.

The library promotion staff at Crowell Junior Books say that I write novels for ages ten and up. When I examine books intended for this audience, my first observation is how few special limitations there seem to be.

There is, for example, no apparent limitation on vocabulary or sentence structure. A writer for *The Washingtonian Magazine* did a reading-level test on my book *The Master Puppeteer*. He reported to his readers that it fell comfortably between the seventh- and eighth-grade levels, which is just where the publisher claims it belongs. But the writer went on to say that he had applied the same test to Erica Jong's *Fear of Flying*. *Flying*, he said, had come out at the sixth-grade level. These are matters beyond my knowledge, but I do know that I spend an inordinate amount of time with my nose in dictionaries trying to develop a vocabulary worthy of my readers.

Okay, okay, you can use big words if you want to. You'll have to admit, the protester cries from the back row, that your subject matter is restricted. I can only speak from experience. My editor has never tried to restrict me. Let me offer a brief and brutal survey of my already published novels for children and young adults. In the first, the hero is a bastard, and the chief female character ends up in a brothel. In the second, the heroine has an illicit love affair, her mother dies in a plague, and most of her companions commit suicide. In the third, which is full of riots in the streets, the hero's best friend is permanently maimed. In the fourth, a central child character dies in an accident. In the fifth, turning away from the mayhem in the first four, I wrote what I refer to as my "funny book." In it the heroine merely fights, lies, steals, cusses, bullies an emotionally disturbed child, and acts out her racial bigotry in a particularly vicious manner.

You may not be surprised to know that I do from time to time receive letters of protest from teachers and librarians. You may be amazed to know that the only element in any of my books that any of these adults has complained to me about is the occasional profanity. Characters in young people's novels should be permitted to do anything, it would seem, except cuss. I can only perceive this as a testimony to the power of words.

But back to subject matter. When I examine a bald recitation of the events depicted in my books, I come away slightly shocked. What could I have been thinking of? Yet, somehow, when a story is coming to life, I'm not judging it as appropriate or inappropriate, I'm living through it. In *The Sign of the Chrysanthemum* Akiko ended up in a brothel not because I wanted to scandalize my readers, not because I'm advocating legal prostitution, but because in twelfth-century Japan, a beautiful thirteen-year-old-girl with no protector would have ended up in a brothel. And the penniless boy who loved her would indeed have been powerless to save her. I didn't want to make Akiko a prostitute, but there was no way out. It did occur to me afterward that I hadn't seen a lot of books for young readers along this line, but twelve years ago, when I was writing this story, I was being torn apart that such a thing did and does happen to children in this world. If we compare subject matter as my friend at *The Washingtonian Magazine* compared reading levels, I note that the adult best-seller at the time my book was being readied for market—the adult best-seller that was breaking every sales record since *Gone with the Wind*—was the story of an overachieving seagull.

If the limitations inherent to my form are not in reading level or subject matter, where are they? I am going to tell you where the boundaries are for me, realizing that you will be able to cite a gate for every fence.

First, a book for young readers has to tell a story. This may seem self-evident, but the truth is some people ignore it because plotting is very hard work. When I'm hearing myself introduced as a "great natural storyteller," it is all I can do to keep from leaping to my feet to object. Great natural storytellers don't spend countless days hewing a story line out of rock with a straight pin, now do they? Yet it's got to be done. I received an anguished letter from a yet unpublished writer, in which she asked, "Isn't there any place for the plotless teenage novel?" I could only think of one. As burdensome as the limitation of plot may seem to be, it is not one I'm willing to circumvent. I simply don't like novels that aren't going anywhere, and I can't imagine many readers who do.

A second limitation on the novel for the young is length. Now there are plenty of exceptions to this one. *Watership Down* and *The Lord of the Rings* were written by the authors as stories for their own children. But these days a novel for the young usually runs under two hundred pages. Unlike plotting, this perfectly suits my natural tendencies. I am one of those people who write short. A great deal of my revision time is spent fleshing out and very little in cutting. When I first began to think seriously about writing, I assumed that this quality of mine would lead me into the world of the short story. So I wrote short story upon short story, selling practically nothing. I think the truth of the matter is that I am not basically a short-story writer. I am a novelist who writes short novels.

This is closely related to what I see as a third limitation. Intricacy, density, design—I'm not sure what to call it, but when I read Mary Lee Settle's *Blood Tie*, Anne Tyler's *Celestial Navigation*, or John Fowles's *Daniel Martin*, I hear a symphony orchestra. When I read my own *Bridge to Terabithia*, I hear a flute solo, unaccompanied. Occasionally, to be sure, you get a decent adult novel along the flute-solo line, but most truly fine adult novels are extremely complex works of art. Some eleven-year-olds are reading Dickens and Austen, but most are not. And I, even when I'm dealing with an almost impossibly complicated situation like the Gempei War in twelfth-century Japan, tend to hear through all the storm and clamor a rather simple melody.

A writer is also limited, you see, by who she is. As Flannery O'Connor wrote to a young writer friend: "There is only one answer . . . and that is that one writes what one can. Vocation implies limitation but few people realize it who don't actually practice an art."[1] So when people ask me why I write what I do, I take comfort from one of my heroines. Flannery O'Connor wrote what she could; I write what I can.

A fourth limitation has to do with characters. They may be any age, and, indeed, any species, but they must be characters a reader can care about. This is another of those limitations I can rejoice in. When I am reading a novel and discover that the author has contempt for the people he has created, I am furious. If he despises these who are flesh of his flesh, what right does he have to inflict them on me? I don't want to waste my energy reading, and certainly not my energy writing about people I hate. Even if I start a book with a satisfying villain, I seem doomed to care for that person before the end.

There is certainly room in the world of books for entertainment, but for the serious writer of fiction for the young there is a fifth limitation, that of theme, for she will want to write not only a story that is going somewhere but a story about something that matters deeply. I would like to share with you the best explanation of the importance of theme in books for young people that I have ever heard. It comes from Jill Paton Walsh's 1978 Whittall Lecture at the Library of Congress.

"When I was young," she says, "my grandfather tried to teach me to play chess, which he deeply loved and wanted to share with me. And he got me horribly confused. Like most good players, he was not really interested in opening games. No sooner did I get far enough to advance a king's pawn timidly two paces than he was telling me about six thousand possibilities in the middle game opened up by such a beginning, and six thousand others by the same act excluded; and the more he spoke the less I understood him.

"How often," she continues, "I recollect that situation when I read adult novels. They are treatises on the complexities of the middle game, written by and for players of some skill. My grandfather was not wrong to point out to me the consequences of an opening game, which does indeed condition the middle game; but he had forgotten to tell me about checkmate, and you cannot play at all unless you know how the game is won and lost, and what will count as an ending. That is why it is necessary in children's books to mirror death, to show a projected end, to teach that nothing is forever, so that the child may know the nature of the game he is playing and may take a direction, make purposeful moves. It is the plain truth that human life is passing, and that we must find what we will value in the world, and how we will live in the light of that."[2]

That is why, you see, I do find the strong themes of my books appropriate for young readers. Like Jill Paton Walsh, I want them to see the nature of the game we are all engaged in so that they may make purposeful moves.

And in the shadow of this rather grand limitation, I find a more personal one. I will not take a young reader through a story and in the end abandon him. That is, I will not write a book that closes in despair. I cannot, will not, withhold from my young readers the harsh realities of human hunger and suffering and loss, but neither will I neglect to plant that stubborn seed of hope that has enabled our race to outlast wars and famines and the destruction of death.

If you think that this is the limitation that will keep me forever a writer for the young, perhaps it is. I don't mind. I do what I can and do it joyfully.

Words

When I told a friend of mine that I was going to tackle the subject of
"words," she asked me quite naturally what I was going to say about
them. "Well," I said, "I think I have something valid to say, I just
haven't figured out what it is, yet." Which, of course, is one of the
problems with words—there they all are—humanity's greatest natural
resource, but most of us have trouble figuring out how to put them
together in a valuable way.

So we blame it on the words. Words are cheap, we say. One picture is worth a thousand words. Silence is golden.

But words aren't cheap. They are very precious. They are like water, which gives life and growth and refreshment, but because it has
always been abundant, we treat it cheaply. We waste it and pollute it
and doctor it. Then, when we take a drink from a city faucet, we
wrinkle our nose and say: "This is terrible water." And we blame the
water because we have misused it.

Words, words, words [cries Eliza Doolittle]
I'm so sick of words.
I get words all day through
First from him, now from you.
Is that all you blighters can do?

Now there is probably not one of us who has not had the impulse in the middle of an interminable committee meeting to leap to his feet like Julie Andrews and sing out this protest, but as one of the blighters with a vested interest in the commodity, I feel the need from time to time to justify myself, especially to myself. I read the newspaper. I watch the eleven-o'clock news. I know as well as anyone else that the International Year of the Child came to an end with countless children starving to death in Cambodia. Children in Northern Ireland are still playing war—and not just pretend. My daily newspaper carries accounts of battered, even maimed, children in my own city. And this fall a six-year-old and a nine-year-old made a serious attempt to hold up a bank. The clerks thought it was cute.

And what am I doing while the world is falling apart? I am sitting in my little study in front of my typewriter trying to find words and put them together. Sometimes I see it as an evasion of responsibility, sometimes as escape, and always as selfishness, since I particularly love what I'm doing. I'm uncomfortably reminded of the story of the old Quaker who, after his first cup of coffee, said: "Anything that tastes this good has got to be a sin."

But granted all this, still I believe that words, too, are necessities—and to give the children of the world the words they need is, in a real sense, to give them life and growth and refreshment.

If sometimes today, I feel myself drowning in verbiage, I can remember clearly how it feels not to have any words. In those months after I went to Japan in 1957, I would often find myself being taken somewhere by Japanese friends, not knowing where I was going or whom I was going to see. When I got to wherever I had been taken, I would find myself surrounded by people who were talking and laughing away, but because I did not know their words, I was totally shut out. As I began to learn a few words, people would try with infinite, exaggerated patience to talk with me. And because my speech was so halting and miserable, they would try to help me, try to put words into my mouth, try to guess what on earth it was I was trying to convey. When I was finally able to get out a sentence near enough to Japanese so that my listeners could grasp what I was driving at, they felt sure I'd appreciate knowing how I *should* have expressed that particular thought, and they would gently, firmly, and ever so politely, take my pitiful little sentence apart and correct it for me.

I'm sorry to report that I was not grateful. I wanted to yell, cry, throw a tantrum. *I am not a fool!* I wanted to scream. If only you could know me in *English*, you would see at once what a clever, delightful person I am. But, of course, I didn't say it. I couldn't say it. I didn't have the minimum daily requirement in either vocabulary or syntax. The first time I saw the play *The Miracle Worker*, I knew what had been happening to me in those days. It was the rage of those starving for words.

In 1961, after four years in Japan, I boarded a jet in Tokyo and landed about twenty hours later in Baltimore. I was met by my parents and one of my sisters and taken home to Virginia. Every night for many weeks I would get out of the soft bed, which was killing my back, and lie sleepless on the floor. I was utterly miserable. "These people," I would say to myself, meaning my own family, "these people don't even know me." The reason I thought my family didn't know me was that they didn't know me in Japanese.

You see, in those four years I had become a different person. I had not only learned new ways to express myself, I had new thoughts to

express. I had come by painful experience to a conclusion that lin-
guists now advance: Language is not simply the instrument by which
we communicate thought. The language we speak will shape the
thoughts and feelings themselves.

Because I remembered so well what it was like not to have words,
it was easy for me to imagine, when I at last became a mother, what
my children were going through when they were first learning to
speak. In my great and just possibly superfluous concern I determined
to help them all I could. I spoke to them from the first in complete
English sentences, just as though they could take in every word I was
saying. I read to them poems and wonderful books, far before an edu-
cator, indeed before any sensible person, would think they could be
ready to understand the words. But in the midst of this richness, when
one of them would stand before me, the little cords straining in his
neck, as he sought to express the still inexpressible, I would wait with
totally uncharacteristic patience, reasoning that if they were to learn
to speak freely and comfortably to me, I must be willing to listen. Nor
would I correct their mistakes. It is rude, I thought, to correct the
grammar of someone who is trying his best to tell you something, no
matter how tall the person might happen to be. And if it was rude for
me, it was certain to be frustrating and discouraging to the speaker.
They would learn quite ꜱoon enough, I reasoned, the difference between the singular and plural form of the verb. All they had to do was
listen. If not to me, to their father.

Well, the other day, the turkeys flew home to roost. One of them
came home from school totally scandalized by a bit of information
from his English teacher. "Do you know what she said?" he asked.
And while I waited for the revelation of his teacher's radical political
or moral philosophy, he continued in the same shocked tone: "She
said I couldn't say, 'Who are you waiting for?' "

"She did?" I asked nervously.

"She said"—he could hardly believe it still—"she said I had to say, 'For whoooooom are you waiting?' "

"I'm afraid she's right."

"Whaaaaat? You think I'm going around saying 'For whoooom are you waiting?' Everybody would think I'd gone nuts."

The grammar lesson was obviously overdue. "No," I agreed. "If you went around saying 'For whooooooom are you waiting?' or even if I had a kid in a book who said, 'For whom are you waiting?' everyone would think we had taken leave of our senses, but, actually, your teacher is right. The correct, formal English is: 'For whom are you waiting?' "

He gave me a look of utter disgust and muttered. "For whoom" several times under his breath, making it sound for all the world like an obscenity. Finally he said, "Why do we have to have proper grammar anyway? Why can't we just go around grunting like the cavemen?"

Now for all my failures as a teacher of English, I want to assure you that my son is not going to give up language and return to grunting. This is the child of ours so in need of language that, perceiving great lacks in English, he invents language and vocabulary to fill the gaps. There is, he perceived, no adequate mild expletive in English. The Japanese have a very nice one—*Ara!*—but he didn't know Japanese. So he invented *bip*. When, for example, you are reading the newspaper and pouring yourself a glass of milk at the same time, and your mother suggests that you may have missed the glass, you can stop, look at the table, and say *bip*. A few years ago he invented *labysan,* which is harder to decode than pig Latin and has the added attraction that no one over the age of ten (except him) can possibly pronounce it.

In other words, he is a genuine human being with the very human drive for language. We humans have had from time unknown the compulsion to name things and thus to be able to deal with them. The name we give to something shapes our attitude toward it. And in ancient thought the name itself has power, so that to know someone's name is to have a certain power over him. And in some societies, as you know, there was a public name and a real or secret name, which would not be revealed to others.

Now, the animals communicate with one another. They give signals of danger or mating calls. But they do not, as far as we know, name things. Jacob Bronowski says that an animal cry is a sentence, whereas in human language we have somehow miraculously broken down sentences into words—words that name objects and actions, which means then we can take these same words and rearrange them, reconstitute them into other sentences with quite different meanings. Because we name, we name ourselves, and we can think of ourselves as separate creatures, apart from nature. We can, therefore, using our vision and our power to create language, develop science and art.

But in this process of naming, of being able to take apart nature, to study it, to communicate about it, in the very process that becomes our glory lies an insoluble paradox. And that is this: Nature is intricately and infinitely connected. The minute I name something and begin to regard it as a separate entity, I break this unbreakable unity. So that which makes it possible for us to seek truths about the universe and about ourselves has within itself the guarantee that we will never be able to find the Truth. Our knowledge must be forever fragmented, because that is the nature of systematic knowledge.

"The world," and I am quoting now, "the world is totally connected. Whatever explanation we invent at any moment is a partial connection and its richness derives from the richness of such connections as we are able to make. . . . The act of imagination is the opening of the system so that it shows new connections."[1]

But what has all this esoteric talk about language and imagina-

tion to do with me—much less with you and why we are all together today?

I find the connection in a very disturbing essay by Joan Didion,
entitled "Slouching Towards Bethlehem." Didion wrote this essay at a
time in 1967 when, in her own words, she felt forced to deal "directly
and flatly with the evidence of atomization, the proof that things fall
apart. I went," she says further, "to San Francisco because I had not
been able to work in some months, had been paralyzed by the conviction that writing was an irrelevant act, that the world as I had understood it no longer existed. If I was to work again at all, it would be
necessary for me to come to terms with disorder."

So Didion went to Haight-Ashbury to live for a while among the
flower children. In her essay she piles up story after story of the children she meets—the flower children so glorified by the media but
whom she regards in a much more somber light.

"We were seeing," Didion concludes, "the desperate attempt of a
handful of pathetically unequipped children to create a community in
a social vacuum. . . . These were the children who grew up cut loose
from the web of cousins and great-aunts and family doctors and life-
long neighbors who had traditionally suggested and enforced the society's values. They are children who have moved around a lot. . . .
They are less in rebellion against society than ignorant of it, able only
to feed back certain of its most publicized self-doubts, *Vietnam, Saran
Wrap, diet pills, the Bomb.*

"They feed back exactly what is given them. Because they do not
believe in words . . . and a thought that needs words is just one more
of those ego trips—their only proficient vocabulary is in the society's
platitudes. As it happens"—and here at last Didion makes her own
connection as well as the one I am trying to make today—"I am still
committed to the idea that the ability to think for one's self depends
upon one's mastery of the language, and I am not optimistic about

children who will settle for saying, to indicate that their mother and father do not live together, that they come from 'a broken home.' They are sixteen, fifteen, fourteen years old, younger all the time, an army of children waiting to be given the words."[2]

Now this essay was written in 1967. No one is worried about the flower children of Haight-Ashbury anymore. They have long since, in a word of our times, "self-destructed."

But there are still children in 1979 waiting to be given the words. I was talking recently to a woman who has the unenviable job of teaching young teenagers to read. These children are characteristically (in the non-word of one expert) "un-verbal." That is, their only proficient vocabulary is in obscenities and other current clichés. And if they are not at home with the spoken language, they are positively at war with the written word. The teacher described for me the anguish of these young people as they try to decode a single sentence. "We have wonderful books," she went on to say. "All designed to help them, to entice them to read. But they won't even open them."

Why won't they open them?

"Because they are books. And these children hate books."

I was in no position to make suggestions. I have always loved books passionately. I, who would never have made the gifted-and-talented program, still taught myself to read, simply because I loved books so much. I have noticed that the fact that I have no right to make a suggestion doesn't necessarily keep me from making one. But in this case, I was a little hesitant. The suggestion I wanted to make was such an obvious one. "Do you read aloud to them?" I asked.

She shook her head sadly. "Sometimes I do. A little. A short section or a paragraph, trying to interest them in something, but the administration frowns on it. They think I'd be simply entertaining these kids when they ought to be working."

I wanted to cry. We both wanted to cry. How can these children ever learn to read—why should they ever *want* to learn to read—if books are enemies to be fought rather than friends who will enrich and broaden and give joy to their lives?

Then I told her about my friend Eddie. And at the risk of bragging, I'm going to tell you about Eddie because he seems to sum up what I'm trying to say and do.

Last spring I had been asked to speak in a junior high school, and I gave those in charge my usual little speech about what I would do and what I expected them to do. For example: I do not sing, dance, or do card tricks; therefore, I will not attempt to entertain an auditorium full of bored children. I will speak to a classroom-size group of students who have read something that I have written and who want to talk with me about it. I don't care a bit if they liked what they read or not, simply that it aroused sufficient interest to make them want to discuss it.

When I was actually in the car on the way to the school, one of the ladies in charge of my appearance began to explain to me that they uh hadn't uh exactly been able to follow out my wishes and uh they hoped I wouldn't be too upset. Their original plan had been for me to speak to the gifted-and-talented program, which was made up of about fifty seventh-, eighth-, and ninth-graders. (I gasped.) But they'd gotten fouled up. It seems that the special reading teacher had read *The Great Gilly Hopkins* out loud to her class, and when she heard that I was going to be at the school, had simply demanded that her class be allowed to horn in on the gifted-and-talented's special event. So there I was with about seventy junior high students to enthrall. Much to my surprise, not to say relief, the session went all right. I wasn't sure who was from the gifted program and who was from the special reading class, the questions were more or less of the ordinary variety. But I did notice a boy in a red sweatshirt sitting several feet away from everyone else in the room who was giving me more than ordinary attention. After the program was over, he came up and hung around until the other students had left, and then he be-

gan to ask me about Gilly. Who was she? Where was she? Then he
wanted to know all the other stories—the things that had happened
that somehow hadn't gotten into the book. It was one of those times
when you know the real question is not being voiced, but I didn't understand what it was. Finally, a teacher persuaded the boy that he
must return to class, and besides, she explained, I had to catch a plane
shortly. When he had gone, the librarian told me that Eddie was a
member of the special reading class who had heard *Gilly* read. Like
Gilly, he was battling his way through a world of trouble. He had
never shown any particular positive interest in books or school until
his teacher had read *Gilly* to the class. And suddenly he had a passion.
He was wild about a book—one of those reluctant readers, or even
nonreaders, who had to this point seen words, not to mention books,
as the deadliest of enemies.

I thought about Eddie for days. Here was a real live Gilly who
not only approved of but actually liked my fictional one. It was
better than having a Japanese like *The Master Puppeteer*. Well, I decided, I'll just send him a copy. Even if he won't ever read it. At least
he will own a book he likes. And that will be one for our side, now
won't it?

Just before *Gilly* won the National Book Award, I got a letter from
Eddie, and as some of you may remember, I read his letter with, I hasten to assure you, his permission, as part of my acceptance speech. But
it feels so good to hear it that I'm going to repeat it.

Dear Mrs. Paterson,

Thank you for the book "The Great Gilly Hopkins." I love
the book. I am on page 16.

> Your friend
> Always
> Eddie Young

And Eddie didn't stop on page 16. He's read the book four times. He's also read *Bridge to Terabithia*, and in his last letter he said he was starting on *The Master Puppeteer*. I rushed off a "Now don't be discouraged by all those long Japanese names" letter to him. I don't know as I write this if he finished it, or even if he's read any other books since he learned that books are not fearsome enemies. I hope he has. I believe he will.

But somebody, you see, had to make the connection for him. Someone had to first give him the words. His teacher did it by reading to him what he would not have, perhaps at the time could not have, read for himself. Then she fought against the administration and the rules of a fussy writer to get Eddie in to hear me speak. She believed that Eddie had a right to the words—that he had a need for the words, even if no one else, not even Eddie, believed that he did.

I love to tell this story because it was my words that Eddie's teacher used. More often it will not be my book but someone else's that works this magic for a child. Indeed, when I told the story of Eddie to my friend, the reading teacher, her face brightened and she told me the story of her own son, who shunned books, even though his mother was a teacher of reading and his father a librarian. Suddenly at nine, not to be outdone by a younger sister, he had picked up a children's classic version of Robin Hood, determined to get through one book cover to cover to prove to his seven-year-old sister that he wasn't as dumb as she thought he was. He read all day and into the night and came to his mother the next morning with tears streaming down his cheeks. It was the best book, he declared, that he had *ever* read. It didn't seem to occur to him that it was the *only* book he had ever read. Of course, it was just the first. But it was there when he needed it.

In all the furor about the right to read and basic education, there is often, it seems to me, something missing. Why are we so determined to teach our children to read? So that they can read road signs?

Of course. Make out a job application? Of course. Figure out the destination of the bus so that they can get to work? Yes, of course. But don't we want far more for them than the ability to decode? Don't we want for them the life and growth and refreshment that only the full richness of our language can give? And when I say this I am saying with Joan Didion that we fail our children if all we give them are the platitudes, the clichés, the slogans of our society, which we throw out whole to keep from having to think or feel deeply.

We cannot give them what we do not have. We cannot share what we do not care for deeply ourselves. If we prescribe books as medicine, our children have a perfect right to refuse the nasty-tasting spoon.

I was always told that I should read the *Odyssey*. It popped up in small doses in English and Latin textbooks as I was growing up. But somehow I never got around to the whole thing until I was forty-six years old. My daughter Mary and I were going on a trip to Greece, and I gave myself the assignment to read the *Odyssey* all the way through from beginning to end. Do you know why the *Odyssey* has lasted for nearly three thousand years? Because it is a simply marvelous story. Why did people keep telling me that I *ought* to read it so I could be an educated person? Was it because they had never read it themselves but had always meant to? I can't imagine anyone who had ever read it, certainly not in Rouse's translation, anyone who had ever really read it, telling someone else to read it because it was good for him. Read it because it's one of the best stories you'll ever read. Read it because it's one of the best stories I ever read.

And when you close Homer, there are the books of Jane Austen and Joseph Conrad, and great fat volumes of Tolstoy. There is the Bible, perhaps the most overprescribed and least taken of any. There is Flannery O'Connor and Anne Tyler. There is William Shakespeare and Jacob Bronowski. There is *The Yearling* and *A Tale of Two Cities*.

There is *The Secret Garden* and *The Wind in the Willows*. There is *Ramona the Brave* and *Where the Wild Things Are*. I have only begun to name what I especially love. There are countless others—really good books. Good or even great because they make the right connections. They pull together for us a world that is falling apart. They are the words that integrate us, stretch us, judge us, comfort and heal us. They are the words that mirror the Word of creation, bringing order out of chaos.

I believe we must try, always conscious of our own fragmentary knowledge and nature, to give our children these words. I know as you do that words can be used for evil as well as good. But we must take that risk. We must try as best we are able to give our children words that will shape their minds so they can make those miraculous leaps of imagination that no sinless computer will ever be able to rival—those connections in science, in art, in the living of this life that will reveal the little truths. For it is these little truths that point to the awesome, unknowable unity, the Truth, which holds us together and makes us members one of another.

National Book Award Acceptance Speech

for <u>The Great Gilly Hopkins</u>

I would like to thank Eleanor Cameron, Robert Coles, and Priscilla Moxom, and the Association of American Publishers, for giving *Gilly* this honor. Thanks also to my friends at Thomas Y. Crowell, especially my editor, Virginia Buckley, who must know that without her I would not be standing here today. And a very special thank you to my children, Lin, John, David, and Mary, who laughed when they read *Gilly*, and to my husband, John, who cried.

I wrote this book because, by chance rather than by design, I was for two months a foster mother. Now, as a mother, I am not a finalist for any prizes, but on the whole I'm serviceable. I was not serviceable as a foster mother, and this is why: I knew from the beginning that the children were going to be with us only a short time, so when a problem arose as problems will, I'd say to myself, "I can't really deal with that. They'll be here only a few weeks." Suddenly and too late, I heard what I had been saying. I was regarding two human beings as Kleenex, disposable. And it forced me to think, what must it be like for those thousands upon thousands of children in our midst who find themselves rated disposable? So I wrote a book, a confession of sin, in which one of those embittered children meets the world's greatest foster mother. Virginia Buckley said that my characters were mythic; a critic being less kind used the word *unbelievable*. I knew when I wrote the book that Gilly and Trotter were larger than life. I did it deliberately, to get attention, like that unknown lover who wrote across the underpass near our house in letters ten feet high, I LOVE YOU, GRACE KOWASKI.

But the wonderful thing about being a writer is that it gives you readers, readers who bring their own stories to the story you have written, people who have the power to take your mythic, unbelievable, ten-foot-high characters and fit them to the shape of their own lives. I met one of these people the other day.

A teacher had read aloud *The Great Gilly Hopkins* to her class, and Eddie, another foster child, hearing in the story of Gilly his own story, did something that apparently flabbergasted everyone who knew him. He fell in love with a book. Can you imagine how that made me feel? Here was a twelve-year-old who knew far better than I what my story was about, and he did me the honor of claiming it for himself. It seemed to me that anyone who liked a book as much as Eddie did should have a copy of his own, so I sent him one. On Saturday I got this letter:

Dear Mrs. Paterson,

Thank you for the book "The Great Gilly Hopkins." I love the book. I am on page 16.

Your friend
Always
Eddie Young

Flannery O'Connor says this about herself when she was Eddie's age: "I was a very ancient twelve. My views at that age would have done credit to a Civil War veteran. I'm much younger now than I was at twelve or anyway, less burdened. The weight of the centuries lies on children. I'm sure of it."

So I, who have grown younger and less burdened with the years, count it a singular grace when what began for me as a confession of sin seems to lift, if only for a moment, the weight of the centuries from some young shoulder. Or, in the immortal word of that ancient seven-year-old William Ernest Teague—*Pow*.

Newbery Medal Acceptance Speech
for <u>Bridge to Terabithia</u>

The day after my early-morning call telling me that *Bridge to Ter-abithia* had won the Newbery Medal, a scene from my childhood kept replaying itself in my head. A chubby-faced eight-year-old is telling her older brother and sister what she desperately hopes is a very funny story.

"Katherine," they ask sweetly when she finishes, "did you make that up all by yourself?"

"Yes." She nods eagerly.

"Sounded like it."

You cannot see my eight-year-old self, but I promise you, she is here tonight as I accept your honor for this funny little wounded story which I made up myself and which sounds like it. It is a marvelous thing to know that it has been heard and not despised. Thank you.

When I say I made it up all by myself, that is not really true. I know how very many people are a part of its making: Lisa Hill, from whose life and death the story sprang; my husband, John, who loved it first; our children, Lin, John, David, and Mary; the Womeldorf family, in which I, like Jesse Aarons, was the middle child of five; the sixth-grade class I taught, or who taught me, in rural Virginia more than twenty years ago; Virginia Buckley, my editor and my friend, along with all my fellow workers at Thomas Y. Crowell; Donna Diamond with her delicate but, at the same time, powerful illustrations. My new friends at Crowell and Harper & Row understand that I need to say a special thanks to Ann Beneduce and Sophie Silberberg, whose love and concern not only for my work but for me have meant so much to my life.

I was told that I could make a long speech, but if I mention everyone who has helped me, we'll be in Chicago until the next blizzard. So, my loving and beloved ones, I am very grateful.

The summer our son David was three years old he fell in love with bridges. I understood just how he felt, being a lover of bridges myself, and coming home from Lake George the whole family took delight in the bridges along the way. We were spending the night with our Long Island cousins; it was well after dark, and everyone was getting cranky by the time the last bridge was crossed.

"When is the next bridge, Mommy?" David asked.

"There aren't any more," I told him. "We're almost at Uncle Arthur's house now."

"Just one more bridge, Mommy, please, just one more bridge," he said, believing in his three-year-old heart that mothers can do anything, including instant bridge building.

"There aren't any more bridges, sweetheart, we're almost there."

He began to weep. "*Please*, Mommy, just one more bridge."

Nothing we said could console him. I was at my wit's end. Why couldn't he understand that I was not maliciously withholding his heart's desire—that there was no way I could conjure up a bridge and throw it in the path of our car? When would he know that I was a human being, devoid of any magic power?

It was later that night that I remembered. The next day I could give him a bridge, and not just any bridge. The next day I could give him the Verrazano Bridge. I could hardly wait.

That is the last and only time I was given credit for building the Verrazano Bridge, but it occurs to me that I have spent a good part of my life trying to construct bridges. Usually my bridges have turned out looking much more like the bridge to Terabithia, a few planks over a nearly dry gully, than like that elegant span across the Narrows. There were so many chasms I saw that needed bridging—chasms of time and culture and disparate human nature—that I began sawing and hammering at the rough wood planks for my children and for any other children who might read what I had written.

But of course I could not make a bridge for them any more than I could conjure one up that night on Long Island. I discovered gradually and not without a little pain that you don't put together a bridge for a child. You become one—you lay yourself across the chasm.

It is there in the Simon and Garfunkel song—

> *Like a bridge over troubled water*
> *I will lay me down. . . .*

The waters to be crossed are not always troubled. The land on the other side of the river may be flowing with joy, not to mention milk and honey. But still the bridge that the child trusts or delights in— and, in my case, the book that will take children from where they are to where they might be—needs to be made not from synthetic or inanimate objects, but from the stuff of life. And a writer has no life to give but her own.

My first three novels were set in feudal Japan, but I never considered them remote from my life. I had left Japan seven years before I wrote the first of them, but in writing them, I had a chance to become almost Japanese again, and if you know me, you know that Muna and

Takiko and Jiro are me as well. Yet of all the people I have ever written about, perhaps Jesse Aarons is more nearly me than any other, and in writing this book, I have thrown my body across the chasm that had most terrified me.

I have been afraid of death since I was a child—lying stiffly in the dark, my arms glued to my sides, afraid that sleep would seduce me into a land of no awakening or of wakening into judgment.

As I grew up, the fear went underground, but never really went away. Then I was forty-one years old with a husband and four children whom I loved very much, my first novel published, and a second soon to be, with a third bubbling along, friends I cared about in a town I delighted to live in, when it was discovered that I had cancer. I could not in any justice cry "Why me?"—for no one had been given more of the true wealth of this world than I. Surely as a card-carrying member of the human race some dues must be paid.

But even though the operation was pronounced successful and the prognosis hopeful, it was a hard season for me and my family, and just when it seemed that we were all on our feet again and beginning to get on with life, our David's closest friend was struck and killed by lightning.

If the spring and summer had been hard, they were nothing compared to the fall. David went through all the classical stages of grief, inventing a few the experts have yet to catalog. In one of these he decided that since Lisa had been good, God had not killed her for her sins but as a punishment for him, David. Moreover, God would continue to punish him by killing off everyone he loved. I was second on the list, right after his sister Mary.

We listened to him and cried with him, but we could not give Lisa back to him, these mere mortals that he now knew his parents to be.

In January, I went to a meeting of the Children's Book Guild of Washington at which Ann Durell of Dutton was to speak. By some chance or design, depending on your theology, I was put at the head table. In the polite amenities before lunch someone said to me: "How are the children?"—for which the answer, as we all know, is "Fine." But I botched it. Before I could stop myself I began to really tell how the children were, leading my startled tablemates deep into the story of David's grief.

No one interrupted me. But when I finally shut up, Ann Durell said very gently, "I know this sounds just like an editor, but you should write that story. Of course," she added, "the child can't die by lightning. No editor would ever believe that."

I thought I couldn't write it, that I was too close and too overwhelmed, but I began to try to write. It would be a kind of therapy for me, if not for the children. I started to write in pencil on the free pages of a used spiral notebook so that when it came to nothing I could pretend that I'd never been very serious about it.

After a few false starts, thirty-two smudged pages emerged, which made me feel that perhaps there might be a book after all. In a flush of optimism I moved to the typewriter and pounded out a few dozen more, only to find myself growing colder with every page until I was totally frozen. The time had come for my fictional child to die, and I could not let it happen.

I caught up on my correspondence, I rearranged my bookshelves, I even cleaned the kitchen—anything to keep the inevitable from happening. And then one day a friend asked, as friends will, "How is the new book coming?" and I blurted out—"I'm writing a book in which a child dies, and I can't let her die. I guess," I said, "I can't face going through Lisa's death again."

"Katherine," she said, looking me in the eye, for she is a true friend, "I don't think it's Lisa's death you can't face. I think it's yours."

I went straight home to my study and closed the door. If it was my death I could not face, then by God, I would face it. I began in a kind of fever, and in a day I had written the chapter, and within a few weeks I had completed the draft, the cold sweat pouring down my arms.

It was not a finished book, and I knew it, but I went ahead and did what no real writer would ever do: I had it typed up and mailed it off to Virginia before the sweat had a chance to evaporate.

There is no span of time quite so eternal as that between the mailing of a manuscript and the reception of an editor's reply. I knew she hated it; that's why she hadn't written or called. It was weird and raw and no good, and she was trying to think of some kind way to tell me that I was through as a writer.

Finally she called. "I laughed through the first two-thirds and cried through the last," she said. So it was all right. She understood, as she always has, what I was struggling to do. And although she did not know what was happening in my life, she did not break the bruised reed I had offered her but sought to help me weave it into a story, a real story, with a beginning, a middle, and an end.

"We need to see Leslie grow and change," she said. And suddenly, from the ancient dust of the playground at Calvin H. Wiley School, there sprang up a small army of seventh-grade Amazons led by the dreadful Pansy Something-or-Other, who had terrorized my life when I was nine and not too hard to terrify.

"You must convince us," Ann Beneduce added, "that Jesse has the mind of an artist." This seemed harder, for I certainly don't have Ann's kind of artistic vision. I started bravely, if pompously, reading the letters of Vincent van Gogh, and when they didn't help, I went, as I often do, to my children.

"David," I asked, feeling like a spy, "why don't you ever draw pictures from nature?"

And my ten-year-old artist-nature lover replied, "I can't get the poetry of the trees." It is the only line of dialogue that I have ever consciously taken from the mouth of a living person and put into the mouth of a fictitious one. It doesn't usually work, but that time it seemed to.

I have never been happier in my life than I was those weeks I was revising the book. It was like falling happily if a little crazily in love. I could hardly wait to begin work in the morning and would regularly forget about lunch. The valley of the shadow which I had passed through so fearfully in the spring had, in the fall, become a hill of rejoicing.

This time when I sent the manuscript off to Virginia I said: "I know that love is blind, for I have just mailed you a flawless manuscript."

In time, of course, my vision was restored. I no longer imagine the book to be without flaws, but I have never ceased to love the people of this book—even the graceless Brenda and the inarticulate Mrs. Aarons. And, oh, May Belle, will you ever make a queen? I still mourn for Leslie, and when children ask me why she had to die, I want to weep, because it is a question for which I have no answer.

It is a strange and wonderful thing to me that other people who do not even know me love Jesse Aarons and Leslie Burke. I have given away my own fear and pain and faltering faith and have been repaid a hundredfold in loving compassion from readers like you. As the prophet Hosea says, the Valley of Trouble has been turned into the Gate of Hope.

Theodore Gill has said, "The artist is the one who gives form to difficult visions." This statement comes alive for me when I pore over Peter Spier's *Noah's Ark*. The difficult vision is not the destruction of the world. We've had too much practice imagining that. The difficult vision which Mr. Spier has given form to is that in the midst of this destruction as well as beyond it, there is life and humor and caring along with a lot of manure shoveling. For me those final few words "and he planted a vineyard" ring with the same joy as "he found his supper waiting for him and it was still hot."

In talking with children who have read *Bridge to Terabithia*, I have met several who do not like the ending. They resent the fact that Jesse would build a bridge into the secret kingdom that he and Leslie had shared. The thought of May Belle following in the footsteps of Leslie is bad enough, but the hint that the thumb-sucking Joyce Ann may come as well is totally abhorrent to these readers. How could I allow Jesse to build a bridge for the unworthy? they ask me. Their sense of what is fitting and right and just is offended. I hear my young critics out and do not try to argue with them, for I know as well as they do that May Belle is not Leslie, nor will she ever be. But perhaps someday they will understand Jesse's bridge as an act of grace, which he built not because of who May Belle was, but because of who he himself had become crossing the gully into Terabithia. I allowed him to build the bridge because I dare to believe with the prophet Hosea that the very valley where evil and despair defeat us can become a gate of hope—if there is a bridge.

In closing, I want to explain the Japanese word on the dedication page of *Bridge to Terabithia*. The word is *banzai*, which some of you will remember from old war movies. I am very annoyed when writers throw in Italian and German phrases that I cannot understand, but suddenly as I wrote the dedication to this book, *banzai* seemed to be the only word I knew that was appropriate. The two characters that make up the word say "all years," but the word itself combines the meanings of our English word *Hooray* with the ancient salute to royalty, "Live forever!" It is a cry of triumph and joy, a word full of hope in the midst of the world's contrary evidence. It is the word I wanted to say through *Bridge to Terabithia*. It is a word that I think Leslie Burke would have liked. It is my salute to all of you whose lives are bridges for the young.

Banzai!

National Book Award
Acceptance Speech
for <u>The Master Puppeteer</u>

A woman asked me recently why I "wasted" my time writing exotic historical fiction for children. I was shaken because I believe that growing up and making responsible choices are universal rather than alien or exotic themes. And then I never set out to write historical novels. I was born in China and I remember the Japanese as an occupying army. The Japanese soldiers came screaming up the beach and across our yard in Tsingtao, practicing, they said, for the invasion of San Francisco. I went to live in Japan when I was twenty-four and I became a child again, for I was suddenly not only illiterate but unable to speak or understand. This time the Japanese taught me things the soldiers on the beach had not. The violence has always been there, but so has the beauty. After I returned to the States I began writing about Japan because I missed being there, and I set the stories in the past because it is easier to see patterns there than in the present.

I am grateful to those of you who looked at my exotic historical novels and have seen something of value. To John, my husband, who made sure I had time to write even though seven years passed without a published word. To my friends at Thomas Y. Crowell, especially Ann Beneduce, who, when I had very nearly sunk in the slough of slush piles, yanked me out and proceeded to publish each volume with care and artistry. I feel sure no one has a more perceptive editor than I have in Virginia Buckley, nor a more gifted illustrator than Haru Wells. Thank you, Crowell, for gambling on exotic historical novels. I hope you are vindicated today.

But even people who don't mind my writing historical novels ask me why I write them for children. I don't write for children, I say. I write for myself, and then look in the catalog to see how old I am. But it's not true that I simply write for myself. I do write for children. For my own four children and for others who are faced with the question of whether they dare to become adult, responsible for their own lives and the lives of others. They remind me of the biblical children of Israel, trembling on the bank of the Jordan. You'll remember that Moses sent spies ahead, who came back to tell of the richness of the land. But ten of the spies advised the Israelites to turn back. The cities are fortified, they said, and the people are giants. It would be better to return to slavery in Egypt or to wander aimlessly in the desert.

I want to become a spy like Joshua and Caleb. I have crossed the river and tangled with a few giants, but I want to go back and say to those who are hesitating, Don't be afraid to cross over. The promised land is worth possessing, and we are not alone. I want to be a spy for hope.

Laying the First Plank

My mother used to say that anyone who could read should never try to clean. I think of this every time I try to clean my study. No scrap of paper can be thrown away without a careful reading. It does tend to ensure lack of progress, but, as the Japanese say, *Shikataganai*. There ain't nothing you can do about it.

I was engaged in this futile activity in late December of 1978. We were to move to Norfolk the next month, after thirteen years in Maryland, and I was determined to leave some of the trash behind. In my bulging file I came across a three-page draft of something that looked vaguely familiar. As I read it, the memory started my pulse thumping in my temple. It was the first plank of *Bridge to Terabithia*.

After I had decided to try to write some story growing out of David and Lisa's friendship, I sat down at the typewriter and for days nothing happened. Finally, I said to myself: "Okay. If you can't write what you want to, write what you can." So I wrote three pages, promptly lost them for three years, and didn't even remember they existed. But it was these pages that apparently had released me to write the book that earlier in 1978 had been awarded the Newbery Medal.

Here they are. Only the spelling and punctuation have been corrected.

I am not sure I can tell this story. The pain is too fresh for it to fall into rational paragraphs, but I want to try. For David, for Lisa, for Lisa's mother, and for me.

The small elementary school that my children attended was closed, and the students moved to a larger elementary school in the next neighborhood. Three of my four children adjusted quickly and happily into their new surroundings, but David, the second-grader, was at sea. David is our third child, and since I was a third child, too, I fancy I can understand the need to be special that seems to possess so many of us who will never be as handsome or clever or as magically old as our brothers and sisters who precede us. When he was three, David was torn between growing up to become a moon monster or a jellyfish, but soon after, he put away childish things and devoted himself to art. It was his art that made him special, so when he came home from the new school to report that "everyone" thought his pictures were "stupid," it was with the classic despair of the misunderstood genius. It was only the compulsory education law that persuaded me to return him to what he perceived to be an insensitive wasteland. It was a grim autumn for him—grim, that is, until he and Lisa found each other.

Here I am very hazy as to the details. It may well be that David's perceptive young teacher saw the child's loneliness and hit upon a plan to relieve it. Or it may have been more like the classic tale—the smile across the crowded room—that brought Lisa catapulting into our lives. I only know that one day David said solemnly, "Me and Lisa Hill are making a diorama about *Little House in the Big Woods*," and from then on David was special again.

I'm trying to remember if it worried me that David had chosen a girl to be his best friend. I hope not, but I can't promise. At any rate, Lisa was the Liberation Movement's dream of the ideal girl. Bright, joy-filled, self-assured—the only girl to invade the second- and third-grade T-ball team. But sharing David's love for animals and art.

"It's your *girl*friend, David," his older brother would say, but David would take the phone unperturbed. Girlfriends were a classification for the ones who chased you on the playground, hoping to grab you and kiss you. Lisa was no more a "girlfriend" than Rose Kennedy is a Playboy bunny.

Lisa was the person you did everything with and told everything to. She laughed at his jokes (the ones his older brother and sister groaned over), and he laughed at hers. They played long, imaginative games in the woods behind her house, and in the late spring they both turned eight years old.

On a bright August afternoon, the phone call came. I listened in disbelief and horror and then quickly bypassed David, reading in the living room, to search out his father. Lisa was dead. Killed by lightning on a summer afternoon.

Somehow I told David and held him while he cried. Knowing in my heart that those tears would be only the first stirrings of a pain that would shake his whole young being.

We took him to the memorial service. He rather resented the two rows of Brownie Scouts. Was he not Lisa's best friend? So he made himself special by drawing a picture, "A funny one, so I won't make her sad," to give to Lisa's mother after the service.

School began, and with it the real work of grief. Other children, uncomfortable with the unaccustomed intrusion of death, teased David. "You're in love with a dead girl," they'd say. And how could he deny it?

He told me later that he tried to cut them out by pretending Lisa were still there. "Lisa and me used to sit in the corner in music class and sing 'Free to Be You and Me' real loud. So I sat there and tried to hear her voice, but there wasn't anybody there. I was all alone." He was sobbing, and so was I.

How can you comfort? We tried, by listening mostly. The school tried. The principal and his new teacher gave him special tasks and assignments calling for his artistic talents. They tried to be patient with his daydreaming and not remind him that last year he had been thus and so.

He kept thinking she would come back. And he would listen for her and watch for her. And then, when the hard truth began to dawn, he began to search within himself the reason for her death.

"I know why Lisa died," he said one night after his prayers. "It's because God hates me. Probably he's going to kill Mary next." (Mary is his beloved younger sister.)

Again, how does one comfort and reassure?

Lisa's mother has tried. She invited several of Lisa's friends to plant the bulbs she and Lisa had ordered together. And when she and David meet, she never fails to give him that assurance of his specialness that Lisa once provided. Lisa's grandmother made it possible for David to have pottery lessons. And perhaps of all the things we tried to do, this physical struggling with the clay was the most healing for him.

But he is not fully healed. Perhaps he will never be, and I am beginning to believe that this is right. How many people in their whole lifetimes have a friend who is to them what Lisa was to David? When you have had such a gift, should you ever forget it? Of course he will forget a little. Even now he is making other friendships. His life will go on, though hers could not. And selfishly I want his pain to ease. But how can I say that I want him to "get over it," as though having loved and been loved were some sort of disease? I want the joy of knowing Lisa and the sorrow of losing her to be a part of him and to shape him into growing levels of caring and understanding, perhaps as an artist, but certainly as a person.

Reading and Writing

Benjamin Disraeli said that "the author who speaks about his own books is almost as bad as a mother who talks about her own children." The fact that I must plead guilty on both counts in no way mitigates the indictment. There are real problems when a writer talks about her own books. You can't talk about them while you're writing them, at least I can't. They're too fragile and would collapse under the weight of your verbiage. Once they're safely written but not yet published might be a good time, but you may be the only person interested in the book at that point. And even if you aren't, it would be grossly un-fair, because no one else would be in a position to talk back. After the book is published, you're already hard at work on another book and can't remember what you said in the previous book or exactly why, so when people ask you questions about it, you begin to develop a kind of mythology about the book. It becomes almost impossible to recall why you said a certain thing the way you did, but as you reflect upon it, you come up with some rather interesting answers, which may or may not be factual. Your critical faculties also begin to come into play.

You read a passage and not only forget why you wrote it but can hardly believe you would have or that your peerless editor could have let you get away with it.

The best people to talk about a book, then, are not writers, but readers. I am no Benjamin Disraeli, but I do have my little philosophies: My philosophy of publication goes something like this: Once a book is published, it no longer belongs to me. My creative task is done. The work now belongs to the creative mind of my readers. I had my turn to make of it what I would, now it is their turn. I have no more right to tell readers how they should respond to what I have written than they had to tell me how to write it. It's a wonderful feeling when readers hear what I thought I was trying to say, but there is no law that they must. Frankly, it is even more thrilling for a reader to find something in my writing that I hadn't until that moment known was there. But this happens because of who the reader is, not simply because of who I am or what I have done.

Recently I was talking with a former college professor of mine, the man, I suppose more than any other, who taught me how to write. We were talking not about any of my books but about Ursula Le Guin's *The Tombs of Atuan*, which I urged him to read. He began to speak about the powerful range of emotion that the book had evoked in him and wondered aloud if it was really suitable for children. "How could a young reader bear it?" he asked me. "I could hardly bear it myself." What I said to him rather inarticulately is the point I'm still fumbling to make. It was that what he had experienced in reading that book was not simply what the genius of the writer had put there (and I do not underestimate the genius), but the whole emotional history of a beautiful sixty-year-old life responding to that story. His creative genius had made a powerful book even more powerful. Dr. Winship is by nature and by discipline a great reader, just as Mrs. Le Guin is by nature and discipline a great writer.

The fact that Dr. Winship is a great reader does not mean that everything he touches turns to gold. He once told a class of dropping a book called *World Enough and Time* after a chapter and a half, concluding that he had neither. So there must be something in the book itself to evoke a powerful response from a reader. It's not hard to recognize that something when a book has it, but to describe what it is or duplicate the effect—ah, there's the rub.

One Sunday night we were watching the episode in the PBS life of Dickens that contained the reaction of the reading public to the death of Little Nell. It was marvelously done, piling scene upon scene of persons all over England weeping unashamedly over what sounded suspiciously to me, my husband, and my eleven-year-old as a clear case of criminal overwriting. I hasten to say we were hearing it entirely out of context, but we were screaming with laughter at the distress of Dickens's readers. How could anyone, much less the entire English-speaking world, have fallen to pieces over the death of a child in a magazine serial? Maybe it was funny because I've never read *The Old Curiosity Shop*. I do remember quite clearly reading through the whole of *A Tale of Two Cities* perfectly dry-eyed, closing the book, going to my bed, and crying inconsolably for a long, long time.

Of course, I've been tricked into crying on more than one occasion by what I can recognize perfectly well as cheap sentimentality, so I don't put any ultimate value on my own tears, taken by themselves. But there are books, some of them by Dickens, that have drawn from me a depth of response that makes me know that this book—no, not this book, these persons (or in several notable cases, these animals) are no longer figments of an author's imagination—these persons are alive in me, part of my life from that time on.

How does a writer do this? I don't know. I really don't know. I'm not trying to be coy. I certainly can't speak for Ursula Le Guin or Charles Dickens. But as the only writer I know well enough to talk about, I feel a need to try to describe a process I don't understand. It's something like a seed that grows in the dark, and one day you look and there is a full-grown plant with a flower on it—or a grain of sand that keeps rubbing at your vitals until you find you are building a coating around it. I think that's why it takes me a long time to write a book. The physical act of setting it down on a page doesn't take so long, but the growth of a book takes time, and most of it happens out of sight like a kind of dream work. And why it should happen inside me instead of inside someone else, I have no idea. It makes no more sense to me that I should be a writer than that I should have curly hair. I am conscious of feeding the process, though even this is indirect. I read, I think, I talk, I look, I listen, I hate, I fear, I love, I weep, and somehow all of my life gets wrapped around the grain. I don't get a perfect pearl every time, but then, neither does the oyster. (The trick is to know which ones to string and which ones to cast away.)

What I'm trying to say is that to me writing and reading are both gifts, neither of which has meaning without the other.

Now the gift of creative reading, like all natural gifts, must be nourished or it will atrophy. And you nourish it in much the same way you nourish the gift of writing—you read, think, talk, look, listen, hate, fear, love, weep—and bring all your life like a sieve to what you read. That which is not worthy of your gift will quickly pass through, but the gold remains. I can feel this metaphor crumbling about my ears, because a sieve is a passive thing and creative reading is not. It can take a modest pearl and set it off by its own experience in such a way that it will give off a luster never imagined by the oyster/writer working away between his shells in the darkness. And the reader will say humbly to the writer: What a beautiful pearl you made! And I hope the writer will be honest enough to know that she has been twice blessed—once with the gift of the pearl and again with the gift of a reader who could receive and cherish what was, after all, simply a natural response to a pain in the stomach.

Excerpts from
<u>A Sense of Wonder</u> and
<u>Gates of Excellence</u>

To read a great novel is to lay yourself open for a conversion experience. . . . And isn't it significant that you have trouble putting that experience into words? Isn't it because the truly great novelists have not changed you by their power to manipulate your intellect so much as they have captured your senses and borne away your emotions? And the true artist is never a manipulator anyway. Although this change has taken place in you beneath the level of rational explanations, it has taken place, not against your will, but with your eager, even joyful, collaboration.

— "A SONG OF INNOCENCE AND EXPERIENCE"

I love revisions. Where else in life can spilled milk be transformed into ice cream? We can't go back and revise our lives, but being allowed to go back and revise what we have written comes closest.

— "YES, BUT IS IT TRUE?"

Why do you write for children? [Lately] when someone asks "Why?" my response has been "Why not?" Because it has begun to occur to me that it is the implied objection that needs defending, not my choice of audience. . . . "No one will ever take you seriously," I'm told by speakers who do not even realize that they have just relegated to nonpersonhood not only me but all the children who read my books and take them quite seriously. But that's because in this country we refuse to take children seriously.   —"WHY?"

Among the more than twice-told tales in my family is the tragic one about the year we lived in Richmond, Virginia, when I came home from first grade on February 14 without a single valentine. My mother grieved over this event until her death, asking me once why I didn't write a story about the time I didn't get any valentines. "But, Mother," I said, "*all* my stories are about the time I didn't get any valentines."   —"UP FROM ELSIE DINSMORE"

Now I have a study with bookcases, files, and an oversized wooden desk. Taped above the desk is a three-by-five card on which I have hand-printed a Greek saying that I borrowed from an Edith Hamilton book. In letters large enough to be read without my glasses, it says:

BEFORE THE GATES OF EXCELLENCE
THE HIGH GODS HAVE PLACED SWEAT

I always type with my back to it. Also out of my line of vision as I work is a *Peanuts* sequence that my typist in Maryland had mounted for me. Snoopy and typewriter are on the roof of the doghouse. "It," says the first frame. Then follow two frames of Snoopy pacing the roof. "It was"—pace. "It was a dark"—two more frames of pacing. "It was a dark and stormy night." In the final frame Snoopy looks up from the machine to observe: "Good writing is hard work."

                                         —GATES OF EXCELLENCE

Source Notes

In Search of Wonder

1. Leon Garfield, "And So It Grows," *The Horn Book* (December 1968), pp. 671–672.
2. A. R. Ammons, "Identity," *The Selected Poems: 1951–1977* (New York: W. W. Norton, 1977), pp. 28–29.
3. Thomas Green, *The Activities of Teaching* (New York: McGraw-Hill, 1971), p. 200.
4. Ibid.
5. E. B. White, *Charlotte's Web* (New York: Harper & Row, 1952), pp. 108–109.
6. Margaret Mahy, "A Dissolving Ghost," *The Arbuthnot Lectures 1980–89*, ALA-ALSC (Chicago: 1990), p. 138.
7. Rachel Carson, *The Sense of Wonder* (New York: Harper & Row, 1965), pp. 42–43.
8. C. S. Lewis, *Surprised by Joy* (New York: Harcourt, Brace and Company, 1955), pp. 16–17.
9. William Howard Tucker, *History of Hartford, Vermont; July 4, 1761–April 4, 1889* (Burlington, VT: Free Press Association, 1889), p. 308.
10. White, op. cit., p. 183.
11. Rabbi Abraham Joshua Heschel, *Man Is Not Alone* (New York: Farrar, Straus, 1951), pp. 40–41.
12. Ibid., pp. 36–37.
13. Carson, op. cit., p. 89.
14. Ammons, op. cit., pp. 27–28.
15. Mary B. Mullett, "Snowflake Bentley," reprinted in *Northern New Hampshire Magazine*, January 1995, pp. 20–21.
16. White, op. cit., pp. 84–85.

The Child in the Attic

1. Frances Hodgson Burnett, *A Little Princess* (originally published 1905).
2. Ibid.
3. Ibid.

The Invisible Child

1. Joseph Conrad, Preface to *The Nigger of the "Narcissus"* (originally published 1897).
2. Katherine Paterson and Stephanie Tolan, *"Bridge to Terabithia": A Play with Music*, Act II, Scene 3 (New York: Samuel French, 1992).
3. Katherine Paterson, *Bridge to Terabithia* (New York: Thomas Y. Crowell, 1977), p. 98.
4. Katherine Paterson, *Preacher's Boy* (New York: Clarion Books, 1999), p. 156.
5. Katherine Paterson, *Jip, His Story* (New York: Dutton Children's Books, 1996), p. 162.
6. Han Nolan, *Dancing on the Edge* (San Diego, CA: Harcourt Brace Jovanovich, 1997).

Missing Persons

1. Rabindranath Tagore, *Gitanjali: Song Offerings* (Wellesley, MA: Branden Books, 2000), pp. 26–27.

Confusion at the Crossroads

1. Anne Carroll Moore, *My Roads to Childhood: Views and Reviews of Children's Books* (Boston: Horn Book, Inc.), 1961.
2. Jacob Bronowski, *The Ascent of Man* (Boston: Little, Brown, 1973), p. 427.
3. Sue Birtwistle and Susie Conklin, *The Making of Pride and Prejudice* (England: Penguin UK, 1995), p. viii.
4. Alexander Pope, *An Essay on Criticism* (1711).
5. Earl Shorris, "Liberal Education as a Weapon in the Hands of the Restless Poor," *Harper's Magazine*, September 1997, p. 50.
6. Ibid., p. 51.
7. Ibid., p. 53.
8. Ibid., p. 56.
9. Sven Birkerts, *The Gutenberg Elegies: The Fate of Reading in an Electronic Age* (New York: Fawcett Books, 1995), p. 228.
10. Ibid., p. 74.
11. Ibid., p. 75.
12. Frances Clarke Sayers, *Summoned by Books* (New York: Viking, 1965), p. 67.

Still Summoned by Books

1. Frances Clarke Sayers, *Summoned by Books* (New York: Viking, 1965), pp. 114–115.
2. Ibid., p. 16.
3. Jacob Bronowski, *The Ascent of Man*, p. 412.
4. William Wordsworth, "Ode: Intimations of Immortality from Recollections of Early Childhood" (Oxford, England: *The New Oxford Book of English Verse*).
5. Sayers, op. cit., pp. 114–115.

6. Huston Smith, *The World's Religions* (New York: Paragon House, 1995), p. 157.

7. Sayers, op. cit., p. 66.

8. Ibid., p. 17.

The Yearling and I

1. Katherine Paterson, *The Great Gilly Hopkins* (New York: Thomas Y. Crowell, 1978), pp. 147–148.

2. Marjorie Kinnan Rawlings, *The Yearling* (New York: Scribner, 1938), p. 467.

3. Katherine Paterson, *Bridge to Terabithia* (New York: Thomas Y. Crowell, 1977), pp. 127–128.

Metaphors to Live By

1. *The Scrake of Dawn: Poems by Young People from Northern Ireland*, chosen by Paul Muldoon (Belfast: Blackstaff Press, 1979).

2. Phillip L. Berman, *The Search for Meaning: Americans Talk About What They Believe and Why* (New York: Ballantine Books, 1990), p. 62.

3. Micah 4:4–5 (Revised Standard Version).

4. Fawn Brodie, *Thomas Jefferson: An Intimate History* (New York: W. W. Norton, 1974), p. 337.

5. Jeremiah 32:14–15 (Revised Standard Version).

Hope and Happy Endings

1. James Holt McGavran, Jr., "Bathrobes and Bibles, Waves and Words in Katherine Paterson's *Jacob Have I Loved*," *Children's Literature in Education* 17 (Spring 1986), p. 3.

2. Bruno Bettelheim, *The Uses of Enchantment* (New York: Alfred A. Knopf, 1976), p. 133.

3. Exodus 3:13 (Revised Standard Version).

4. Exodus 3:14–15.

5. Wolfram von Eschenbach, *Parzival*, trans. A. T. Hatto (New York: Penguin, 1980).

6. Katherine Paterson, *The Great Gilly Hopkins* (New York: Thomas Y. Crowell, 1978), p. 147.

7. Ibid., p. 148.

The Story of My Lives

1. Ashleigh Brilliant, Hallmark Cards, 1975.

2. Henry Martin, *The New Yorker*, August 5, 1985, p. 24.

3. Deuteronomy 26:5–10 (Revised Standard Version).

4. Flannery O'Connor, "The Nature and Aim of Fiction," *Mystery and Manners*, ed. Sally and Robert Fitzgerald (New York: Farrar, Straus and Giroux, 1969), p. 68.

5. Romans 9:13 (King James Version).

6. Katherine Paterson, *Jacob Have I Loved* (New York: Thomas Y. Crowell, 1980), p. 215.

Do I Dare Disturb the Universe?

1. Henrik Ibsen, quoted in Robertson Davies, *One Half of Robertson Davies* (Middlesex, England: Penguin, 1978), p. 124.

2. Marie Winn, "Where Have All the Children Gone?" *The Virginian-Pilot/Ledger-Star*, June 5, 1983.

3. Alan Paton, *Cry, the Beloved Country* (New York: Scribner, 1950), p. 3.

4. Eudora Welty, *The Eye of the Story: Selected Essays and Reviews* (New York: Vintage Books, 1979), p. 152.
5. Genesis 3:4–5 (King James Version).
6. Welty, op. cit., p. 153.

Ideas

1. J. R. R. Tolkien, *The Return of the King* (New York: Ballantine Books, 1965), p. 385.
2. Jill Paton Walsh, telephone conversation with author, June 11, 1988.
3. Rainer Maria Rilke, *The Notebooks of Malte Laurids Brigge*, trans. Stephen Mitchell (New York: Vintage Books, 1985), pp. 19–20.

Sounds in the Heart

1. Gerard Manley Hopkins, "God's Grandeur," *The Harper Anthology of Poetry*, ed. John Frederick Nims (New York: Harper & Row, 1981), p. 446.

Creativity Limited

1. Flannery O'Connor, *The Habit of Being: Letters* (New York: Farrar, Straus and Giroux, 1979), p. 221.
2. Jill Paton Walsh, "The Lords of Time," Whittall Lecture, Library of Congress, November 13, 1978. Published in the *Library of Congress Quarterly* (Spring 1979).

Words

1. Jacob Bronowski, *The Origins of Knowledge and Imagination* (New Haven: Yale University Press, 1978), p. 109.
2. Joan Didion, *Slouching Towards Bethlehem* (New York: Dell, 1968), pp. 122–123.

Permissions